GIFTKILLERS

GiftKillers

How Satan Plans to
Kill your Spiritual Gifts,
Steal your Joy
and Destroy your
Life's Purpose

Dr. Michael Miller

PALMETTO
PUBLISHING
Charleston, SC
www.PalmettoPublishing.com

Paperback ISBN: 979-8-9864136-0-0

THANK YOU

To my family, friends and patients for listening
to me talk about my book for decades…

It saved me thousands of dollars in therapy! ☺

To My Mother

Thanks for always telling me
I could be anything I wanted to be.

TABLE OF CONTENTS

INTRODUCTION

In my line of work you see thousands of people in physical pain. For over 36 years my Chiropractic practice has given me a unique opportunity to share what I've learned about people who are in pain. People tend to be more real with you when they are hurting and often struggle with the question, "Is life worth the pain?" They will often open up about their deep problems when they are in pain. I've heard Chiropractors are called "Psychologists with hands" and I agree.

Having served over 25 years on Tres Dias Christian retreats, I've seen many people's spiritual pain. The weekends are designed to help people drop the baggage of life and go serve their families and church. They deal with the same question, "Is life worth the pain?" These weekends are very real as they deal with Satan's attacks. There are many speakers, both preachers and regular people like myself, who give specific talks. These talks usually include real testimonies about their life. The speakers are open about the bad things they did and how Jesus saved them. Their testimonies show how all humans have failed and how we all need a Savior, Jesus Christ. Seeing how others struggled with life and overcame it with Jesus allows people to accept God's grace and forgiveness, drop their baggage and follow Christ.

By serving on more and more weekends I noticed patterns in the "pain" people were suffering. I noticed similar personalities had similar "pain." Jim and Joe had similar personalities and had the same "pain." Pete and Paul are alike in their personalities but they were different from Jim and Joe. Pete and Paul had the same "pain" but it was different from Jim and Joe's "pain." My science-oriented brain wanted answers so I asked God for the "Battle Plans" Satan uses against us to cause the "pain" in people's lives.

God was patiently waiting for me to ask for those "Battle Plans" and He began to pour information into me. It was like drinking from a firehose! He opened up the hose and poured the plans into me over the next twenty years. I know that like me, if you will take the time to learn these "Battle Plans" and take proper actions, they will help you stand firm in your spiritual battles. Not only will knowing these plans help protect you from Satan's attacks, they will show you what your Creator made you to be and what your purpose is here on Earth.

Because of my previous studies of personality traits, my first thoughts were Satan used the weak spots of personalities to attack us. Over the years I observed he attacked the weak spots of spiritual gifts. He knows the specific weaknesses of each spiritual gift God gave us and does his best to destroy us with that knowledge. Isn't it like Satan to try and destroy what God created?

Scripture describes Christians as the Body of Christ and some parts of the body have weaknesses which may not affect others. An eye may be blinded by a bright light but the ear is unaffected. Yet a loud sound may deafen the ear and the eye will remain unaffected. Unfortunately you can be an easy target when you fail to learn your weaknesses and arm yourself against Satan's attacks. Sunglasses and ear plugs could have easily prevented the problems with light and sound. My prayer for you is the knowledge in this book helps you realize your purpose in Christ and equips you for the battles in your life. I also pray you will share this information and help protect others from the attacks they face in their lives.

The journey to learn our purpose and put it into action will take some time but will be totally worth the effort. It will not easy but it will be filled with joy-filled rewards from the Father. Becoming more aware of the Spiritual Battle going on around us helps us realize that many of the trials we face are targeted at keeping us from becoming what we are created to be. God has a plan for our life and He does work all things for good for those who love Him.

Know Your Creator
Trust Your Creator
Be What He Created You To Be

When we realize God has the best plan for our life, we will want to hear from Him, trust Him and follow Him. We need to know what He created us to be by learning the spiritual gifts He has blessed us with and how to use them to build up the Body of Christ. This is your journey of trusting Him.

"Talk with God, no breath is lost.
Walk with God, no strength is lost.
Wait for God, no time is lost.
Trust in God, you will never be lost."
Unknown

CHAPTER ONE
WHY AM I HERE?

"For we are God's handiwork, created in Christ Jesus to do good works, which God prepared in advance for us to do."
Ephesians 2:10

Are you struggling with being *"God's handiwork"* as you seek direction and purpose in your life? You may believe you have a purpose but feel as if God is keeping it a secret from you and not helping you achieve your goals. Worse, you may have fallen victim to Satan's schemes and are trapped in sins which are destroying your life and the lives around you. These sins can make you feel unworthy to be *"God's handiwork."* Many people, including Christians, struggle with the question, "Why am I here?" Even if you know God created you for a purpose you can still feel like God skipped over you when He handed out the directions for your life.

It borders on insanity when the world asks a 17-year-old what they want to do for the rest of their lives. We've all been there. What life experiences equipped us to answer a question which will impact the remainder of our life at such a young age? Sometimes we feel forced to answer and spend tens of thousands of dollars and years of our life in college just to find out it wasn't the job for us. We either work out the rest of their lives in a miserable job or quit to do something else. Most of us never took the time to learn who God created us to be and instead chose a random popular path. These poor decisions can lead many to bad life choices from low self-esteem and depression.

We all desperately need to know what God created us to be and to follow His plan for our life to find our purpose. I hope and pray you've reached a point in your life where you are seeking a purpose and direction which will be pleasing to God. If you are, then you're in the right place!

I pray this book shows you how to determine your life's purpose and direction. I pray you get to know the Creator who calls you His *"handiwork!"* I pray even harder for you to trust your Creator so you can clearly see "Whose" you are and become the best possible version of what He created you to be. I hope you begin to see yourself through His eyes so you'll begin to know the plans He *"prepared in advance for us to do."* I pray the peace of God covers you as you begin this journey of discovery about yourself and your future.

SEEKING GOD'S PLAN FOR YOUR LIFE

> *"For I know the plans I have for you,"* declares the Lord, *"plans to prosper you and not to harm you, plans to give you hope and a future."*   Jeremiah 29:11

You may think you are so messed up God could never use you in His plans. It may be the sins of your past or some on-going sins. It may be how badly you were treated in the past or sins which were forced upon you that make you feel unworthy of God's plans. In any case you feel unusable in God's hands.

> *"Don't let past mistakes keep you from seeking God"*[1]
> Billy Graham

By knowing God and knowing He has a plan for your life you will begin to realize your past does not define your future. Never let what you have done or what was done to you become bigger than what Jesus did for you on the cross. It's not what happened to you that makes you who you are; It's what God created you to be. Life is not just about escaping from pain!

Jeremiah 29:11 is a very popular Scripture because it states God has *"plans to prosper you and not harm you, plans to give you hope and a future."* The word *"prosper"* really bothered me every time I read this passage. I am not a fan of teaching people to pray harder so they will get the pink Cadillac they've always wanted. God doesn't care what you drive but He does care about you taking meals to those in need and transporting people to church and doctors. So I looked up the word and get this, it's the Hebrew word "shalom" and means a complete peace. This totally changed my attitude about this Scripture. It is not about getting more of what you want it is about gaining the complete peace of God!

This world does not offer anything anywhere close to this kind of peace. It is always demanding more and more of you, your time and your money. Can you imagine receiving God's perfect peace! Jeremiah goes on to say...

> *"Then you will call on me and come and pray to me, and I will listen to you. You will seek me and find me when you seek me with all your heart."* Jeremiah 29:12-13

Do you need someone to call on who will listen to your needs during the darkest times of your life? Do you need an anchor to weather the storms of your life? What do you crave more, the perfect peace of God or more stuff when you are struggling through the trials of your life? Seek Jesus with all of your heart and you will find Him and His perfect peace. Keep your eyes on Him in the storms and stay focused on the plan He has for your life. Jesus wants you to look to Him and see the hope filled future you have with Him. God is good all the time and all the time God is good.

SEEKING GOD'S GOODNESS EVEN IN HARD TIMES

> *"And we know that in all things God works for the good..."*
> Romans 8:28

Here is another well repeated Scripture. It is spoken over and over when people are going through hard times. While speaking with a patient suffering through the tragic loss of her son she told me she was sick of people quoting this verse to her as she grieved. His death was consuming her life. She was having trouble processing *"all things"* and struggling to understand his death at such an early age. As she came in for several visits I asked her about the good times she and her son had together and did my best to speak light into her life. I eventually got her to laugh again and start rebuilding her life one good thing at a time.

Over the years, patients like this one have come back and said the words I shared with them changed their lives. To be honest, many times I give messages and later have no idea what I said. Sometimes I state the obvious like they are alive for a reason and are loved by Jesus. We all live in a broken world where God says it rains on the just and the unjust and bad things happen to good people. I tell them they still have a purpose no matter what they have been through, but Satan wants them dead or at least ineffective to carry out God's purpose for their life.

I remind them to stop listening to the voices telling them how bad they are and how a "nobody" like them would never be used by God. I urge them to focus on what the Creator of the Universe thinks about them. Many Christians might read a Scripture on a coffee mug or wall art and stop there. I beg them to read God's Word deeply to learn more about Him and His purpose for their life. Many people stop at the word *"good"* in Romans 8:28, but God did not stop there:

> *"And we know that in all things God works for the good of those who love him, who have been called according to his purpose."* Romans 8:28

This verse is like a beautifully sewn tapestry. When looking at the finished side it is pleasing to the eye and full of color and design. Turn the tapestry around and look at the backside. It's almost unrecognizable from the front. There are knots in the strings and the colors barely make sense. Much like your life, God will use the knots for His good to make a beautiful tapestry for *"those who love Him."* You may not discover all the "whys" in your lifetime but I believe God's Word and His promises. He always tells the truth. It has taken many years for me to not only believe this but to experience it in my own life. Whatever has happened to you, in some way, it *"works for the good."* You need to allow Him to work through you *"according to His purpose"* for your life. You need to know Him, trust Him and be what He created you to be.

ANSWERING THE MOST IMPORTANT QUESTION

Let's jump feet first into the deep end of the pool. You cannot ask yourself "Why am I here" until you answer the most important question in your life, "Is there a God?" The purpose of your life is directly affected by your answer to this question. If the answer is, "There is no God" then there is no real purpose to life.

If there is no God then humans are simply an accident from Cosmic Flatulence! A gas exploded then it condensed down to form planets and stars. This belief forces a human to agree their great, great, great, great... grandparents were rocks and water and they formed slime. The slime somehow formed amino acids, then protein strands and then creatures from those chemicals. Those creatures walked out of the water and eventually, over billions of years, became a human. Welcome to the world of the survival of the fittest! The only goal in life is to get what you can, can what you get and poison the rest! The purpose of life is out-running and out-smarting everyone around you to survive another day.

Without God there are no morals, no justice, no rights and no purpose and life is meaningless as everyone scratches and claws their way to the top. Success is only measured by the worldly standards of wealth, possessions and power over others. You have no rights as a human being other than to be manipulated and enslaved by others.

If you say, "Yes, there is a God" you can begin to seek your purpose in this infinite universe. You were created with not only a physical body but you have thoughts, reasoning and the ability to love. You were also created with a human spirit which can connect with God to understand why you are here. You can distinguish between good and evil and desire what is good, right and just. If God made the universe and you in it, He must have a purpose for you to be here. If God allowed you to be here then you must have value to Him.

Perhaps a better question than "Why am I here?" is to ask God, "Why did you create me?" If a potter makes a clay pitcher he intends it to serve liquids. If you are made to be a hammer you need to work with nails. If you are a hammer in a room full of bolts you will live a very unhappy and unfulfilled life until you find the nails you need to be working with. God created our purpose and knowing God shows us our purpose.

NO GOD - NO PURPOSE
KNOW GOD - KNOW PURPOSE

In the following chapters you will learn why you are here and begin see God's Will for your life. You will discover what He created you to be and find your purpose by using the spiritual gifts God gave you. You'll learn why it has been so hard to live in this world as you feel attacked at every corner. Learning to be ready for those attacks will help you defeat the enemy who is dead set on destroying your life and God's purpose for you.

This is a journey of discovery about you and your relationship with God. It is not a quick microwave recipe or a 12 step program to maturity in Christ. Please do not get in a hurry other than to learn all you can about your Creator and the plans He has for your life. You will need to learn "Whose" you are in Christ and build on His foundation.

By building a relationship with God you will discover your spiritual gifts and how they shape your purpose and give you meaning. Your relationship with Him will allow you to communicate with Him so He can guide you. You will need to grow your Faith in Christ and move from infant milk to the maturity of meat so you can become a functioning part of the Body of Christ. Most of all you will need to learn about your enemy and how he plans to take you down. You can fight him and stand firm against him with God's help. You no longer have to fight on your own! It's a lot to take in but it is doable one spiritual step at a time.

A NECESSARY FIRST SPIRITUAL STEP!

"Whoever belongs to God hears what God says. The reason you do not hear is that you do not belong to God."
John 8:47

The next few paragraphs are necessary because non-believers will not understand the spiritual battle ahead of them. The chapters which lay ahead will not make sense to someone who doesn't have a relationship with Jesus Christ. Without a relationship with Jesus how will you know His voice? How could you ever know His purpose for your life without being able to listen to Him?

"The person without the Spirit does not accept the things that come from the Spirit of God but considers them foolishness, and cannot understand them because they are discerned only through the Spirit." 1 Corinthians 2:14

If you said there is no God then you will not understand this book. This book is for the followers of Christ. If Jesus is not your Lord and Savior, you will never be able to have the peace of God and hear the plan He has for your life. If you are not a Christian and feel an urge to know Jesus Christ as your Lord and Savior ask Him to come into your heart right now.

"If you declare with your mouth, 'Jesus is Lord,' and believe in your heart that God raised him from the dead, you will be saved. For it is with your heart that you believe and are justified, and it is with your mouth that you profess your faith and are saved." Romans 10:9-10

Ask Jesus to become the Lord of your life. You need to realize everyone has sinned, including you. We've all messed up and that's why we all need a Savior. There are no fancy words to say other than inviting Jesus into your heart. Believe Jesus is the Son of God, He died for your sins and He rose from the dead so His sacrifice will allow you to be in heaven with Him for eternity.

If you prayed for Jesus to be the Lord of your life, pray again for God to send you a believer and ask them what to do next. It should be water baptism and joining a church. I rejoice with you on your decision and look forward to meeting you in heaven one day. Mostly I look forward to hearing the stories of new believers finding their purpose through the spiritual gifts God gave us!

"I tell you that in the same way there will be more rejoicing in heaven over one sinner who repents than over ninety-nine righteous persons who do not need to repent." Luke 15:7

As believers we rejoice with you for becoming a Christian. It is the single most important decision you will ever make in your life. It's not going to be easy but it is going to be worth it! Buckle up for the ride of your life and enjoy the journey God has laid out for you. He loves you dearly and has a plan for your life!

"We have received too much from God to allow ourselves opportunities for unbelief. We have received too many gifts and privileges to allow a grumbling, murmuring heart to disqualify us of our destiny."[2] -Francis Frangipane

Believers, please pray right now for these simple paragraphs to lead people to Christ. Pray for Godly people to come into their lives to help mentor them to know and trust our Lord. Pray you are available to become their mentor and help them grow in Christ. Pray they become the best version of what God created them to be!

"Before I formed you in the womb I knew you, before you were born I set you apart..." Jeremiah 1:5

If God knew you before you were even formed *"in the womb"* then He has a purpose for your life and you have value to Him! Yes, this is a book about spiritual gifts but it's more about using them in your life's journey to mature in Christ. Most books on spiritual gifts are like reading a dictionary. You have spiritual gift "A" and you are good at these things. You have spiritual gift "B" so you're good at these other things. Discovering your spiritual gifts lets you see how the Creator of the Universe made you. It's how you find your purpose and how God created you to walk with Him. Prepare yourself for a journey and be ready for the unexpected and the miraculous as you and God travel together. He has so much to show you and it was inside of you all along.

"I have been crucified with Christ and I no longer live, but Christ lives in me. The life I now live in the body, I live by faith in the Son of God, who loved me and gave himself for me." Galatians 2:20

If Christ lives in you, how much space do you allow Him to have? Have you put Him in your spare bedroom and never allow Him in the living room or your bedroom? How much space to you think He wants? Jesus loves you so much He wants all of you. He wants to bless every room in your home. Jesus is not redecorating; He is there for a complete renovation from the foundation to the roof. He wants to be a part of your total restoration. Allow Him into every room in your home and start your first steps on your Spiritual journey about learning your purpose and the plans he has for you.

Stop wondering if God can use you, because He died for you! Look at what Jesus sees inside of you, He sees Himself! Listen to what God has to say about His purpose for your life and become what God created you to be; a blood bought sinner turned saint with a purpose from God. You will discover how the God-given spiritual gifts you have are directly connected to your purpose. Learning how God intended for you to use them is extremely important in finding out why you are here.

"There is no one who is insignificant in the purpose of God."[3]
Alistair Begg

PONDERING POINTS

"Whose" are you?

Do you have a purpose?

How do you get to know God?

How do you trust God?

Does God have a plan for your life?

What is your biggest struggle with becoming what God created you to be?

Are you of value to God?

Do you feel unworthy to serve God?

What's keeping you from following God?

What do you fear?

CHAPTER TWO

WHY ARE SPIRITUAL GIFTS IMPORTANT TO YOUR PURPOSE

"Now concerning spiritual gifts, bretheren, I do not want you to be ignorant."　　　1 Corinthians 12:1 NKJV

God knew from the beginning we would be *"ignorant"* about spiritual gifts and we live up to those sad expectations. The wording here can mean not to know but it implies to willfully "ignore" learning about the gifts. Sadly, most of us have ignored finding out about our spiritual gifts and statistics show how good we are at ignoring them. Learning about our spiritual gifts could clear up much of the confusion found among Christians struggling with their identity in Christ.

In February 2009 Barna, a trusted Christian polling group, surveyed Christians about their Spiritual Gifts. Their poll, *"Survey Describes the Spiritual Gifts That Christians Say They Have,"* asked Christians if they had heard about spiritual gifts. 68% answered yes and were asked to describe their spiritual gifts. The poll revealed five types of Christians and their ideas about their gifts. 28% (of the 68%) said they have no gift at all. 21% (of the 68%) said they had false gifts not found in Scripture like having a house, a job, a sense of humor, happiness, and health. 15% (of the 68%) did not know their gift. The fourth group was the remainder of the 68% familiar with their Spiritual gifts. The fifth group was the 32% from the original group of Christians who had never heard about Spiritual Gifts.

Even with Paul's warning the polls show Christians are clearly *"ignorant"* about spiritual gifts just as Scripture states. The poll showed almost 64% of Christians who have heard about spiritual gifts were confused about them. Add the number of Christians who had never heard about spiritual gifts and it showed 75% of Christians are *"ignorant"* about them!

It is clear Paul is warning you about the importance of knowing your spiritual gifts. Do you know your spiritual gifts? Do you know how to use your spiritual gifts? Are you ready to be "willingly smart" and learn what your gifts are and how to use them?

Stop making excuses for being "willingly ignorant" about your spiritual gifts! Look to God for answers about the confusion of the spiritual gifts He gave you. Then listen to God and He will teach you how to use your spiritual gifts. Become what He created you to be; an eager Christian learning how to use the spiritual gifts God gave you.

WE HAVE AN ENEMY WHO WANTS US TO BE IGNORANT

Satan knows spiritual gifts will grow your Faith and build up the church. He also knows they are weapons that can be used against him and his attacks. He will use everything within his power to stop you from using your gifts. He is the master of confusion and takes great pride in the Barna polls showing his work is having the desired effect of keeping you *"ignorant"* about your spiritual gifts. Satan's goal is to keep you off course and misinformed about your top spiritual weapons. Stop now and pray for God to help you better understand the Spiritual Gifts He has given you. Ask God to show you clear directions on how to use them to better your life and the lives of others.

BE BETTER THAN THE WORLD

"Do not conform to the pattern of this world, but be transformed by the renewing of your mind. Then you will be able to test and approve what God's will is—his good, pleasing and perfect will."   Romans 12:2

We've all watched friends or family fall victim to Satan's schemes? Many people will start by pushing away from the good people around them as they fall into his traps. We've watched Satan drag them away from anyone who could help as they burn bridges with friends and family and fly head-on into their destruction on purpose.

I've seen Sunday school teachers leave their wives and children through adulterous affairs. They step away from their family only to chase worldly gratification. They create a path of destruction which will affect generations because of their fleeting fleshly desires. I'm going to tell you something straight up; God will never tell you to do something like this. This is from Satan! You are called to be different from the world; actually you are called to be better than the world.

I've seen friends turn to sex, alcohol and drugs and destroy their life along with those closest to them. I've noticed a very strange turn-about after one spouse has an affair and destroys the marriage. For some crazy reason the other spouse will have an affair with a married person. I'm going to tell you something straight up again; God will never tell you to do something like this. This is from Satan! You do not have a Get-out-of-jail-free card to use since it happened to you.

There is a strange tendency to become the very thing we hate? Someone who was abused may become the abuser. Another says they will never drink alcohol because of an alcoholic family member but they become an alcoholic. Many of those in prison have a parent or family member who served time. Why do we become the very thing we hate? Why do we become the parent who we swore we'd never be? What are the plans Satan uses against us to turn us into the very things we hate?

There are connections and patterns to the evil that happens to you and it is based on your spiritual gifts. This is the reason for "Why Spiritual Gifts?" Each gift has its strengths and weaknesses. Satan focuses on those weak spots like a heat-seeking missile to destroy your ability to use your spiritual gifts. This usually leads to a life full of depression, fear and self-destruction along with feeling insignificant and joyless.

Satan loves to push you down and keep you there. One tactic he loves to use is to divide and conquer. He uses this age old trick to separate you from the people who can help you and pick you up when you fall. Watch out for being pulled away from the very people God put into your life who can help you. Do not allow Satan to control your life and keep you from your purpose and the plans God has for your life! Satan is doing the best he can to delay his eternal punishment by keeping you from building up the Kingdom of God with your spiritual gifts.

A STEP TO FIGHTING BACK

I've watched Satan win too many battles and destroy friends and family's lives. It's time we started fighting and taking back what is rightfully ours. We need to quit being ignorant about spiritual gifts and learn how to use the power found in those gifts to take back what Satan stole. Sometimes the fight starts with simple life decisions like who we hang around with.

> *"Do not be misled: "Bad company corrupts good character."*
> *Come back to your senses as you ought, and stop sinning; for*
> *there are some who are ignorant of God—I say this to your*
> *shame."*   1 Corinthians 15:33-34

A beginning step in your maturity is to get away from the *"bad company"* around you who constantly tempt you into sin. At 14 years old I started hanging out with a "friend" who showed me how easy it was to shoplift. My Mom and I were not well off and I had very little so I began to shoplift items from some local stores. I was caught at a Zayre department store stealing, of all things, a KISS Live album.

Because of my age, their policy was to call the parents and turn me over to them but they could not contact my Mom. They called the police but they were too busy with calls to take me to Juvenile Detention. They delayed a bit and decided to take me in themselves but on the way out of the store I asked if they would try to call my Mom one more time and they did. Mom had just gotten home with groceries and had to immediately come get me. Fortunately I did not go to Juvenile Detention but it was a hard night with my Mom. She told me she did not raise me that way and she was very disappointed and she grounded me severely. I came to my senses out of fear and never hung out with that "friend" again.

Bad company will fill your mind with poor decision-making which will lead to regret and shame. Misery always loves company and they will do their best to drag you into sin to make themselves feel better about their sins. Stop chasing sin; it will never be satisfied and it will always want more.

Do your best, with God's help, to run from the sins which are destroying your life. You will never be completely sinless here on earth but you can sin-less because Jesus will make a way for you to choose a better path. Take back your mind and your body by seeking good company and have a life filled with the peace and joy of God who already lives within you.

"Examine yourselves to see whether you are in the faith; test yourselves. Do you not realize that Christ Jesus is in you—unless, of course, you fail the test?"
2 Corinthians 13:5

To change the actions which are destroying your life you must be willing to take a deeper look inside yourself. You may be terrified to see what is buried deep inside yourself. I was! Are the wounds so deep and calloused you know there will be great pain just to open them up again? Do you feel unworthy to serve a God who loves you because of those old wounds? Why would Christ choose to live inside of you if He wasn't capable of restoring you!

WHEN I WAS SAVED

I walked down the aisle of a small country church when I was 12 years old to be saved. I love to say my Mamaw helped me with a "drug" problem because she always "drug" me to church every time I visited her! My Mamaw, who made the best food on the planet, made sure I went to church every time I visited her. Since my Mom's idea of a hot breakfast was toasting my pop-tarts I was always excited to go to church with my grandmother and be well fed.

One of my favorite meals was her breakfast of homemade biscuits with sorghum syrup, fried fat-back and scrambled eggs. She also had the best cornbread dressing and fried squash. At church she always had chewing gum and Ludden's Cherry Cough Drops on hand for any occasion but they were mostly to keep us kids quiet in service. Her patience and prayers finally paid off when I gave my heart to Jesus in that old country church next to the railroad track in Montevallo.

Unfortunately I had no church home and a complete lack of any discipleship other than an occasional trip to church with my Mamaw. My Dad had left my Mom and me when I was nine and I had no positive male role models in my life. I had my fire insurance and I became the best heathen I could. Satan took advantage of this opportunity and crept into my life because I did not fill the empty places in my mind with Godly things. I was self-centered and looked mostly to my own survival and pleasures. It took decades to get serious about a relationship with Jesus.

Please, stay in church and feed your soul on God's Word after getting saved. Find good Christians to help guide you on your life's journey. I could write a book on what not to do after you get saved. I lost years of my life but even worse is the path of destruction I left in other people's lives. I look back at the positive influences I could have had on others but I selfishly encouraged bad behaviors in the ones I knew. I wish I could apologize to every one of those people. Please find good company and work together to become more like Christ.

MY STEPS BACK TO GOD

Fast forward nearly 20 years. It was the time in a marriage to have a child and my biggest goal was to not to be the father my father was to me. I figured the answer to my goal was to be a better spiritual man. Keep in mind I did not want to go to church with hypocrites. I'd been hurt by so many people I had major trust issues at this point in my life. I felt I could do this spiritual thing on my own so I thought the best place to begin was to read the New Testament.

After reading though the New Testament and not understanding the Book of Revelation, I asked God to help me understand. It was like God jumped for joy and He gave me a thirst for researching Revelation. After a lot of study I slowly began to understand some of it and I'll give you my best interpretation; I read the end of The Book and we win!

Within a few months the most influential man in my life was born, my son. It's funny how God gets our attention. God saw something in me even though I could not see it in myself. He ignited a spark in me to start moving forward with my life. I could not see the big plans He had for me so He only showed me one step at a time. Helping the kingdom was so far from my mind during this time of my life. I was just trying to be a good dad, a good husband, a good Chiropractor and somehow rebuild my life by returning to Him. But God had a plan for my life just like He has a plan for your life!

Over a decade ago I was about to fly to Sacramento to serve on a Tres Dias men's weekend. I told my 15 year old son if anything happened to me I wanted him to know he was the best man I had ever known. My son is not perfect but he has a good head on his shoulders and he has made so many better choices than I had at his age. The small steps of Faith I started decades ago have proven to be a great journey in my life, God is good!

By giving you this part of my testimony it can help you understand there are steps in God's plans for you and your life. These steps can take quite a bit of time. Usually the reason for more time is because of the lack of obedience. I know, because I was disobedient! Sometimes you may not understand why God is having you do something but stay with Him every step of the way. There is a plan for each of the steps in your life and one day you will look back and understand!

> *"Jesus replied, 'You do not realize now what I am doing, but later you will understand.'"*   John 13:7

Jesus was trying to wash the Disciple's feet and they didn't understand what He was doing. They had no idea he was about to die on the cross for them and He wanted to show them a true act of humility and servanthood so they could follow His example.

> *"Now that I, your Lord and Teacher, have washed your feet, you also should wash one another's feet. I have set you an example that you should do as I have done for you. Very truly I tell you, no servant is greater than his master, nor is a messenger greater than the one who sent him. Now that you know these things, you will be blessed if you do them."*
> John 13:14-17

When things do not fit our way of thinking we tend to ignore them and see no value in them. The iconic scene in the *Karate Kid* movie comes to mind when the Master is teaching the student to "wax on" and "wax off." Soon the student grumbles about it being a waste of time but the Master had a plan which involved small steps in the student's life. The waxing helped the student use the motions he had learned to defend himself in battle. When the student realized the Master had a plan he became a better student and listened more carefully to the Master's instructions. Allow God to work with you step by step, month by month and year by year.

Listen to the plans the Creator of the Universe has laid out for you before you were born! Follow Him and grow your Faith through His mercy, grace and the gifts He gave you.

> *"But grow in the grace and knowledge of our Lord and Savior Jesus Christ. To him be glory both now and forever! Amen."*   2 Peter 3:18

I stopped long enough to get saved and then wasted decades of my life. When I looked at the wreckage of my life I decided to become a better man and asked for wisdom from God. I listened for the next steps God had planned for my life. These first steps included reading the Bible, attending church and Sunday school. I went through specialty classes and eventually taught them a few times.

I continued my Christian growth with Promise Keeper's, joined an accountability group and led a men's ministry at church. When Tres Dias came into my life it helped my spiritual gifts grow to levels I could never have imagined. Now I find myself writing a book about Satan's Battle Plans. Keep in mind this came after 20 years of not following Jesus and another 24 years after I decided to follow Him. Learning how to use your spiritual gifts will take time so prepare for a life journey. It is not a run to the super market to pick up a gallon of milk; it's a lifelong marathon with Christ.

> *"I remain confident of this: I will see the goodness of the Lord in the land of the living. Wait for the Lord; be strong and take heart and wait for the Lord."*
> Psalm 27:13-14

My journey has taken most of my life but I can see *"the goodness of the Lord in the land of the living!"* There was a lot of waiting and training but it's worth the all the effort. I've experiences miracles and lives changed because of waiting on the Lord. God wants to work through you to change the world and He is willing to be patient with you. Are you willing to be patient with Him?

Waiting starts with stopping. If you're busy trying to fix everything under your own power you'll have a difficult time looking at the bigger picture and the bigger problems. Sometimes being busy is not of the Devil, it is the Devil. When you finally stop to look around listen for God's instruction for His plan to fix the problem. Stopping, looking and listening are essential for building up the spiritual gifts within you to be used to expand God's Kingdom.

KNOWING WHEN TO STOP, LOOK AND LISTEN ON YOUR JOURNEY

Your journey is taken one step at a time. It's a lifelong journey and each step builds on itself to help you mature in Christ. Be careful about getting in a rush. Enjoy the journey and be sure to look around at the miracles God is doing every step of the way. But be sure to heed the warnings as you cross new intersections.

RAILROAD CROSSINGS

Life's journey is a lot like a railroad crossing. Many crossings have red flashing lights, clanging bells and crossing guards to lower down for our protection. It's obviously dangerous to cross the intersection as the train comes down the track blowing its horn. Yet some people zig zag through the crossing thinking the risk is worth saving a few minutes of their life.

Sometimes crossings just have sound and lights and many people zoom across the track while the train is coming. Most country road crossings have no lights, no bells and no arms to block the road. Our safety totally depends on us seeing the railroad crossing sign and doing what we were taught when we learned to drive; Stop, Look and Listen.

These three words save many lives but some people still ignore the signs and rush across the tracks without even a second glance. Getting away with it time after time makes the problem worse because they never learn from their mistakes unless there is a close call or they are hit by the train. We all have dangers we face in our lives. Do we rush in a zig zagged course to save a few minutes of our life? Do we ignore warnings and randomly take chances hoping danger never hits us? Or do we wait patiently for a sign to go forward and use "Stop, Look and Listen" in our own spiritual lives to make Godly decisions. How do we use these three actions in our Spiritual journey?

STOP:

"…Stop doubting and believe."   John 20:27

Stop for a moment and remember "Whose" you are. Never forget God has a purpose for you and your life. Stop listening to the voices who say you have no value and believe the One who sees your eternal value. You need to stop trying to figure out everything in your life, stop doubting yourself and simply believe in Him and His purpose for your life.

"Overhearing what they said, Jesus told him, "Don't be afraid; just believe."   Mark 5:36

Believing in Jesus as the Son of God was easy for me and I never knew of a time I did not believe Jesus was the Son of God. I was saved at twelve years old in my Mamaw's old country church but trusting God was one of the hardest things I've had to learn in my life. I am a doer and a fixer and I want to put a wrench on every aspect of my life and repair it. I was a firm believer in the saying, "If you want something done right you've got to do it yourself."

God will allow you to keep fixing everything until you finally can't do it alone. He will allow you to completely wear yourself out trying to do it all under your own power just to get you to be still. Stopping terrified me, I was afraid of being still and seeing who I really was. Stop and realize who God is in your life and how much He loves you! Stop trying to do everything yourself and believe in a God who will help you.

> *"...Be still, and know that I am God..."*
> Psalm 46:10

Sometimes stopping can be a regular quiet time with God. Use this time to read His Word, speak with Him and listen. Read for depth not distance. Think of your life as a marathon, not a sprint. Pace yourself, so you're never seen wearing a "Burned out for Jesus" T-shirt. You want to finish the race; not necessarily win. God has already won the race for you so thank Him for who He is and what He has done and what He will do in your future.

> *"The Lord will fight for you; you need only to be still."*
> Exodus 14:14

LOOK:

> *"After this I looked, and there before me was a door standing open in heaven. And the voice I had first heard speaking to me like a trumpet said, 'Come up here, and I will show you what must take place after this.'"* Revelation 4:1

Many times when an angel appears in Scripture with a message, the person receiving the message drops to their knees and bows their head. Then the angel would say to the person, "Get up, and do not worship me." It can be difficult to look around when you are staring at the ground. Keep your eyes open and look to heaven for your answers not the world.

In Revelation God is trying to reveal a message to John to look and see the *"door standing open in heaven"* then God says to John, *"come up here."* If you are not constantly looking for God then how will you find the answers for your life's journey? How will God *"show you what must take place after this?"*

God has a plan for your life and you only need to look to Him and follow His plan. Keep your eyes open and focused on Him. Eventually you will start seeing through the eyes of God much like the song "Give Me Your Eyes" by Brandon Heath. When you see what God sees, if only for a moment, you can see the importance of the needs of others.

> *"Do nothing out of selfish ambition or vain conceit. Rather, in humility value others above yourselves, not looking to your own interests but each of you to the interests of the others."* Philippians 2:3-4

Stopping can help you look clearer at *"the interests of others."* Running around being so busy with worldly chores can cause you to miss the important things right in front of your eyes. If you stop and look, you may see something to help your own life. You may also see the needs of others and do something to fill those needs. Either way you are building up God's Kingdom.

This verse is very personal because it reminds me of my Mamaw and the day she passed away. I was with my Mamaw for her last breath and I called my wife to tell her the news. She pulled in to pick up our son at his Christian School and he was crying and being consoled by his teachers as he walked out to the car. When he sat in the car my wife told him his Mamaw passed away. My son said, "I knew she had passed away because God told me she would die today while I was in morning chapel."

I questioned my son later about chapel and he told me they were going over this Scripture in Philippians and it reminded him of his

Mamaw. This Scripture was truly her verse. I remember her going to feed the "Old Folks" when she was 80 years old. She always had many unfinished projects of her own because she would stop what she was doing to help others. When my cousin and I painted her home, she had at least 4 different colors on the house where she would start and then stop to help someone in need.

My Mamaw found joy in using the spiritual gifts God gave her to serve others. She was always looking for ways to bless others through her gratitude of what Jesus did for her. Be sure to stop and look at the needs around you and ask God how you can help those needs. An old saying states, "It's nice to be important but it's more important to be nice."

My Mamaw looked for ways to be nice! In the book *"Experiencing God,"* Henry Blackaby taught a very important life lesson. Look to see where God is working and get involved. God will show you where to find joy in serving Him if you will just stop and look. Ask Him for the plans He has for your life and where you should serve based on the way He created you. Look to help others but also look to God and rejoice in what He has done for you. Look for ways to become what He created you to be.

If I had not joined a Christian men's organization where I looked and saw God working, this book would have never been written. I rejoice over the needs of others being met through this organization. I rejoice even more that the pain and suffering of other's lives can be carefully crafted into a plan which helps people avoid the same pitfalls in their own lives. I pray this book helps you avoid those pitfalls.

> *"I suddenly saw that all the time it was not I who had been seeking God, but God who had been seeking me. I had made myself the centre of my own existence and had my back turned to God."*[4]
> -Bede Griffiths

This quote described me for decades. God never left me, I drifted from Him. It is difficult to see something behind you as you walk away. It is essential to turn around and look to God for answers. He is waiting for you to turn to Him so He can give you a hug and share the wonderful life He has in store for you. I am humbled that the God of the Universe seeks me!

LISTEN:

"The word 'listen' contains the same letters as the word silent."[5]
-Alfred Brendel

Listening seems more about forcing others to listen to our problems. We are like the examples in Psalms of people crying out to the Lord to listen to their dire situations. They wanted help from God but ignored the Fatherly advice in Proverbs for a better life. Many Old Testament prophets warned people to listen to God and turn away from their sins. Unfortunately being silent, listening to God and doing what He says is rare.

"We will not listen to the message you have spoken to us in the name of the Lord!" Jeremiah 44:16

Unfortunately, they usually did not to listen to the warnings and they ended up in disastrous situations. They didn't want to listen to God and fix their own problems. They wanted God to fix their problems so they could continue living a life of sin. They were so caught up in their own sins they were blinded to being able to understand the end result of those sins. How well do you listen to God about your sins leading to your destruction? Do you allow God to help you repent and reject those old sins? Do you listen to Him and understand what He wants you to do?

"Jesus called the crowd to him and said, "Listen and understand." Matthew 15:10

Listen to what God has in store for your life. Yes, there will be times you will need to ask God to listen to you but always give Him your ears following your requests. An old saying states, *"Overwork your ears if you want to, but give your tongue a vacation."* You need to listen to Jesus and understand Him because He has a plan for your life and He knows what is best for you!

> *"While he was still speaking, a bright cloud covered them, and a voice from the cloud said, "This is my Son, whom I love; with him I am well pleased. Listen to him!"*
> Matthew 17:5

Jesus showed up to be baptized by John the Baptist and received a literal glowing message from the Father to listen to the Son He loves. With a recommendation like that, don't you think He may have some pretty good advice for you?

> *"My sheep listen to my voice; I know them, and they follow me. I give them eternal life, and they shall never perish; no one will snatch them out of my hand."*
> John 10:27-28

You need to listen and train yourself to hear God so you can follow Him. Ok, don't freak out because you say you cannot hear God! It will take several pages of instruction just to get you started on this journey. Hang in there and remember this is a one-step-at-a-time journey! The best way to hear God is to get to know God and His Word.

While at a Christian retreat my table group was discussing the Holy Spirit. It was a crowded room and most tables had finished their discussions and the room was getting loud from the chatter. I then heard a friend from across the room speak. I could make out what he said over the background chatter and I expressed to the group this is what it feels like to hear from God. If you have a friend you spend a great deal of time with you will know their voice. It is the same with God; only by spending time with Him will you know His voice. Listening comes in many forms but it comes best from knowing God better. Stop, look, and listen, then follow Him to become what He created you to be.

> *"Do not merely listen to the word, and so deceive yourselves.*
> *Do what it says."*   James 1:22

James really gets to the bottom of things quickly without any fluff. I look at his book of the Bible as a no-nonsense mini-Bible. His first four verses go kind of like this; I'm James, Hello, enjoy the ludicrous hogwash you are going to encounter because it's going to toughen you up and make you a better Christian. WOW! Nice to meet you too, James. Obviously James is a doer and probably could not stand committees wasting time trying to decide how to complete a project. I could see James going out to *"do what it says"* and finish the project while others were arguing over the details.

> *"The Bible reveals the Father's overall plan for the world and*
> *provides general guidelines for life. But how can we know His*
> *specific plans for us? Listening to God is essential to walking with*
> *God."*[6]   -Charles Stanley

You need to not only read God's Word; you need to study His Word in order to understand Him better. Go to church and hear God's Word. Go to Sunday school and dig deeper into God's Word with others. Go to your quiet place and spend time in God's Word to grow your relationship with Him. The more you understand the easier it is to listen to God and His plan for your life. Be sure to pray but don't forget to listen to His answer and *"do what it says."*

> *"If any of you lacks wisdom, you should ask God, who gives*
> *generously to all without finding fault, and it will be given*
> *to you."*   James 1:5

Slow down and simply ask for wisdom and then listen. The wisdom you seek is what God has had planned for you before he created the universe. Remember it's real hard to get a hug from Jesus when you are running by Him. Stop to enjoy a hug and look at how much He loves you then listen to His advice and follow Him. Let Him show you have to use your spiritual gifts to grow your Faith.

It took many years of getting to know God better and receive spiritual healing. Through those years I realized how much He actually loves me. I began to trust Him more and this trust grew my Faith in Him. I stopped focusing so much on my own needs and began looking at other's needs. I began to see needs in the lives of my brothers and sisters in Christ around me.

I wasn't completely clear what all the needs of others were so I asked for wisdom and then I listened. Despite the sinner I am, God showed me how Satan attacks our weaknesses based on our spiritual gifts. God generously gave me those plans. He laid out Satan's "Battle Plans" for how he tries to kill our spiritual gifts, steal our joy and destroy our life's purpose.

I asked for the plans and I followed Him to write this book so I could be a doer of the Word and share those plans with you. How will you listen and become a doer of God's Word? Are you willing to put in the time and effort to learn how Satan plans to attack you each and every day of your life? Do you want a heads up about how to prevent those attacks? Do you want to know your purpose and discover why you are here?

Stop being ignorant about the spiritual gifts God gave you and look around. Are you surrounded by bad company who is corrupting you? Are you listening to the world or God to discover your purpose for being here? Do you think the world or God will help you remove the sin which is leading to your destruction? Become what God created you to be; a Christian using their spiritual gifts to follow God's plan for their lives.

If God had told me 20 years ago that this book would take this long to write, I would have told Him to find someone else. Fortunately I stayed the course through many a storm and finished the work He laid out for me. Through all the demonic attacks I still feel blessed to share this with you. My Faith has grown by leaps and bounds through following Him!

"God never loses sight of the treasure which He has placed in our earthen vessels."[7]   -Charles Spurgeon

"So then, just as you received Christ Jesus as Lord, continue to live your lives in him, rooted and built up in him, strengthened in the faith as you were taught, and overflowing with thankfulness. See to it that no one takes you captive through hollow and deceptive philosophy, which depends on human tradition and the elemental spiritual forces of this world rather than on Christ."
Colossians 2:6-8

PONDERING POINTS

On a scale of 1-10 rate your knowledge of spiritual gifts?
Do you know your spiritual gifts?
Do you believe most people know their spiritual gifts?
Have you ever been influenced by "bad company?"
Have you seen men or women of God fall to Satan's attacks?
What did you do to get away from "bad company" in your life?
Who had the biggest "Christian" influence on your life?
What was it like when you accepted Jesus into your Heart?
Was there a moment in your life which pointed you to Christ?
What are some areas you felt like you have grown in Christ?
What are some areas you feel weak in your Christianity?
What are ways you should STOP?
What are ways you should LOOK?
What are ways you should LISTEN?
What fears keep you so busy you cannot stop, look and listen?

CHAPTER THREE

HOW TO BEGIN HEARING FROM GOD

"The Lord said, 'Go out and stand on the mountain in the presence of the Lord, for the Lord is about to pass by.' Then a great and powerful wind tore the mountains apart and shattered the rocks before the Lord, but the Lord was not in the wind. After the wind there was an earthquake, but the Lord was not in the earthquake. After the earthquake came a fire, but the Lord was not in the fire. And after the fire came a gentle whisper."   1 Kings 19:11-12

What the world needs is an amplifier for the *"gentle whisper"* of God. Some believers have some major hearing problems but there is nothing wrong with their ears. They hear what they want to hear and ignore the rest. They are so busy with the worries, riches and pleasures of life they only hear parts of the message. They may even completely miss God's plan for their life all together.

Christians who are unfamiliar with God's voice will accept any message that is not of Him. Sadly the voice they hear may have a lot of truth in it but the questionable 1% lie is accepted because the majority of the message feels right. Eventually the voice keeps pushing the Christian off course until they are trapped in sin. Only when the Christian looks back will they realize all of the opportunities they had to change their course and keep themselves out of the mess they're in now. If only they had known God's voice and listened to Him and not the 1% lie!

GOD'S RADIO SIGNAL

God desires to communicate with you all the time but do you hear Him? Think of a radio picking up a broadcast signal from a distant city. The radio is you trying to hear God's voice, the signal. First, plug the radio into a power source. This is getting saved and connecting to God's power through the Holy Spirit. Second, you need to know how to operate the radio. This is building a relationship with your Creator and learning how He communicates with you through Bible study, church and sharing with other believers. Third, you need to be on the right channel to hear from God. If you are slightly off the real station, the signal can be completely gone or another station could bleed through and gives you the wrong information from the enemy.

Even when you are on the right station there can be static and interference. Background static, caused by the worldly issues in your life, makes the words difficult and sometimes impossible to understand. The static covers God's voice and represents the worries, riches and pleasures of the world. They scream for attention and are never satisfied. It clutters our life with "busy-ness" of no eternal value and pulls us away from God's voice.

Interference is the voices from other channels trying to take you off course. Satan will throw everything at you to destroy anything good in your life but it is usually slow and calculated. Interference usually happens due to a weak signal from drifting away from God's signal. The signal is being broadcast fine but the radio travels further away from the station and begins to pick up another station. This messages Satan broadcasts are designed to mislead and create confusion.

The message of interference is sin but sometimes it's not obvious. The message sounds so tempting it makes you think doing something a little off course wouldn't hurt anything or anybody. Unfortunately your thoughts turn into actions and your actions turns into habits and your habits destroy you and those around you. You need to cut through the static and interference of your life and focus on the main signal from our Creator. If you know your Creator, you can trust the signal from Him and be the person He created you to be.

EXAMPLES OF STATIC AND INTERFERENCE:

WORLDLY STATIC	**SATAN'S INTERFERENCE**
Occasional social drink	Alcohol and Drug abuse
Flirting and second looks	Sex outside marriage
Loving Sports	Idol worship
High Work Ethic	Neglect of Family
Worry	Panic and Paralyzing Fear
Accept Foul language	Cussing openly which destroys God's message
Entertaining Movie	Accept nudity then pornography

There are many more examples of Worldly Static and Satan's Interference. Each of us has weaknesses that need to be recognized in order to avoid the destruction that can come from them. We need to reduce the Worldly Static through our choices by taking our thoughts captive and develop a mind like Christ. We need to know how our specific spiritual gifts are attacked by Satan and how to begin hearing from God to recognize good from evil and choose His goodness over the World's evil.

We need to reduce Satan's Interference by putting on the Armor of God and being ready for the fight. Even with Armor we cannot fight alone. Surround yourself with loving people of God and share the truth together. When you need to hear from God, the best way to have a clear signal is to stay close to the source. Stay in God's Word, stay with God's people and listen carefully to the plans He has for you. He has some amazing days planned for your future, you only need to listen and follow!

2-STEPS TO KNOWING WHEN GOD IS SPEAKING TO YOU

1) 100% of the time when God speaks to you, it will never go against His Word.

2) 99% of the time when God speaks to you, you'll probably not want to do it!

The first rule is pretty simple to understand. God is never going to tell you to sin. The second rule sounds funny but I can't tell you how many times God has asked me to do something when I was completely exhausted and I thought the timing was terrible. But this is one of the ways I know it's of God and not of me.

While editing my book, two preachers questioned the second step and asked if the 99% was too high. I told them I jokingly came up with the number to make a point but after running the numbers I actually felt it was pretty accurate. If the world is only about 30% Christian and only 25% attend church regularly and less than 20% are involved in serving at their church then less than 98% of the world is not "wanting" to follow God's Will.

Add to that number to the percentage of Christians who are called to preach or teach and they "bargain" with God for less responsibility like being a greeter or parking attendant at church. The number could easily reach the "99% of the time" as it becomes very obvious most people do not want to do what God calls them to do. Imagine what it's like for God to accomplish His will with the 1%? The 1% still needs to eat, work and sleep. I doubt God has even a small percent of a percent to work with when dealing with all of us to accomplish His perfect will.

BEING OBEDIENT WITH GOD'S TIMING

So I ask, are you a Christian by Culture, Belief or Obedience? If you call yourself a Christian because your parents and grand-parents were Christians you are a Cultural Christian. There is no relationship with God. If you believe Jesus is the Son of God but do not practice your religion with church attendance and serving others you are a Believing Christian. You have a place in Heaven but you are not producing any fruit on Earth. Your life here is empty and lacking true joy in knowing you helped others into heaven. The Obedient Christian follows the plans God has for them and helps build up the Body of Christ. They have rich amounts of fruit in their life from helping build up the Kingdom of God. They know what true joy is when God uses them to build up others and bring people to Christ.

SALVATION ARMY

Several years ago I came out of our local grocery store and a lady was ringing the bell for Salvation Army. After dropping some money in the bucket I went to my truck, cranked it and put it in reverse. God impressed upon me to go and pray for the lady.

I was tired, hungry and it had been a long day at work. All I wanted to do was to go home, make a sandwich and go to bed. I made a smart remark back to God and said, "What's it about anyway?" Then I heard the word, "Family!" so clear I looked in the back seat of my truck.

Being the most awesome spiritual person I know I jumped out of my truck and ran in to pray for the lady and her family. Actually I was the disobedient 3 year old Child of God and I choose to ignore Him and went home. Over the next several days I was woke up at 3:00 am every morning and found myself praying for this woman's family. Nearly a week of this went by and I finally had enough and grumpily decided to go back to the grocery store and pray for her family.

I don't know why I knew but I knew she'd be there that night. Sure enough she was there ringing the bell. I walked up to her, shared the story and asked her if it made any sense. She looked at me like I hit her in the face with a brick and she said, "My son was put in prison a couple of weeks ago." Immediately I felt a massive weight of guilt fall over me for allowing this poor lady to suffer an additional week. God not only knew what was going on in her life but He actually cared enough about her to let her know He knew about the circumstances.

You cannot be like Jonah who did not want to tell Israel's enemies at Nineveh to turn from their wickedness. Jonah was allowed to say no but God allowed him to spend three days in a fish's belly and get back with Him. While in the fish Jonah prayed for God to help him and then he repented and began to praise God. Jonah delivered God's message and the people of Nineveh repented.

> *"He [Jesus] replied, 'Blessed rather are those who hear the word of God and obey it.'"*   Luke 11:28

This encounter with God taught me a valuable lesson about obedience and God's timing. When you hear from Him, do what He says and do it as quickly as possible. If you have a problem with step #2 for hearing from God you may be spiritually constipated. You need some Biblical Metamucil to move yourself out of the way and let God move through you! Remember, more of Him and less of you. More of you tends to clog the pipes, more of Him frees up the flow of His power. Learn this step toward maturity quickly so God can flow through you. In order to hear from God you need to be a willing and obedient vessel and He will work miracles through you.

> *"The willingness to obey every word from God is critical to hearing God speak."*[8]
>
>   Henry T. Blackaby, Hearing God's Voice

God has used angels, visions, and miracles to speak to His people. He will speak to you through His Word but He can use many other means to communicate with you. He can use circumstances, music, preaching or other Godly people to get a message to you.

He may even speak to you in His voice or speak to you through thoughts and dreams. God can use anything in the universe to get your attention. He even used a donkey to get a message across to Balaam for his disobedience in Numbers 22:21-39. Do your best to get away from the Worldly Static and Satan's Interference and dwell on Godly thoughts throughout the day.

FINDING THE PEACE OF GOD

"Rejoice in the Lord always. I will say it again: Rejoice! Let your gentleness be evident to all. The Lord is near. Do not be anxious about anything, but in every situation, by prayer and petition, with thanksgiving, present your requests to God. And the peace of God, which transcends all understanding, will guard your hearts and your minds in Christ Jesus. Finally, brothers and sisters, whatever is true, whatever is noble, whatever is right, whatever is pure, whatever is lovely, whatever is admirable—if anything is excellent or praiseworthy—think about such things. Whatever you have learned or received or heard from me, or seen in me—put it into practice. And the God of peace will be with you." Philippians 4:4-9

Do you *"think about such things?"* Are you willing to *"put it into practice"* what He says when you get His message? I've worked on this book for almost 20 years and poured my life into it even through a horrible year in 2020. It was one of the worst years of my life yet I had a peace *"which transcends all understanding."* The following year I did not have the same *"peace of God."*

One day, while struggling to understand what was happening; my friend quoted the part of this Scripture about *"think about such things"* as he had done dozens of times before. I was to the point of ignoring my friend when he quoted this Scripture but this time he mentioned the *"peace of God"* and it caught my ear. As he spoke with someone else I looked up the verses on my phone and received the answer as to why I was no longer at peace. I had been thinking, studying and writing things of God intensely for many years but now things were different.

COVID had shut down the Christian retreat where I served regularly. I had given my book out to a dozen friends for their opinions and corrections and waited months for their replies. I worked on the corporate side of publishing with ISBN numbers, formatting, copyrights, references, the website, and the printing. I decreased my time with God and drifted from Him. I lost His peace but I did gain it back as I pushed forward to finish the book and restored my regular relationship with Him.

We all struggle with staying in God's presence for extended amounts of time. I wonder how long we can stay close to God as Satan tries to lure us away. How long can we listen to preaching, read Scripture and sing praises to God? How long can we serve others? The reminder is that our life is a marathon and not a sprint. Pace yourself and make Jesus your example in all circumstances. Think on the things of God and keep making good decisions that will mature you in Christ. This will reduce the static and help you hear and understand Him better.

LOOKING BACK TO SEE FORWARD

There will be patterns in the steps God lays out for you because He always has a plan for your life. In the book *Experiencing God*, Henry Blackaby spoke about God's plan for your life and how to recognize the direction He is taking you. It asks you to look at your past and see the mile markers where God helped you change directions in your life. By looking back at those markers from the past you can see the direction

God is taking you now. Looking back helps us understand His plan is a lifelong process and change doesn't happen overnight. In many cases it takes many years of God working with us and through us to achieve His purpose for our life.

> *"The Lord makes firm the steps of the one who delights in him; though he may stumble, he will not fall, for the Lord upholds him with his hand."*   Psalm 37: 23-24

Our goal is to become as Christ-like as possible one step at a time. In order to be like Him we need to learn more about Him and the more we know Him the more we trust Him. The more we trust Him the more we become what He created us to be right up to the time we enter heaven with Him. We should strive to become better Christians every day and build on what God has already done in our lives. God wants us to be fearless in our pursuit of Him. Remember, no "Burned out for Jesus" T-shirts!

GOD CAN LOVE THE FEAR OUT OF US

> *"For God did not give us a spirit of timidity or cowardice or fear, but [He has given us a spirit] of power and of love and of sound judgment and personal discipline [abilities that result in a calm, well-balanced mind and self-control]."*
> 2 Timothy 1:7 AMP Amplified Bible

One of my greatest fears was public speaking. During a demonstration speech in College I made Bananas Foster for the class. Unfortunately the portable single eye cook top was not very hot and it took a lot longer than I expected to heat up the large amount of dessert. I ran out of material to talk about and there was a lot of dead air space. I was graciously given a decent grade for a very poor performance but I give the delicious dessert the credit. When in doubt, feed others!

When I opened my practice I was invited to become a member of our local Rotary club and soon made vice president. My responsibilities were to invite speakers to our meetings, give announcements and introduce the speakers in front of the small club every week. The President un-expectantly resigned from the club two months later making me the president. I was not ready to be president but God had a plan. I still got up every week and made the announcements and introduced speakers but now I had to give out yearly awards in front of hundreds of prominent citizens from Montevallo.

I had to give awards to Brenda Schneckenburger and Brittany Beiersdoerfer whose names are forever etched into my permanent memory. I was, to say the least, terrified to mess up their names! To top off the evening I was to follow the Mayor, Ralph Sears. I thought to myself, "Great, I get to follow a man who has spent decades on radio, owned a radio station and has been Mayor for the last hundred years." I heard him speak at many functions and he was a very smooth public speaker.

Mr. Sears moved to the podium like a pro and proceeded to make his announcements and then, to my amazement, he messed up! He laughed it off and moved on. At that moment my butterflies began to fly in formation. If this man could mess up and laugh about it, I could easily do the same. That was the moment God had planned for me to conquer my fear of public speaking because He had plans for me.

By the way, I made it through the speech with a good opening joke and pronounced the names correctly. Since then I have shared my Faith in front of several groups. Looking back I can see where God worked in my life even though I was not walking close with Him during this time in my life. God loves me so much He would not leave me where I was at and He continued to work on me to prepare me to speak in front of others for His glory.

> *"I will instruct you and teach you in the way you should go;*
> *I will counsel you with my loving eye on you."*
> Psalm 32:8

God instructed me and taught me the way I should go. He continued to work with me and help shape me when I did not know what was best for my own life! Are you at a stage where you are willing to become what your Creator created you to be? Are you willing to take the steps He knows are best for your future? By the way, I was not following God at this time in my life but He still has His *"loving eye on me"* because He loves me and knew my potential.

You may be a little anxious to hit the road and discover your purpose. By working on a solid foundation in Christ you will learn how much God loves you. Moving from the realization you were broken and needed a Savior to rebuilding yourself through God's help will be one of your most important steps in maturing your Christian walk. Enjoy this time as God does a Spiritual restoration on you. Get to know Him better and let Him love on you so you can hear His voice.

If you are like me, you'll need several knocks to the head before you realize God is speaking to you. He is gracious and will most likely give you several messages through different areas to confirm the action He desires from you. If you are listening you'll get the instructions. The more I got to know God the more I learned His voice. The more I listened the more I trusted Him and the more I trusted Him the more I followed Him.

> *"'If anyone has ears to hear, let them hear.' 'Consider carefully what you hear,' he continued. 'With the measure you use, it will be measured to you—and even more.'"*
> Mark 4:23-24

I've reached the *"and even more"* part of hearing from God and I have an urgency to get the message of this book out to believers as soon as possible. I joke about being 12 months pregnant with this book but it's how urgent I feel to share this information with you.

Earlier I asked, ""Why Are Spiritual Gifts Important to Your Purpose"
My heart is heavy watching people being destroyed by Satan. We all
need the plans on how to avoid Satan's attacks and to help others with
attacks on their lives. Most Christians have a very poor understanding
of spiritual gifts. Books and sermons rarely tackle the warnings about
the spiritual gifts and almost never discuss the way Satan attacks their
weaknesses.

> *"There are different kinds of gifts, but the same Spirit
> distributes them."*   1 Corinthians 12:4

You are called to be a part of the Body of Christ because you cannot do
it alone. You need to work together with other Believers for the greatest
good because the gifts are all from the same Spirit. The spiritual gifts are
designed to build up the Body of Christ and bring others into the Body.
The spiritual gifts are needed to unify the church rather than divide it.
We need to all finish this race together.

FINISHING THE RACE

> *"For I am already being poured out like a drink offering,
> and the time for my departure is near. I have fought the good
> fight, I have finished the race, I have kept the faith. Now
> there is in store for me the crown of righteousness, which the
> Lord, the righteous Judge, will award to me on that day—
> and not only to me, but also to all who have longed for his
> appearing."*   2 Timothy 4:6-8

The last thing you say with your last breath may start an avalanche
of Christ's work that will spread through many generations. Will you
know what to say in your last breath? Will you hear God in those last
few seconds of your life? Will your life make a difference?

"His master replied, 'Well done, good and faithful servant!
You have been faithful with a few things; I will put you
in charge of many things. Come and share your master's
happiness!'"   Matthew 25:21

This is what I yearn to hear when I take my last breath and come face to face with Jesus, **"Well done, good and faithful servant?"** Don't you want Jesus to say you made a difference with your life? If God is trying to do something different in your life it doesn't mean it's wrong. As long as the message stays the same the delivery can be completely different. It has been said, *"The definition of insanity is doing the same thing over and over again and expecting a different result."* Our churches do not sing Gregorian chants so we need to sing a new song to reach the lost! We need to change the delivery of the message in order to reach the new generations but keep the message the same.

PRAISE MUSIC

I was at a friend's home one evening when his elderly Mother said they needed to leave. She went on to say, "We're going to a revival" in a slow sad Eeyore voice. She sounded like she was going to her own funeral so I asked her, "Why so gloomy?" She said, in the same voice, "There will probably be praise music." I told her I was blessed to grow up with old hymns and the praise music and I enjoy them both. I told her I love *I'll Fly Away, Mansion over the Hilltop, Take my Hand Precious Lord,* and *Peace in the Valley* but these type songs all have something in common. They all say, "Kill me now and take me home!"

I asked her to try something different while she was at the meeting. I asked her to listen to the words of the praise music and not the modern beat of the music. Listen to what the song is saying in its lyrics. I explained that most praise songs are simply worshiping God and being in His presence. Other praise songs give us actions to build up God's Kingdom. I explained God wants us to be living out our best Christian life up until our last breath. It's ok to be grateful for the eternity we have been given but it's much more important to finish what God prepared for us to do while here on earth.

I saw her a short time later and asked if she followed my suggestion about listening to the words of the praise music. With a big grin she thanked me and gave me a grateful hug. I felt like I gave her a little boost to finish the race the Lord had laid out for her.

You need to stop doing the same things over and over again expecting life to change. It's like running around a track and falling into a pothole in the track. You get up, brush yourself off and start running again only to fall in the same hole again. If you never fix the pot holes in your life then why are you surprised when you fall? You need to conquer your fears and allow God to replace those fears with His loving purpose for your life!

STOP and ask God to reveal what spiritual gifts you have been given by Him.

LOOK for ways you can help build up the Body of Christ. Be cautious and look for the traps Satan will set for you to keep you from doing good works.

LISTEN to the *"gentle whisper"* from God for instructions on His plans for you.

BE WHAT GOD CREATED YOU TO BE and do what He is calling you to do. Follow Him into a life filled with the joy from being used by your Creator and becoming a *"well done good and faithful servant."*

"Nevertheless, each person should live as a believer in whatever situation the Lord has assigned to them, just as God has called them. This is the rule I lay down in all the churches." 1 Corinthian 7:17

PONDERING POINTS

What hinders you from hearing from God?

What is the "Worldly Static" in your life?

What worries, riches and pleasures of the world keep you from hearing from God?

What is "Satan's Interference" in your life?

Has God ever asked you to do something?

Were you obedient to God's calling?

Has God ever asked you to do something you didn't want to do?

Have you ever not done what God asked you to do?

How did you feel when you did not do what God asked of you?

Have you ever received multiple messages from God?

Has God worked in your past to bring you here today?

Is doing the same thing over and over again driving you insane?

What will you say with your last breath?

What's keeping you from being a *"good and faithful servant?"*

What are the ongoing attacks you face on a regular basis?

What fears keep you from hearing God's voice?

CHAPTER FOUR

WHAT ARE SPIRITUAL GIFTS?

"Each of you should use whatever gift you have received to serve others, as faithful stewards of God's grace in its various forms. If anyone speaks, they should do so as one who speaks the very words of God. If anyone serves, they should do so with the strength God provides, so that in all things God may be praised through Jesus Christ."

1 Peter 4:10-11

Spiritual gifts are God-given abilities to fulfill the mission of the church through love. They are given freely by God's grace to build up, encourage and comfort the church to glorify Him.

DO ALL CHRISTIANS HAVE SPIRITUAL GIFTS?

In chapter two you saw the confusion surrounding spiritual gifts. There was even a large group of Christians that thought they had no gift at all. Scripture clearly states ***"Each of you should use whatever gift you have received to serve others."*** It doesn't say for the special few that received a gift from God, it says ***"Each of you."*** We all have spiritual gifts.

"We have different gifts, according to the grace given us."
Romans 12:6

Here the words ***"We"*** and ***"us"*** are used, not "some" or "a few" which indicates God has given all of us spiritual gifts to build up His Kingdom. The Greek word for gift is Charisma which comes from the word Charis meaning grace. These gifts are blessings of undeserved favor from God.

They are given to us by God through His grace for us to show His grace and love to others.

> *"All these are the work of one and the same Spirit, and he gives them [gifts] to each one, just as he determines."*
> 1 Corinthians 12:11

The spiritual gifts come from the Holy Spirit and God gives them as He chooses. God knew what would be best for us before He formed us in the womb and He knows what spiritual gifts would be best for us to become what He created us to be.

> *"I wish that all of you were as I am. But each of you has your own gift from God; one has this gift, another has that."*
> 1 Corinthians 7:7

Without question, all Christians have spiritual gifts! Scripture remains clear that *"each of you has your own gift from God."*

> *"There are different kinds of gifts, but the same Spirit distributes them. There are different kinds of service, but the same Lord. There are different kinds of working, but in all of them and in everyone it is the same God at work. Now to each one the manifestation of the Spirit is given for the common good."*
> 1 Corinthians 12:4-7

It's clear there are different spiritual gifts and *"the same Spirit distributes them."* It goes on to individualize the spiritual gifts by saying *"Now to each one the manifestation of the Spirit is given for the common good."* Clearly God wants you to know you have spiritual gifts.

If you think you don't have a spiritual gift from God it boils down to feeling unworthy of receiving a gift from Him. Remember, you are worthy and you have value because He wants to be with you in heaven for an eternity. Stop looking at the way Satan condemns you; he is trying to get you to focus on your flaws. Look at the way God sees you through Jeremiah.

> *"'For I know the plans I have for you,' declares the Lord, 'plans to prosper you and not to harm you, plans to give you hope and a future. Then you will call on me and come and pray to me, and I will listen to you. You will seek me and find me when you seek me with all your heart."*
>
> Jeremiah 29:11-13

The God of the Universe has *"plans to give you hope and a future."* Follow His plans step by step. Sure, you are going to stumble but get back up and keep going. You'll find amazing joy when you use your spiritual gifts to build up the Body of Christ. The joy from a job well done you will grow your Faith and help you find purpose and fulfillment in your life. If God made you to be a hammer get out of the room of bolts and find some nails! Ask God what you were created to be and ask Him to show you where you need to be.

HOW LONG DO SPITITUAL GIFTS LAST?

> *"for God's gifts and his call are irrevocable."*
>
> Romans 11:29

God gave freely His gifts and promises to the patriarchs of Israel and never broke His covenant with them no matter what they did. In the same way, when you accept the invitation to believe in His Son you are guaranteed salvation and a place in heaven.

God's gifts give you your abilities but His calling gives you your identity in Christ. Your spiritual gifts were freely given to you through God's grace and He will not take them away. They are yours forever and you have the freedom to use them in any way you see fit, good or bad. This is free will but our relationship with Him helps us use them for good.

My son was given a much wanted 1999 Isuzu Vehicross as a gift for his 16th birthday. This unique vehicle was 12 years old when it was purchased for him and he greatly enjoyed his new ride. Could his gift be taken away by the giver? In this case it very well could have been taken away in a heartbeat if rules were not followed. This is not how God gives spiritual gifts. You have the choice of how and when you would like to use your gifts. But God will allow consequences for our bad choices. An example with the Vehicross would be my son driving recklessly and it leads to an accident.

My son had the ability to run drugs in his vehicle but is that pleasing to the one who gave it to him? Not at all! My hope is that he uses it wisely for school, work, recreation and safely transporting friends and family. In the same way God wants a loving relationship with Him so you can use your gifts unselfishly for your entire life. This is where you will find your purpose and joy in life.

THE DIFFERENCE BETWEEN A TALENT AND A GIFT

"Now to the one who works, wages are not credited to him as a gift, but as an obligation."   Romans 4:4

Spiritual gifts are given to us for our lifetime and we can use them in any way we like. They are given through grace which has no strings attached. They are given for you to *"work"* for a living. The reward or *"wages"* for working with your talents simply takes care of your debts or *"obligations"* from daily living expenses. This is not *"credited"* as a gift, which is a blessing from your relationship with God.

"However, to the one who does not work but trusts God who justifies the ungodly, their faith is credited as righteousness."
Romans 4:5

A person who uses their talent, acquired by their work, receives a reward to make a living. But those who rely on Faith and put their trust in God will have righteousness given to them. This shows our Faith, not our works, gives us the *"righteousness"* needed to enter heaven.

If a man enters into a contract to perform a service he is owed for his service. It is neither a gift nor favor to pay him, he has earned his wages. If a man could work out his own righteousness then God would owe that man salvation. That would go against the following verse:

> *"And if by grace, then it cannot be based on works; if it were, grace would no longer be grace."*
>
> Romans 11:6

God's grace undeservingly purifies us for Heaven through righteousness. This is accomplished simply by our Faith and trust in Him. Once this happens, our love for God allows our talents to be used as spiritual gifts so we can give back to Him for all He has done for us.

> *"For the kingdom of heaven is like a man traveling to a far country, who called his own servants and delivered his goods to them. And to one he gave five talents, to another two, and to another one, to each according to his own ability; and immediately he went on a journey. Then he who had received the five talents went and traded with them, and made another five talents. And likewise he who had received two gained two more also. But he who had received one went and dug in the ground, and hid his lord's money. After a long time the lord of those servants came and settled accounts with them. "* Matthew 25:14-19 NKJV

The man here has absolute ownership over his servants. He gives out *"talents"* to increase his kingdom based on their abilities while he was gone for a long time. The NIV Bible calls the talents "bags of gold" and two of the servants doubled their gold and the other one hid his gold in the ground.

"So he who had received five talents came and brought five other talents, saying, 'Lord, you delivered to me five talents; look, I have gained five more talents besides them.' His lord said to him, 'Well done, good and faithful servant; you were faithful over a few things, I will make you ruler over many things. Enter into the joy of your lord.' He also who had received two talents came and said, 'Lord, you delivered to me two talents; look, I have gained two more talents besides them.' His lord said to him, 'Well done, good and faithful servant; you have been faithful over a few things, I will make you ruler over many things. Enter into the joy of your lord.'" Matthew 25:20-23 NKJV

When the servant doubled their talents, **"His lord said to him, 'Well done,** good and faithful servant; you were faithful over a few things, I will make you ruler over many things. Enter into the joy of your lord.'"** Chapter 25 of Matthew is about the *"kingdom of heaven."* The heavenly side of this parable describes what happens when we do good things with what we have been given.

"Then he who had received the one talent came and said, 'Lord, I knew you to be a hard man, reaping where you have not sown, and gathering where you have not scattered seed. And I was afraid, and went and hid your talent in the ground. Look, there you have what is yours.' But his lord answered and said to him, 'You wicked and lazy servant, you knew that I reap where I have not sown, and gather where I have not scattered seed. So you ought to have deposited my money with the bankers, and at my coming I would have received back my own with interest. So take the talent from him, and give it to him who has ten talents. For to everyone who has, more will be given, and he will have abundance; but from him who does not have, even what he has will be taken away. And cast the unprofitable servant into the outer darkness. There will be weeping and gnashing of teeth.'" Matthew 25:24-30 NKJV

God gives people their talents so they will have abilities to survive in this world. Each of the three servants used their talents to work for their food, clothing and housing. Only two decided to do more for the Master and gift back their talents to him. The third servant made excuses for his lack of work. How many people make excuses for becoming a Christian? They say, "Christians are Hypocrites and judgmental so why would they want to be one of them?" They continue with God being hard on Christians by telling them what they can and can't do.

The servant even knew the Master explored new areas to expand His Kingdom yet he was too lazy to even take the gold to the bank for interest. Unfortunately there is a time where everyone will be accountable for what they did with the talents given to them by God. If they never developed a relationship with Him their talents will be taken away and they will be casted *"into the outer darkness. There will be weeping and gnashing of teeth."* This image of the parable is the hopeless and grieving side of Hell.

So a talent and a gift are one in the same. The talent of Helps can build a house for a paycheck yet it becomes a gift when used to build a home for those in need through Habitat for Humanity. Someone with the talent of Teaching can draw a salary teaching students but they could use it as a gift to teach Sunday school or produce a blog to teach about Jesus. What makes the gifts special is when the members of the Body of Christ work together toward a common goal to build up the church. This is when our talents become our gift back to God.

THE BAD AND UGLY SIDE OF TALENTS

"All of us have become like one who is unclean, and all our righteous acts are like filthy rags; we all shrivel up like a leaf, and like the wind our sins sweep us away."
Isaiah 64:6

Without a relationship with God all of our *"righteous acts"* are like monthly minstrel rags to Him. Our God-given talents are only of value when they are used to Glorify God and build up the Body of Christ. Imagine if each Christian brought one person to Christ; we could have another 2 Billion Christians in the world!

But look at the dark side of gifts for a moment. Could someone sell Satan with their sales talent of Evangelism? It's done every day in satanic worship groups. Could the talent of evangelism sell their selves to form a cult? Could someone with a helps talent be given a hammer and build a temple to another god such as Buddha? They could also use it to build a stage for a dirty play or even murder someone with the same hammer.

If our selfish spirit is not reunited with God, then we can do bad things with our talents and abilities. By being united with God we have the Holy Spirit to train us to do better with our lives. Everything we were given by God can be used against His church. As bad as it hurts Him for his creation to have no Faith in Him, He still allows us the freedom of choice. We can either believe in Him or believe in something completely different or even nothing at all. God gave us talents and our spiritual gift is using those talents to build up God's Kingdom. By His grace they were given to us and by our appreciation for what He did for us on the cross, we give our gift back to Him.

Who do you love more, the world or God? Who are you more obedient to, the world or to God? A talent used for worldly works has no eternal value but when it becomes a spiritual gift used for God's Kingdom it can have endless possibilities. A selfless use of our talent is our gift back to God and with God involved there will be eternal rewards that can never be measured by any amount of time or money. Someone with the spiritual gift of Leadership may be able to lead soldiers into battle during times of war and come home to lead missionaries into dangerous situations to spread the Gospel of Christ. What is an eternity in heaven with God worth? Is it worth doing what God asks in order for someone to be in heaven with Jesus?

BE OBEDIENT TO GOD'S CALL

Some Spiritual gifts may just pop-up in your life. God has given you gifts to encourage and build up the Body of Christ. He will invite you to participate in His joy and His glory; you only need to accept His invitation.

Imagine working hard setting up tables for the Mission Team's dinner to make the place look perfect. Your goal is for the event to express God's love toward these people who are on the front lines for the church. You love to work behind-the-scenes to bless others and you really do not care to be in the spotlight. You simply enjoy just being a fly-on-the-wall. You fear speaking in front of people but during the dinner you feel like God is telling you to speak to one of the missionaries about spiritual matters. This is way out of your comfort zone.

You finally get up the nerve to share the message God gave you for them. Then the Holy Spirit intercedes and both of you end up crying together. The message you delivered was an answer to their prayer. You may not be an expert in the gift of Prophecy or Encouragement but you were a willing vessel to give a message to someone in need at just the right time. God saw you were available and willing and He wanted you to comfort them in their time of need.

Times like these can bring out Spiritual gifts through our obedience that was previously hidden within you. God knows He planted them there before you were born because He knew you would need them. All they needed was some good soil to produce a fruit-filled crop. Your willingness to serve God allowed your gift to break ground and bloom in that moment. Never be afraid to accept God's invitations, they will bless you and others.

"All these are the work of one and the same Spirit, and he distributes them to each one, just as he determines."
1 Corinthians 12:11

STOP thinking you have no spiritual gifts from God. Be a willing and available vessel and He will show your spiritual gifts to you.

LOOK for the ways you are good at serving others but always be available to the individual needing to hear from God.

LISTEN For God's voice to nudge you toward the gifts He has freely given you.

BE WHAT GOD CREATED YOU TO BE and look for the talents God placed within you and use them to build up the Body of Christ and express your gift back to God.

HOW TO ASK FOR SPIRITUAL GIFTS

Jesus says, "If you, then, though you are evil, know how to give good gifts to your children, how much more will your Father in heaven give good gifts to those who ask him!"
Matthew 7:11

You cannot purchase nor earn a spiritual gift but it doesn't mean you can't ask God to give you one. You shouldn't be afraid to ask for gifts because God wants to give you good gifts. But consider my Son's first vehicle. Did he have the experience to handle a new Ferrari? Was he ready for a high performance race car? There may be a Ferrari of a spiritual gift within you but you will need to learn how to drive it! It may look cute when a 16 year old cranks up and drives away in a new Ferrari but it usually will not end well.

"It is not great gifts that God blesses so much as it is great likeness to Christ."[9]   Robert Murray McCheyne

Be sure to ask to become more like Christ when you ask for another spiritual gift. It's good to be an experienced driver especially when it comes to using the gifts. But the fuel that runs the spiritual gifts is love.

"Follow the way of love and eagerly desire spiritual gifts, especially the gift of prophecy"   1 Corinthians 14:1

God wants us to *"desire"* His gifts but he also wants us to *"follow the way of love"* when it comes to asking for spiritual gifts. In other words what is the motive behind your desire for a gift? Years ago this very verse prompted me to ask for the spiritual gift of Prophecy and I eventually received the gift. When I say I received the gift, I actually opened the gift that was already inside of me.

I needed a lot of training to use it correctly. I had to be willing to put in the time to mature into my spiritual gift. It took years just to get a small grasp of how to use the gift. I never realized what was in store for me with this spiritual gift. At first it was difficult because of the "deep cleaning" necessary for me to hear God more clearly. The process of having to put into action the very things I spoke into other people's lives took its toll. I had to "do" the very thing I was asking others to do as I was tested and retested. If you plan to be a messenger for God then you need to start acting like the one who sent you in the first place!

TEACH GOD'S TRUTH THROUGH YOUR SPIRITUAL GIFTS

I remember the words I spoke into my son's High School Bible teacher's life. I explained to the teacher that Bible class was the main reason my son attended a Christian school. The reason I spent $5000 a year, with an additional $1500 in fuel costs to drive him to school, was because I wanted my son to hear about God while there. I felt the Bible class was the focus of the entire school and should be treated with the most respect. The Bible teacher should be the best, most punctual, most fun, most strict, most fair, most excited, most responsible, most everything positive a teacher could possibly be because Scripture states that teachers of the Word are held more accountable for their actions. The same goes for me; if I give a message to someone that shows them how to avoid sin then I should be willing to live my life in the same manner.

"Not many of you should become teachers, my fellow believers; because you know that we who teach will be judged more strictly. We all stumble in many ways. Anyone who is never at fault in what they say is perfect, able to keep their whole body in check. When we put bits into the mouths of horses to make them obey us, we can turn the whole animal. Or take ships as an example. Although they are so large and are driven by strong winds, they are steered by a very small rudder wherever the pilot wants to go. Likewise, the tongue is a small part of the body, but it makes great boasts. Consider what a great forest is set on fire by a small spark. The tongue also is a fire, a world of evil among the parts of the body. It corrupts the whole body, sets the whole course of one's life on fire, and is itself set on fire by hell."

James 3:1-6

Wow, James gets right to the point. Obviously James is big on the truth and how the truth is spread throughout God's Kingdom. I once told an audience I was going to show them the strongest muscle in the body. I asked them to stand up, bend forward at the waist, bend backwards, stand straight and raise your arms, now sit down. I then explained how my tongue was the strongest muscle in the room that day. It moved several tons of people with very little effort.

James wants us to know how important it is to teach the truth. You may write, speak, or sing but all of these require you to get the most truthful message out to others. Overall having the gift of Prophecy has been a blessing for me and others. The hardest thing to learn was obedience in the moment and having to practice what I preach. I had to realize there are small windows of opportunities associated with spiritual gifts that show the power of God. His Words and His timing are important so don't miss the still, small voice because that is where you will find the truth!

FOUR RED LETTER A'S

While serving on a Tres Dias weekend I was asked for a favor. The man asking was going through the weekend and I did not know him from Adam. He told me he had been praying and needed some verification. He then asked me to tell him what he was praying about. Truthfully the first thing in my head was, "I'm thinking of a man's name in China, what's his name?"

I had never used my gift in this way before, but I was crazy enough to say, "Yes." When I said yes to his request I immediately saw four red letter "A's" in my head and I knew exactly what they meant. I told him I would get with him after the next activity. I bargained a little with God and said I would soften the third letter "A" and I really did not want to go to the fourth letter "A."

About 30 minutes later I called him aside and asked if he was ready. He had such a carefree look on his face when I began. I started with the first letter "A" and asked if he was Angry with God, himself or both. He looked a bit more serious and said, "Both." I proceeded to the second letter "A" and I asked if Alcohol was a new problem or and an old problem that had come back. He had a shocked look on his face and responded, "A new problem." For the third letter "A" I softened up the word Adultery and asked him if lust had gone too far.

He began weeping uncontrollably on my shoulder and told me he had an affair on his first wife and lost the marriage. Later, his second wife had an affair and they divorced. He was in a very bad place in his life and was struggling. As we shared our lives, he told me how he and the second wife had trouble getting pregnant but they managed to finally get pregnant through the aid of doctors. After the breakup, his wife texted him and told him not worry about the baby because she had taken care of it. The fourth red letter "A" was Abortion.

The weekend was a huge blessing for the man who bravely asked a question to a stranger. He found out, without a shadow of a doubt, why he was there. God still loved and cared for him even though he was a sinner.

> *"Let us not become weary in doing good, for at the proper time we will reap a harvest if we do not give up. Therefore, as we have opportunity, let us do good to all people, especially to those who belong to the family of believers."*
>
> Galatians 6:9-10

Saying "Yes" to God can be some of the hardest steps you will ever take but it's what changes you and others. With business it's all about location, location, location but with God it's about timing, timing, timing! I often have to remember that I asked for this spiritual gift and God is in control. If you plan to ask for a gift, expect God to show you how to use it. I'm not trying to scare you, just stating the facts. You may be tired, hungry and extremely busy but God wants to use you at the exact right moment. You need to always say, "Yes Lord!"

> *"Then I heard the voice of the Lord saying, 'Whom shall I send? And who will go for us?" And I said, "Here am I. Send me!"'*
>
> Isaiah 6:8

HOW LONG DOES IT TAKE TO USE SPIRITUAL GIFTS?

> *"Are all apostles? Are all prophets? Are all teachers? Do all work miracles? Do all have gifts of healing? Do all speak in tongues? Do all interpret? But eagerly desire the greater gifts."*
>
> 1 Corinthians 12:29-31

I hope you will be inspired to *"eagerly desire"* and ask for spiritual gifts. Ask God for strengthening and training of spiritual gifts already present in you but remember there are steps involved. Some gifts come quickly but most will need building up much like muscles need exercise to grow in strength. Gifts require many things like discipline, obedience, and Faith. You wouldn't show up for a marathon without ever running around the block.

There is a time for training so stick to a spiritual routine and follow the steps God has for you. Stay in the Word, pray, listen, attend church, and spend time with others discussing Scriptures. Do not be disappointed if it takes time for your gift to be used in the ways you were expecting. Small victories will lead to bigger victories. There is a lot to be said for maturity among believers while using their gifts. We have enough religious fanatics who do more harm than good so always stay close to God and remember the 100% rule; hearing from God is always Biblical! Trust Him with what He has given you and do your best.

Jesus says, "Whoever can be trusted with very little can also be trusted with much, and whoever is dishonest with very little will also be dishonest with much. So if you have not been trustworthy in handling worldly wealth, who will trust you with true riches? And if you have not been trustworthy with someone else's property, who will give you property of your own?"
Luke 16:10-12

We need to show God and others we are being obedient with the little jobs that God entrusts us with. We need to be mentored by people we trust while practicing our gifts. We need people in our lives that will hold us accountable to do the right things and be honest with us when we mess up. Ask God to place the right people in your life for this very purpose.

DO YOUR JOURNEY WITH OTHER CHRISTIANS

"Two are better than one, because they have a good return for their labor: If either of them falls down, one can help the other up. But pity anyone who falls and has no one to help them up."
Ecclesiastes 4:9-10

Going through this world alone is like a chicken wandering through the woods filled with wolves. There will be a big target on your back and you'll easily be destroyed. There are times when we may need to be alone to rest and recharge with God but we should not give up meeting together. Being alone with God for a quiet time and finding direction is fine but be sure to share your journey with others. Being alone all the time is dangerous especially when it draws you away from God and other people who can help you grow in Christ.

> *"I am the vine; you are the branches. If you remain in me and I in you, you will bear much fruit; apart from me you can do nothing."*　　　John 15:5

Attending Sunday school, Promise Keepers or Fourth Day movements like Tres Dias, Walk to Emmaus or Cursillo can help you bond with other believers. These bonds could become a much needed Accountability Group for you and others to grow and encourage one another.

Being alone is dangerous but living apart from Jesus is even worse. Spiritual gifts work better when members of the Body of Christ work together in unity. With Him you can accomplish so much for the Kingdom but Satan would love to find you alone so he can take you down. Don't ever think you can do this world alone. God designed us to be an army fighting Satan together for the greater good!

> *"Humble yourselves, therefore, under God's mighty hand, that he may lift you up in due time. Cast all your anxiety on him because he cares for you. Be alert and of sober mind. Your enemy the devil prowls around like a roaring lion looking for someone to devour. Resist him, standing firm in the faith, because you know that the family of believers throughout the world is undergoing the same kind of sufferings. And the God of all grace, who called you to his eternal glory in Christ, after you have suffered a little while, will himself restore you and make you strong, firm and steadfast. To him be the power for ever and ever. Amen."*
> 1 Peter 5:6-11

You are part of a *"family of believers"* going up against an enemy *"looking for someone to devour."* As a Christian being alone is not a good idea. Having a family trained as an army covering your back is a much better idea. Stay the course and follow God's plan for your life and cover others back while you are fighting.

In *"due time"* Jesus can *"restore you"* from Satan's destruction in your life. Place your burdens on Him, seek humility and grow your Faith by getting to know Jesus better *"because he cares for you."* Stand firm against Satan with your family of believers and grow your Faith so Jesus can show His strength through your weakness.

Stay together, stay calm, stay focused and stay patient while waiting for God to train you to use your spiritual gifts. Look for mentors who are more mature with their gifts to help you with your gifts. Grow in Christ and let *"God's mighty hand"* work with you to *"make you strong, firm and steadfast."* Look to Him for your hope.

"But now, Lord, what do I look for? My hope is in you."
Psalm 39:7

Keep your hope focused on the Lord and be patient with the maturing of your spiritual gifts. He may be training you in a specific gift that He knows will be of more use in the Kingdom than you think. God keeps your best interest at heart and knows what you and others need over what you think you want. God knows you can spread yourself thin and become less effective with your gifts and eventually experience spiritual burn-out. God said, "No" to me when I asked for another gift and simply said, "I am training you in prophecy." Be willing to accept "no" from God knowing He knows your future better than you.

HOW DO WE MATURE OUR SPIRITUAL GIFTS?

Most Christians are deeply confused about spiritual gifts. Instead of spending the needed time to train and educate themselves about their gifts they simply ignore them. Satan smiles when he sees this because he knows Christians will be a whole lot less effective for God's Kingdom when they're ignorant about spiritual gifts.

> *"So Christ himself gave the apostles, the prophets, the evangelists, the pastors and teachers, to equip his people for works of service, so that the body of Christ may be built up until we all reach unity in the faith and in the knowledge of the Son of God and become mature, attaining to the whole measure of the fullness of Christ."* Ephesians 4:11-13

"Christ himself" gave us spiritual gifts *"to equip His people for works of service"* and He wants us to use those gifts to build up the Body of Christ. He also gave us goals of unity, knowledge and maturity. Imagine if all Christians had unity, knowledge, and the maturity of Christ and used their spiritual gifts to build the Kingdom of God! Ephesians continues:

> *"Then we will no longer be infants, tossed back and forth by the waves, and blown here and there by every wind of teaching and by the cunning and craftiness of people in their deceitful scheming. Instead, speaking the truth in love, we will grow to become in every respect the mature body of him who is the head, that is, Christ. From him the whole body, joined and held together by every supporting ligament, grows and builds itself up in love, as each part does its work."*   Ephesians 4:14-16

The knowledge of Christ keeps you from falling for *"deceitful scheming"* while *"speaking the truth in love"* will help you mature from the infant stage of your Christian walk. Unity holds the many parts of the Body of Christ together and each part has a responsibility to work for the common good.

The way to overcome the fear of public speaking is to speak in front of others. The way to become a pilot is to learn how to fly a plane. If you want to race cars you need to learn to drive a car first. Christians come together from all walks of life to form the Body of Christ and work together to build up their gifts which will build up the church.

> *"Just as a body, though one, has many parts, but all its many parts form one body, so it is with Christ. For we were all baptized by one Spirit so as to form one body—whether Jews or Gentiles, slave or free—and we were all given the one Spirit to drink. Even so the body is not made up of one part but of many."* 1 Corinthians 12:12-14

We are many parts under one God and His one Spirit guides the many parts just as our brain commands our body parts. When working together in unity much can be accomplished for the church.

> *"...Holy Father, protect them by the power of your name, the name you gave me, so that they may be one as we are one."* John 17:11

Being one unified Body of Christ was Jesus' prayer for us before He died on the cross. What gives power to our spiritual gifts is the unity among believers. Our gifts primary power is to build up the church together. So how do we mature our spiritual gifts? Through unity in Christ and other Christians!

THE PURPOSE OF SPIRITUAL GIFTS IS TO HELP...

...build up the Body of Christ
...us be used by God for the common good
...us share our Faith with others
...spread God's Word all over the world
...bring People to Christ and fulfill the Great Commission
...unify the Church into 1 Body, 1 Faith, 1 Hope and 1 LORD
...train Christians to become effective with their spiritual gifts
...educate Christians in the truth of the Gospel of Christ

…Christians know who they and "Whose" they are

…lead you and others toward becoming more like Christ

…believers mature and find peace, joy, purpose and direction

…encourage God's people

…see God's plans for people's lives

…us focus on Jesus during the storms in our lives

…bring us into worship

…show God's Mercy and Grace to others

…distinguish between good and evil

…us see the needs of others

…serve others in need

…repair broken Christians

…heal others mental, physical and spiritual needs

…those who cannot help themselves

…comfort the church

…expand God's Kingdom

…Christians stand firm against Satan

…show people the Power of God

…bring Glory to God

You are this list! Are you serious about getting rid of the ignorance surrounding spiritual gifts and their power? Are you willing to learn how to use your spiritual gifts? Are you eager to build up the church with your gifts? Knowing Jesus is maturity, unity is maturity and distinguishing good from evil is maturity. Becoming more like Christ is the ultimate act of maturity so seek maturity in Him!

> *"Since you are eager for gifts of the Spirit, try to excel in those that build up the church."*   1 Corinthians 14:12

STOP and ask God to help you learn about your spiritual gifts but more importantly ask how to put them into action to build up the church. **LOOK** for opportunities to mature in Christ by simply getting to know Him better and allow Him to move you out of your comfort zone.

LISTEN for Satan when he tries to sneak in and disrupt the Body of Christ through his lies. Gather with others and do your best to put out the fires he tries to start.

BE WHAT GOD CREATED YOU TO BE and humbly follow the steps God has laid out for you and receive unimaginable joy from being used of God to change lives. Seek maturity and become the Kingdom builder He created you to be.

"Be completely humble and gentle; be patient, bearing with one another in love. Make every effort to keep the unity of the Spirit through the bond of peace. There is one body and one Spirit—just as you were called to one hope when you were called—one Lord, one faith, one baptism; One God and Father of all, who is over all and through all and in all."

Ephesians 4:2-6

"To place ourselves in range of God's choicest gifts, we have to walk with God, work with God, lean on God, cling to God, come to have the sense and feel of God, refer all things to God."[10]

-Cornelius Plantinga

PONDERING POINTS

Do you have any talents that the Church could use?

Has God ever moved you out of your comfort zone?

What did "being out of your comfort zone" feel like?

Do you have a spiritual gift? (Hint, the answer is yes!)

Have you asked for a spiritual gift and received it?

Why is teaching held to such a high standard?

Are you willing to say, "Here I am, send me?"

Can you wait while God trains you in your spiritual gifts?

Why is it important to have other believers in your life?

What is the purpose of your life?

What fears keep you from learning about your spiritual gifts?

CHAPTER FIVE

WHAT ARE THE SPIRITUAL GIFTS FOUND IN SCRIPTURE?

"We have different gifts, according to the grace given to each of us. If your gift is prophesying, then prophesy in accordance with your faith; if it is serving, then serve; if it is teaching, then teach; if it is to encourage, then give encouragement; if it is giving, then give generously; if it is to lead, do it diligently; if it is to show mercy, do it cheerfully."
Romans 12:6-8

We all have *"different gifts"* according to Scripture. Some may be flashier than others but we all have gifts, plural. Some serve behind-the-scenes while others stand in the spotlight.

"Now you are the body of Christ, and each one of you is a part of it. And God has placed in the church first of all apostles, second prophets, third teachers, then miracles, then gifts of healing, of helping, of guidance, and of different kinds of tongues. Are all apostles? Are all prophets? Are all teachers? Do all work miracles? Do all have gifts of healing? Do all speak in tongues? Do all interpret? Now eagerly desire the greater gifts."
1 Corinthians 12:27-30

Don't worry if you are not in the spotlight. You will discover more about yourself than you ever thought possible as you continue to learn about your spiritual gifts. You are part of something much larger than yourself. This is not just about you and your gift; it's about your relationship with your Creator and what He created you to be. If there is little to no relationship with Jesus then there will be little to no use of your spiritual gifts. Draw close to Him and learn how to use your spiritual gifts with the potential He sees in your special blend of gifts. Do not let Satan scare or confuse you. God gave you your gifts and He has a plan for you to use them.

> *"Now to each one the manifestation of the Spirit is given for the common good. To one there is given through the Spirit a message of wisdom, to another a message of knowledge by means of the same Spirit, to another faith by the same Spirit, to another gifts of healing by that one Spirit, to another miraculous powers, to another prophecy, to another distinguishing between spirits, to another speaking in different kinds of tongues, and to still another the interpretation of tongues. All these are the work of one and the same Spirit, and he distributes them to each one, just as he determines."* 1 Corinthians 12:7-10

Again, "Spiritual gifts are God-given abilities to fulfill the mission of the church through love. They are given freely by God's grace to build up, encourage and comfort the church to glorify Him."

> *"So Christ himself gave the apostles, the prophets, the evangelists, the pastors and teachers, to equip his people for works of service, so that the body of Christ may be built up..."* Ephesians 4:11-12

Jesus gives us Spiritual Gifts *"so that the body of Christ may be built up."* Learn as much as possible about your gifts but learn about other gifts as well to help build up other people's gifts. Being familiar with their gifts can help you understand them better. You'll be able to help them along their life's journey and together you can expand and build up God's Kingdom. We are all under the same Spirit so discover your gifts, discover other's gifts and discover the possibilities God has planned for you and others.

THE 20 SPIRITUAL GIFTS LISTED IN SCRIPTURE

God's Word speaks about spiritual gifts often and lists them several times in Scriptures. There are 20 different gifts listed and no one list has all 20 gifts. Confusion has come from the different lists and different Bible translations using different words to describe the same gifts. To reduce this confusion, let's stay with the 20 spiritual gifts listed in Scripture and use the list below. The asterisk shows the different translated words. Here are the 20 Biblical spiritual gifts in alphabetical order with their other translated names and Scriptural references:

Administration or Governments* or Guidance* [c]
Apostleship [c,d]
Discernment of or Distinguishing* between Spirits [b]
Encouragement or Exhortation* [a]
Evangelist [d]
Faith [b]
Giving [a]
Healing [b,c]
Helps [c]
Leadership or Ruling* [a,c]
Mercy [[a]
Ministry or Serving* or Service* [a,d]
Miracles or Miraculous Powers* (Working* or Effecting*) [b,c]
Pastor or Shepherding* [d]
Prophecy [a,b,c,d]
Teaching [a,c,d]
Tongues (Different Kinds* or Various Kinds* or Diverse*) [b,c]
Tongues (Interpretation) [b,c]
Word or Message* of Knowledge [b]
Word or Message* of Wisdom [b]

[a] Romans 12:6-8   [c] 1 Corinthians 12:27-30
[b] 1 Corinthians 12:7-10   [d] Ephesians 4:11-12

The real problem is not the different translated names; it's ignoring how to use the gifts God gave you. To avoid confusion the first name of the gift in this list will be used in the book.

> *"But to each one of us grace has been given as Christ apportioned it. This is why it says: When he ascended on high, he [Jesus] led captives in his train and gave gifts to men."*   Ephesians 4:7-8

Let's unwrap the gifts Jesus gave you! This chapter is designed to help you identify your God-given spiritual gifts and take the steps toward using them. Taking the spiritual gift Test will help you start your journey toward your purpose and what God created you to be.

The end of this chapter gives a list of talents and how they can be placed into their proper spiritual gift category. An example would be someone gifted with singing or playing music. They may not see their spiritual gift listed but their talent can easily fit in the Biblical category of Ministry because they love to make others feel warm and welcome for a purpose. Helping bring about worship is definitely a Ministry gift. Their musical talent may even fall under Encouragement by building up others through the words of their music. If they write their own songs they could be a Teacher or use a Prophetic gift to give Biblical messages in their lyrics.

> *"For just as each of us has one body with many members, and these members do not all have the same function, so in Christ we, though many, form one body, and each member belongs to all the others."*   Romans 12:4-5

We are one Body of Christ with many parts. All the spiritual gifts are important but some believe one gift is more important than another. This has caused great divisions among denominations and this is of the enemy. Satan knows we have the power to cause great damage to his schemes through unity in Christ. He will do everything he can to confuse and divide the body in order to carry out his mission of killing, stealing and destroying. Our unity is found in following the Holy Spirit and focusing on what God wants, not what we want.

"There are different kinds of gifts, but the same Spirit."
1 Corinthians 12:4

All of these spiritual gifts come from the same Holy Spirit. Use your God-given gifts to unite, not divide, the church. Learn to appreciate all the spiritual gifts in all their varieties. There is great power in the unity of Christians and this is why Jesus prayed this to His Father for us!

"I in them and you in me—so that they may be brought to complete unity. Then the world will know that you sent me and have loved them even as you have loved me."
John 17:23

GIFT KILLERS
SPIRITUAL GIFT TEST

Directions for discovering your Spiritual Gifts:

Now it's time to take the spiritual gift Test. This is the beginning of finding yourself and discovering your purpose and why you are here. Try not to be overwhelmed with the large amount of information about spiritual gifts. There are many levels to each gift. Not all with Leadership run church organizations; they may run a household. Not all Teachers are standing in the pulpit preaching God's Word; they may be teaching their own children about God. Not all Evangelists travel the world; they may simply share Jesus with their family, friends, and neighbors. There's an old question, how do you eat an elephant? It applies to spiritual gifts… simply take one bite at a time. Take your first bites by discovering what you were created to be and work from there. This journey will take time so be patient.

Read each of the next 120 "Life Situations" and write a number between 0-4 in front of each situation that best describes how it relates to you. Use the following scale:

0 - Never true 1 - Rarely true 2 - Sometimes true
3 - Mostly true 4 - Always true

As you read, be yourself and go with your first thought. This is not about impressing others or trying to be something you are not. Simply answer how true the situation is in your life right now. Try not to overthink your answers. You may also take the spiritual gift test online at GiftKillers.com when the website is active.

120 LIFE SITUATIONS

1. ____ I see the "big picture" of projects and help organize the things needed for an institution or ministry to reach their goals.
2. ____ I have a heart to reach the lost in hard and extreme locations.
3. ____ I have the ability to sense if a person is good or evil and know whether to hang around them or not.
4. ____ I enjoy building others up with encouraging words and people are drawn to me to hear words that lift them up when they are having a tough time.
5. ____ I have a heart for the lost along with an urgent desire for them to share in the inheritance of being a child of God by leading them to Christ.
6. ____ I am able to trust God completely through tough situations for His provision and help.
7. ____ I find joy in cheerfully sharing my time, resources and money to meet the needs of others and glorify God.
8. ____ My prayers for people to be healed are often answered.
9. ____ I'm not much for committee meetings and would rather meet people's physical needs as soon as possible rather than talk and plan about it.
10. ____ I am able to recruit and motivate others to accomplish goals they did not know they could do and help them find their potential in Christ.
11. ____ I am sensitive to people who are hurting, unloved and undeserving and I desire to help them by showing them Christ's love.
12. ____ I love helping a group feel warm and welcome for the purpose of building them up in Christ.
13. ____ I have used God's Word to speak into a person's life or situation and saw an unusual series of events supernaturally repair the problem.

14. ____ I find joy in gently correcting and bringing a person back who has fallen away from the church and lost their Faith.

15. ____ People come to me for advice all the time and I feel like I am a mail-person for God when I point them back to His Word and His truth.

16. ____ I put in a lot of study time when asked to teach others and get excited about how God's Word will change people's lives.

17. ____ I believe that praying in the Spirit is important to the church and me.

18. ____ I have given an interpretation for someone speaking in an unknown tongue.

19. ____ I sometimes supernaturally receive specific pieces of information from God about people or situations that I could not have known on my own.

20. ____ I regularly put knowledge into action and provide wise advice to others to build them up and put them on the right path.

21. ____ I am a good planner for organizing ministries, missions, church classes, or church activities.

22. ____ I am a bit of a dreamer when it comes to my ideas to reach the lost and many think my ideas are a bit extreme.

23. ____ I tend to get a first impression about the people I meet about whether they are good or bad and as I get to know them longer my first impression was right most of the time.

24. ____ I am drawn to give hope to the hopeless so I tend to listen to others and help council them with comforting words through their hard times.

25. ____ I am comfortable speaking about Jesus and can clearly share the Gospel with others at any time and any place.

26. ____ I depend on God for direction in all areas of my life, even the impossible.

27. ____ I am able to help those in serious financial need at just the right time and I have no expectation of repayment when I help them.

28. ___ I often find myself praying for those suffering from illness.

29. ___ I see the physical needs of others and find joy in doing projects that help them at just the right time.

30. ___ I can easily have a vision and set goals for the purpose of building up the Body of Christ.

31. ___ I am a good listener and have compassion to spend my time comforting people who are lonely and suffering.

32. ___ I feel discipleship, fellowship, worship and activities for all ages are very important to building up the church and I am drawn to these areas of ministry.

33. ___ When people say miracles have stopped I look to God's greatest miracle of allowing us to spend an eternity in heaven with Him.

34. ___ I like to provide real life practical ways for others to grow their Faith in Christ and show them how to protect themselves from false leaders and evil influences.

35. ___ When giving advice I can sound harsh because it's usually about correction and following God's Will for their life but my words have helped many people.

36. ___ I can put together study material and outlines to help others understand God's Word in a clear, easy and organized manner.

37. ___ I feel as if my prayers are effective in Spiritual battles for others and my own life.

38. ___ I seem to be called to give the meaning to an unknown tongue in front of groups of people at church.

39. ___ The messages I receive from God about others are perfectly timed to help bring about solutions for the circumstances at hand.

40. ___ People see me as an "old soul" because I can usually size up a situation and rightly divide the truth from lies and speak wisdom into the situation.

41. ___ I try to be as efficient as possible and use time, resources and finances with care while preparing a way to reach a goal for a group or organization.

42. ____ I understand that God's grace and forgiveness extends to all parts of the world and I have the desire to start new ministries and new churches to reach them.

43. ____ I can tell when someone is a phony and I know their true motives even when most people think they are a great person.

44. ____ I feel like God gives me the right things to say at just the right time to offer Christ's love to others.

45. ____ I tend to relate well with non-believers and do not mind sharing my story with them in order to bring them to Christ.

46. ____ I tend to be an optimist even in hard times and know God will be glorified.

47. ____ I do not mind giving up a higher standard of living to help give to church ministries which help people in need.

48. ____ I tend to give good specific advice for those in need of healing.

49. ____ I am generally good with my hands in areas like construction and repairs or remodeling and decorating.

50. ____ I am better at leading a group of people rather than being in charge of organizing the things needed to complete a task.

51. ____ I do not mind serving with acts of love and kindness to those who are unloved by others.

52. ____ I can work behind the scenes to help with details others may miss so the project can move forward to bless others.

53. ____ I have fasted and prayed very specific prayers to help free others from demonic strongholds in their lives.

54. ____ I do not put up with sin but I can meet a person where they are at and bring them back to Christ in a loving way.

55. ____ God's Word is the measuring stick for my life and I study it deeply to understand His mysteries and truths so I can share them with others when they ask for my advice.

56. ____ When I study God's Word, I enjoy using reference material like commentaries along with Greek and Hebrew dictionaries to gain a deeper understanding of Scripture.

57. ____ I believe when I pray in a different tongue in front of a group the words are an encouragement from God when they are interpreted.

58. ____ When I interpret a heavenly tongue the message almost always is to edify and build up the church body.

59. ____ People often agree with the information I was given by God to be the truth and it allows me to speak to their heart because they know God is involved in the conversation.

60. ____ People tend to come to me for Godly advice for problem solving and I show them how to put God's truth into action.

61. ____ I am better at organizing and taking care of things rather than leading people.

62. ____ I desire to reach others for Christ no matter where they are and no matter their ethnic background.

63. ____ I generally pray well for spiritual warfare for myself and others.

64. ____ I feel like relationships are important and I spend time keeping those relationships going because I am concerned about their spiritual welfare.

65. ____ I am strong in my Faith even in the middle of many unbelievers and look at the situation as an opportunity to spread the Gospel.

66. ____ I do not mind taking a leap of Faith to move forward when I sense God calling me despite how others around me feel.

67. ____ I have a heart to see the church grow and I enjoy donating to the church building projects or missionary work.

68. ____ I often know the root cause of someone's illness and give a specific message as to how to remove what is blocking the healing of their physical, spiritual or mental ills.

69. ____ I am generally a background worker who is dependable, on time, responsible and follow a project through to completion.

70. ____ I tend to fill in when there is a lack of leadership and quickly lay out a plan of action that others want to follow

71. ____ I find joy in visiting the sick who are home bound, in the hospital or in a nursing home.

72. ____ I am very dependable and committed to finish a project and I do not mind using my time and talents to bless others so they feel like they belong and not alone.

73. ____ I believe there is great power in God's Word. All I need to do is be still to listen for specific instructions and act on them so God can work miracles in people's lives.

74. ____ I tend to take on the responsibility to protect other people and keep them safe so they can grow in their Faith.

75. ____ I can confront others about the sin in their lives and offer practical and real life ways to follow God's Word to repentance and a way out of their sin.

76. ____ I can bring the Bible to life and make it relevant to people's daily lives so they can grow in their Faith.

77. ____ I have spoken in a different tongue and it was interpreted by another believer.

78. ____ I feel it is Biblical and necessary to have an interpretation to an unknown tongue when it is spoken in a group of people or a congregation.

79. ____ God can give me a supernatural message about another person that is very private and I use it carefully to gently correct them and turn them back to God.

80. ____ I can take a perfectly timed supernatural message from God about a person or situation and use it to speak wisdom into that situation or person's life so they take the path with the least damage.

81. ____ I am good at the details of a long term plan and can plan the steps needed for a large project to reach its completion.

82. ____ I seem to adapt well when I am in different environments and relate well to different cultural groups of people.

83. ____ I desire for others to be free of their demonic bondage of sin that is hindering their lives.

84. ____ I see the God-given potential in other people and I do not mind taking time to help build up their life and become a better Christian.

85. ____ Bringing others to Christ seems natural to me and I do not mind sharing my Faith with non-believers.

86. ____ I believe God is working daily in all of our lives and He will use me in the great and small things as long as I am faithful, obedient and available to Him.

87. ____ I believe that God blessed me with more than I need so I can be a blessing to others.

88. ____ I lay my hands on and anoint others with oil when I am asked for healing prayers.

89. ____ I feel it important to "keep up" the church with maintenance, repairs and landscaping to keep the church functioning properly.

90. ____ I enjoy deciding where we need to go and who is needed to make it there in the most efficient way possible.

91. ____ I do not mind sharing God's love and mercy with the outcasts of society that are ignored by others like addicts, inmates and the homeless.

92. ____ I do not mind using my home and resources to offer church fellowship or Bible study.

93. ____ I have prayed for God to intervene in the impossible like divorce, suicide, addictions and terminal illnesses and God miraculously showed up and His name was glorified.

94. ____ I am committed to serving a group of children or adults and help them find their purpose and meaning in Christ.

95. ____ I see all of the brokenness in the world like potholes, dents in cars and grass that needs mowing yet it allows me to see broken people that need help from God to be fixed.

96. ____ I can take large amounts of information from Scripture and condense it down to manageable bite-sized nuggets in order for others to understand God's Word.

97. ____ I feel at peace while praying in a heavenly tongue.

98. ____ I feel at peace when unknown tongues are spoken and interpreted correctly.

99. ____ God has given me messages of warning for the path a person is on and I have shared the information with them to help them choose a better path.

100. ____ I can easily see how Biblical principles relate to people's real life situations and how those principals can help build them up in Christ.

101. ____ I can make the needed corrections as a project moves forward because I can see upcoming potential problems.

102. ____ I have a strong desire to go on difficult missions to reach the lost for Christ

103. ____ I have been given specific actions to do by God and when I did them something miraculous happened.

104. ____ I find joy in lifting up the weak and down-hearted with words and provide encouragement for the discouraged to point them to Christ.

105. ____ I tend to move conversations to the topic of Jesus as much as possible and I get excited about the opportunity to talk about Him.

106. ____ Others have trouble understanding my calmness in adverse situations but their Faith seems to be lifted when they are around me.

107. ____ I give of my resources out of my love for what Christ did for me and I enjoy giving anonymously so God gets the credit.

108. ____ I understand there is more to healing than the physical realm and there are demonic forces that can keep a person oppressed and unable to heal.

109. ____ I do not mind being a helper or doing jobs that others think are routine and less important.

110. ____ People naturally follow my leadership due to my confidence in the vision God gave me for direction.

111. ____ I am cheerful, gracious, available and loving to people because I see their value and purpose to God but I can become so sympathetic I can feel their pain.

112. ____ I am good at finding the perfect gifts or cards for others because I put a great deal of thought into what would be pleasing to them.

113. ___ I have experienced God's name being glorified and people's Faith growing because of following specific actions I received from Him.

114. ___ I like to guide others as a sort of "life coach" in their long term growth to become more like Christ through Godly relationships, Spiritual growth and emotional support.

115. ___ I sometimes feel as if a pattern of life is laid in front of me and I know what will happen to a person if they choose a certain path in their life, good or bad.

116. ___ I feel a huge responsibility to teach God's Word with integrity, truth and correctness because of the influence it has on people's lives.

117. ___ When I pray in private I sometimes pray in a heavenly language and feel like the Holy Spirit prayed for me.

118. ___ I believe that a correct interpretation of a heavenly tongue is an important way God can encourage an individual or the church body.

119. ___ I have received supernatural messages about others while praying for them and it allows me to pray more specifically for their needs.

120. ___ I tend to stay calm in difficult and confusing situations and do not mind offering practical Biblical solutions to the problems.

DISCOVERING YOUR SPIRITUAL GIFT

When you finish rating the life situations from 0-4, write your number choice with the matching Life Situation number in the columned chart on the next two pages. Please be careful, the chart is spread out over two pages and the numbers go from one page to another.

Then add each column of your numbers from top to bottom and place the total at the bottom of the chart in the blank box above each letter.

1.	2.	3.	4.	5.	6.	7.	8.	9.	10.
21.	22.	23.	24.	25.	26.	27.	28.	29.	30.
41.	42.	43.	44.	45.	46.	47.	48.	49.	50.
61.	62.	63.	64.	65.	66.	67.	68.	69.	70.
81.	82.	83.	84.	85.	86.	87.	88.	89.	90.
101.	102.	103.	104.	105.	106.	107.	108.	109.	110.
A	B	C	D	E	F	G	H	I	J

A: Administration
B: Apostleship
C: Discerning of Spirits
D: Encouragement
E: Evangelist
F: Faith
G: Giving
H: Healing
I: Helps
J: Leadership

K: Mercy
L: Ministry / Serving
M: Miracles
N: Pastor
O: Prophecy
P: Teaching
Q: Tongues - Diverse
R: Tongues - Interpretation
S: Word of Knowledge
T: Word of Wisdom

11.	12.	13.	14.	15.	16.	17.	18.	19.	20.
31.	32.	33.	34.	35.	36.	37.	38.	39.	40.
51.	52.	53.	54.	55.	56.	57.	58.	59.	60.
71.	72.	73.	74.	75.	76.	77.	78.	79.	80.
91.	92.	93.	94.	95.	96.	97.	98.	99.	100.
111.	112.	113.	114.	115.	116.	117.	118.	119.	120.
K	L	M	N	O	P	Q	R	S	T

Find your four highest totals of the columns. Use the alphabets at the bottom of the chart to find your spiritual gifts. Write your top four spiritual gifts from high to low in the lines below:

1. _____   2. _____

3. _____   4. _____

The following page lists the spiritual gifts in alphabetical order with the page number for its "good" description found in Chapter 6. The list also gives you the piece of the Armor of God that is related to each spiritual gift.

Use this list to write down each piece of the Armor of God which relates to your top four spiritual gifts. An example would be the spiritual gift of Prophecy is related to the Belt. Helps is related to the Sandals, Leadership is the Helmet and so on.

1. _____   2. _____

3. _____   4. _____

Now with the knowledge of your top four spiritual gifts and the piece of Armor related to them continue to the next chapter.

CHAPTER SIX

SPIRITUAL GIFT DEFINITIONS (THE GOOD)

Discovering Your Spiritual Gifts

This chapter is a dictionary of the good things related to each of the 20 Biblical spiritual gifts. Read about your top spiritual gifts from the spiritual gift test. The end of this chapter has a list of other talents that fall under the Biblical spiritual gifts. If you did not see your "talent" listed in the 20 spiritual gifts, go to the last 3 pages of this Chapter and look at the list of Talents that fall under spiritual gifts. This list may help you find how your talents are related to specific spiritual gifts.

After reading your spiritual gift descriptions in this Chapter, read Chapter 7. Here you will learn how the Armor of God is related to your spiritual gifts. The Chapters that follow are about each piece of Armor and tells the Good, Bad and the Ugly of the spiritual gifts in their group. These chapters will help you to discover how Satan plans to kill your spiritual gift, steal your joy and destroy your life's purpose in the process. These chapters will help you learn how to stand firm against his attacks. You will need to read the Chapters related to your top spiritual gifts. Here are the Chapters and their piece of Armor.

When finished with the Chapters related to your spiritual gifts I would ask everyone to please read Chapter 12 to the end of the book. Even if you did not score high in the gift of Faith, the purpose of this book is to grow your Faith and Chapter 12 will help you. Faith shields all of the other gifts and helps you use them more efficiently and with greater power. Chapter 13 helps you learn how to use the Sword of the Spirit which is God's Word. You will need it to put the knowledge you have gained into action and become what God created you to be! Finally, Chapter 14 is a few final words before leaving on your greatest quest, your life's purpose.

SPIRITUAL GIFT DEFINITIONS
ADMINISTRATION:

This spiritual gift is described as a person steering a ship called a helmsman. They are not necessarily the Captain of the ship but they are responsible for the safety, supplies and direction of the ship. They need to get in and out of ports safely and stay on course for their destination. They are needed in both calm and rough seas to adjust for wind, weather and currents. They need a steady course that uses the rudder of the ship very little in order not to create drag. This can reduce the speed and efficiency of the ship. Administration is a leader of "things" needed to accomplish a mission but they need a good bridge crew. Without them there would be no goals being carried out for the mission of the church.

> *"Then we will no longer be infants, tossed back and forth by the waves, and blown here and there by every wind of teaching and by the cunning and craftiness of people in their deceitful scheming. Instead, speaking the truth in love, we will grow to become in every respect the mature body of him who is the head, that is, Christ. From him the whole body, joined and held together by every supporting ligament, grows and builds itself up in love, as each part does its work."* Ephesians 4:14-16

This spiritual gift of Administration is the unsung hero of the body of Christ. It is part of the *"supporting ligaments"* that help hold the body together and keep it going in a Godly direction. This Scripture perfectly describes the duties of a helmsman. They are to stay the course and not be blown off course by the winds of evil. They are to spread truth and love to help build up the church and grow better Christians.

The person with this gift is a task oriented person on a mission that focuses on the big picture. This gift enables a person to take large projects and break them down into manageable pieces. They understand the "Big Picture" but also understand saving time and money through the handling of small details. They stay with the project for the long haul and have no problems with the long term planning of an organization's future goals, projects, finances and information gathering.

> *"Now he who supplies seed to the sower and bread for food will also supply and increase your store of seed and will enlarge the harvest of your righteousness. You will be enriched in every way so that you can be generous on every occasion, and through us your generosity will result in thanksgiving to God."*   2 Corinthians 9:10-11

Those with this gift know how to grow seed, harvest them and deliver them to another continent if necessary. The people gifted with Administration are efficient, effective and driven by a strong sense of duty to accomplish a job that creates opportunities for Christians to use their spiritual gifts. They know, deep in their heart, they are freeing up others to do more abundant ministry work. They may not be the "frontline soldier" but they do make a way for the frontline to be supplied with the tools to build up God's Kingdom. They know the "what, when and where" of the vision or goal and are more "task" focused than "people" focused. They strongly believe in the future of the church to help people become better Christians through the process. Remember they are more about being a leader of "things" rather than leading "people."

At my church there is an associate Pastor who fits this description very well. He is quietly and efficiently working in the background to make sure all of the "Church" is running like a well-oiled machine. He has an obvious passion for the Lord and does his best to keep the church on mission. I give him praises for the unsung hero work he accomplishes in the back ground, especially when no one is looking!

To be effective in the gift of Administration you need to:

STOP and pray first. Ask for the most efficient way to glorify God with what you have at hand.

LOOK at all the options, access the situation and formulate a Godly plan that seeks simple solutions.

LISTEN to good council for good advice but always be open to the Holy Spirit.

BE WHAT GOD CREATED YOU TO BE and put the plan into action with a clear vison and reachable targets but be ready for needed changes.

> *"Everyone will be forgotten, nothing we do will make any difference, and all good endeavors, even the best, will come to naught. Unless there is God. If the God of the Bible exists, and there is a true reality beneath and behind this one, and this life is not the only life, then every good endeavor, even the simplest ones, pursued in response to God's calling, can matter forever."[11]* Tim Keller

APOSTLESHIP:

This spiritual gift is not to be confused with the "office" of the original Apostles. There is a calling on all of us to express this gift because it means to be an ambassador for Christ. This means we are called to be Christians everywhere and in every moment of our life and be like Christ to others. But this gift represents a more extreme form of vision oriented evangelism.

"Whoever claims to live in him must live as Jesus did."
1 John 2:6

Jesus was always obedient to the Father and He always glorified the Father. If we claim to be Christians we are held to the same standards. When Jesus was asked what the greatest commandment was, He summarized the Ten Commandments into two of the greatest commandments. Once again, if we claim to be Christians we are held to these commandments.

Jesus replied: "'Love the Lord your God with all your heart and with all your soul and with all your mind.' This is the first and greatest commandment. And the second is like it: 'Love your neighbor as yourself.' All the Law and the Prophets hang on these two commandments."

Matthew 22:37-40

Then Jesus gave us a third type of commandment in the form of the Great Commission. Here we are told to go tell others about Jesus and teach them to be obedient to His commands.

"Therefore go and make disciples of all nations, baptizing them in the name of the Father and of the Son and of the Holy Spirit, and teaching them to obey everything I have commanded you."   Matthew 28:19-20

Simply put, we need to love God, love others and tell them about Jesus! Being Ambassadors for Christ we are told to live like Jesus and to tell others about Him. Doesn't it make sense that we are all called, at different levels, to express the gift of Apostleship?

Apostle means a messenger; we are called to be a messenger to others for the purpose of spreading the Gospel. Apostle is from two words meaning "to send off." In addition the Latin for Apostle is translated "Missio" which is where we get the word missionary. Aren't we all called to be on mission to tell the good news of our Lord and Savior Jesus Christ? It may be our neighbor across the street or a total stranger across the world but distance doesn't matter when telling others about Jesus. We just need to be willing to share Jesus with others.

"Then I heard the voice of the Lord saying, "Whom shall I send? And who will go for us?" And I said, "Here am I. Send me!" He said, "Go and tell this people..."

Isaiah 6:8-9

This Scripture perfectly describes the heart of the person with the spiritual gift of Apostleship. They are willing to drop everything and say, *"Here I am. Send me!"* There appears to be three levels of the *"send me"* Christian. The first is every Christian's commandment to tell the people in their circle about Jesus. This may include family, friends and people at work. The second is missionaries with a calling to go to other areas of the world and tell strangers about Jesus. The third is an extreme version of the spiritual gift of Apostleship. There are a very few who fall within this third version.

The third version of the gift of Apostleship is the type of person that says they were told by God to stand on a street corner in Hong Kong on a certain day at a certain time. They were obedient and flew to Hong Kong and met someone at that very corner and a ministry grew from their obedience to God. This extreme version requires trust and obedience when listening to God's voice and following His plans for their life. They are pioneers and visionaries for spreading the Gospel. They have an incredible ability to cross cultural, economic and geographic boundaries to reach others for Christ.

Those with the spiritual gift of Apostleship need to be paired up to someone that can help achieve their vision. I like to give the worldly example of Walt Disney. Walt was the dreamer and visionary but he could not have built the Disney Company without his older brother Roy. Roy was a brilliant administrator and dealt with the banks and every day running of the company. This gave Walt the freedom to dream. Those using the spiritual gift of Apostleship need a good support person like Roy to help make their visions become realities to build God's Kingdom.

To be effective in the gift of Apostleship you need to:

STOP everything and do what God says to do.
LOOK for God in all things; He is always at work to build up His Kingdom.
LISTEN for extremely specific instructions from God.

BE WHAT GOD CREATED YOU TO BE, and be obedient to His calling on your life in order to create amazing ministries.

> *"Don't be afraid to give up the good to go for the great."*[12]
> -John D. Rockefeller

DISCERNING OF SPIRITS:

This is an amazing spiritual gift but it is like the description I gave earlier of giving a 16 year old the keys to a Ferrari. It is a powerful gift that comes with great responsibilities. It is not the gift of discernment, as many believe; it is the gift of Discerning or distinguishing between Spirits. It is the supernatural ability to rightly determine what is of God and what is not. This gift allows the user to recognize Satan and his demons at work!

The gift of Discerning Spirits allows a person to have a very unique look at the world we live in. They realize there is an unseen world where the real battle is fought, the world of angels and demons. I have a friend that has this gift and his is very powerful. His gift so intrigued me it prompted me to ask 24 pastors the question, "Can a sane person see and or hear angels and or demons?" 18 of them said yes without a moment of hesitation, the other 6 appeared taken back by my question. You would have thought I was asking for their Social Security number and personal passwords. They questioned me as to why am I asking such a question and eventually said their answer was no.

> *"Jesus called his twelve disciples to him and gave them authority to drive out impure spirits and to heal every disease and sickness."*   Matthew 10:1

Scriptures clearly show encounters with angels and demons throughout the Bible. They are found in the Old and in the New Testament before and after the resurrection of Jesus. John Blanchard mentioned in his book, *"Demons; Servants of Satan"* that 19 out of 27 New Testament books mentioned demons. I believe the answer to the question I posed to 24 pastors is a very clear, "Yes!" God gave a few people the ability to know when they are around angels and demons.

The word for Spirits means moving air like the wind or breathing. It is used to describe the Holy Spirit along with other spiritual beings such as angels and demons. This gift allows a person to rightly distinguish between a good spirit and a bad spirit even if they look very much alike.

> *"As you go, proclaim this message: 'The kingdom of heaven has come near.' Heal the sick, raise the dead, cleanse those who have leprosy, drive out demons. Freely you have received; freely give."*   Matthew 10:7-8

Jesus gave authority to Christians to drive out demons and heal the sick. We need people who can rightly see the difference between what is good and what is evil. This gift powerfully reveals what is going on behind the scenes and can be very useful in determining people's motives.

> *"The Spirit clearly says that in later times some will abandon the faith and follow deceiving spirits and things taught by demons."*   1 Timothy 4:1

We need people to help us avoid false teachings and point out *"deceiving spirits"* so we do not *"abandon the faith."* The user of this gift can see, feel and hear the spiritual realm. They can see and feel what is good and what is bad. I give the example of a tree being blown by the wind. Most people see the tree bending to the force of the wind but the gift of Discerning Spirits allows a person to see, feel and hear the wind. This is a very emotionally driven gift that can quickly get to the root of a problem. They make decisions with their heart and emotions more than their mind. When logic is fooled supernatural emotions can see the light or the darkness.

> *"And no wonder, for Satan himself masquerades as an angel of light."*   2 Corinthians 11:14

If Satan can come to us as *"an angel of light"* and fool us into going the wrong direction, we need people to test the spirits. They can give us the correct information to choose the best direction. Satan can make something seem so "right" that many will miss the small deception and follow him into the snare of sin. Being able to distinguish between good and evil can be like telling the difference between a left and a right hand. Satan is a master of masquerade and we need people to *"test the spirits."*

> *"Dear friends, do not believe every spirit, but test the spirits to see whether they are from God, because many false prophets have gone out into the world."*
>
> 1 John 4:1

This gift allows people to be excellent judges of the character and motives of other people. They are the testers of the spirits and have a strong desire to free people from the bondage of Satan.

> *"You, dear children, are from God and have overcome them, because the one who is in you is greater than the one who is in the world. They are from the world and therefore speak from the viewpoint of the world, and the world listens to them. We are from God, and whoever knows God listens to us; but whoever is not from God does not listen to us. This is how we recognize the Spirit of truth and the spirit of falsehood."* 1 John 4:4-6

Those with Discerning Spirits recognize the viewpoint of the world and *"the spirit of falsehood."* They may even have visions or dreams to rightly discern spiritual issues. We desperately need this gift operating in the church today because this gift identifies the enemy! This spiritual gift is the emotion of the Body of Christ and operates on feelings. This is the opposite of Prophecy which operates as the Logic of the Body of Christ.

To be effective in the gift of Discerning Spirits you need to:

STOP hiding from your gift and embrace the gift God gave you.
LOOK for those being deceived and trapped by Satan's snares.
LISTEN to God for what your role should be in their deliverance
BE WHAT GOD CREATED YOU TO BE, identify the bad spirits and relay the information to those who can help. Do not tackle this alone, the Disciples were commanded to go out two by two.

"Discernment is not a matter of simply telling the difference between right and wrong; rather it is telling the difference between right and almost right."   -Charles Spurgeon

ENCOURAGEMENT or Exhortation:

Have you ever had a person truly encourage you at just the right moment in your life? My Mom always told me I could be anything I set my mind to be as I grew up. She regularly encouraged me and others to become the best versions of ourselves. People with the gift of Encouragement have the ability to come along side someone and motivate them to become what God created them to be at just the right time with just the right words. They know the perfect things to say to build up others for personal growth and they see the potential in people to become greater than what they are now.

Those with this spiritual gift are moved into action when they see someone who is beaten down by life and is not living their life to their fullest. I watched my Mom encourage her secretary to become a Chiropractor and she did. I heard so many compliments about my Mom's teaching in a local community college. They always said she was much more than a professor because she genuinely cared for her students. I watched her encourage positive change in her small town through the chamber and service organizations because she saw the potential of her little town. She was always on the lookout to build someone up!

"Encouragement is awesome. It (can) actually change the course of another person's day, week, or life."[13] -Chuck Swindoll

The gift of Encouragement puts love into action through words. They comfort and motivate people toward positive changes by applying God's Word to their lives. They are the messengers of hope and can help with the social, physical and spiritual needs of others by letting them know they are loved and cared about.

"But the seed on good soil stands for those with a noble and good heart, who hear the word, retain it, and by persevering produce a crop."   Luke 8:15

They plant seeds of God's Word on good soil and delight in a good crop produced through their actions to others. They love seeing a harvest when the seed produces a crop that produces more seeds. Their good works continue on from simply encouraging a person to be the best version of what God created them to be.

"But encourage one another daily, as long as it is called "Today," so that none of you may be hardened by sin's deceitfulness."   Hebrews 3:13

I believe we are all called to encourage each other but some are given a special ability to do it with excellence. While attending a Christian men's group meeting at a friend's barn I challenged the men to a task of encouragement. After a man shared some deep hurts in his life I asked the men to line up in front of him and face him. I then asked each man to encourage him with the word "trials." This man had suffered a great many trials and each man came face to face with him and spoke life into him with words of encouragement. I asked how many men had received that much encouragement in the last week, no one raised their hand. In the last month, same answer. In the last 6 months, one person raised their hand. How do we function in this world with so little to no encouragement?

"God created us to thrive on encouragement from others."[14]
-Willie Robertson

We greatly need people with the gift of Encouragement to speak life into others. It has been said that a word of encouragement during failure is worth more than an hour of praise after success. There is something in every one of us that the world needs and a person with this gift can help bring it out.

To be effective in the gift of Encouragement you need to:

STOP worrying about just your own needs.
LOOK for opportunities to lift up others in need of a good word.
LISTEN to God for the specific words they need to hear.
BE WHAT GOD CREATED YOU TO BE, and build up the Body of Christ with your words.

"So never lose an opportunity of urging a practical beginning, however small, for it is wonderful how often in such matters the mustard-seed germinates and roots itself."[15]
-Florence Nightingale

EVANGELIST:

We have all met that outgoing person who never meets a stranger and seems to have no fear of speaking in front of people. They can jump into any conversation with confidence and can communicate with many different types of people all at the same time. They can appear to have a salesman style of speaking and be very persuasive to get you to join their point of view.

"Have you no wish for others to be saved? Then you're not saved yourself, be sure of that!"[16]   -Charles Spurgeon

The spiritual gift of Evangelism is a supernatural ability to connect with others to share the good news of Jesus Christ. The word Evangelist actually means a bringer of the good news. They have a unique ability to have the sinner repent and motivate the Christian to do more for God's Kingdom. Their messages are usually simple and to the point because their hearts burden for the lost and they want their message understood completely. Their messages cut through the junk of the World and penetrate the soul of individuals even if they are in a group.

"So Christ himself gave the apostles, the prophets, the evangelists, the pastors and teachers, to equip his people for works of service, so that the body of Christ may be built up until we all reach unity in the faith and in the knowledge of the Son of God and become mature, attaining to the whole measure of the fullness of Christ." Ephesians 4:11-13

The ultimate job of the Evangelist is **"that the Body of Christ may be built up."** Think of them as body builders for Christ. Their job is to deliver a clear message of the death, burial and resurrection of Christ while telling why Jesus died for us.

"I tell you that in the same way there will be more rejoicing in heaven over one sinner who repents than over ninety-nine righteous persons who do not need to repent."
Luke 15:7

It's as if the Evangelist can hear the angels **"rejoicing in heaven"** as people are saved from their message. They know that the Kingdom of God is without end so they want everyone to share in God's infinite inheritance.

"Preach the word; be prepared in season and out of season; correct, rebuke and encourage—with great patience and careful instruction. For the time will come when people will not put up with sound doctrine. Instead, to suit their own desires, they will gather around them a great number of teachers to say what their itching ears want to hear. They will turn their ears away from the truth and turn aside to myths. But you, keep your head in all situations, endure hardship, do the work of an evangelist, discharge all the duties of your ministry."   2 Timothy 4:2-5

The Evangelist should be ready at any time and any place to deliver the message of Christ. They also need to be a person that stays close to God in order not to panic but to listen and carry out the work of God's instructions. Their ability to listen to God for a message is their super power so they always need to keep their ears tuned to God's voice.

"My job as a Christian is not to get people to heaven when they die, it's to get heaven to people while they're alive"[17]
-D.R. Silva

To be effective in the gift of Evangelism you need to:

STOP running into the same brick walls and find your purpose. Tell people the good news of Jesus Christ!
LOOK for those in need of a Savior.
LISTEN for how God wants you to speak to the lost people in need of a Savior.
BE WHAT GOD CREATED YOU TO BE, a salesman for the greatest story ever told!

"God sends no one away empty except those who are full of themselves."[18]   Dwight L. Moody

FAITH:

Have you ever been jealous of the person who keeps calm in almost every circumstance? They seem to know everything is going to work out all right. They simply wait on God to show up and do His thing and always trust God to handle the problems at hand. The Spiritual gift of Faith is a supernatural ability to be calm in the presence of a crazy world and trust God in all circumstances. Their future is full of hope in Jesus Christ and they love to share that hope with others.

> *"Now faith is confidence in what we hope for and assurance about what we do not see."* Hebrews 11:1

Faith is like having oil in an engine. There is going to be friction when an engine runs but the oil reduces the friction and reduces the damage being done to the engine. Even though we do not see the oil inside the engine we have Faith it will protect the engine. Faith reduces the friction between us and the world. It doesn't make the problems go away; it simply puts the problems into an eternal viewpoint. Faith smiles at problems because it sees the possibilities for God to work. Faith laughs at impossibilities because they know God is about to do the miraculous.

> *"...because it is by faith you stand firm."* 2 Corinthians 1:24

The spiritual gift of Faith allows a person to know God is for them through all the trials and circumstances of their life. Their peace, hope and trust of Jesus defy normal understanding as they inspire others to trust God with their own lives. They literally pour out their Faith into other people during times of distress. They are extreme optimists for God and know all things work for the pattern of good in the believer's life.

A person with the spiritual gift of Faith is usually a very humble person that relies on God daily to move about their lives in absolute freedom. They have a quiet joyful nature and seem satisfied and fulfilled with life.

"Be on your guard; stand firm in the faith; be courageous; be strong. Do everything in love." 1 Corinthians 16:13-14

Faith is not being slothful for God and doing nothing while neglecting our duties as Christians. Faith is making a stand with God to work through all of our circumstances. Faith is still required to be on guard against Satan's attacks and to be courageous and strong. Peter had enough Faith to get out of the boat and begin walking on water but he took his eyes off Jesus and sank. Peter flinched! Faith is not flinching when Satan attacks; it is standing firm knowing God has our lives in His hand.

"And without faith it is impossible to please God, because anyone who comes to him must believe that he exists and that he rewards those who earnestly seek him."
Hebrews 11:6

Knowing and trusting God pleases Him. Our Faith is not in our Faith; it is with God's faithfulness. God wants us to become less self-centered and more God-centered so we can have complete peace through Him.

"The issue of faith is not so much whether we believe in God, but whether we believe the God we believe in."[19]
-RC Sproul

"In fact, this is love for God: to keep his commands. And his commands are not burdensome, for everyone born of God overcomes the world. This is the victory that has overcome the world, even our faith. Who is it that overcomes the world? Only the one who believes that Jesus is the Son of God."
1 John 5:3-5

The person overflowing with the spiritual gift of Faith realizes **"His commands are not burdensome."** They know God already has **"overcome the world"** and our Faith in Jesus and His love for us binds us to that victory. Some people seem to have this type of Faith naturally from birth and others tend to develop it through trials and tribulations. Others strengthen and grow their Faith through learning God's Word and putting it into practice. I'm a bit of a hybrid of all three. All my life I knew Jesus was the Son of God but the many trials in my life challenged my Faith. I failed miserably through those attacks but I eventually began to study God's Word and He lifted me up and out of the dark prison of my own making.

Even during my time of studying the Bible I felt my Faith take some hits. During these studies I learned I needed to stand firm in my Faith and press on toward the goal. When I did not received an answer to a question I would push harder for the answer. If I had not continued the pursuit of God's answers I know Satan would have won battles in my mind. God gave me so many jewels of knowledge when I kept digging into Scripture.

What was meant for evil to destroy my Faith only helped to build it up even more. What was really happening was my relationship with God was growing and strengthening as I realized His Word is very real and very accurate. I finally found something in my life I could use as a solid foundation to build my life upon. If you find yourself taking hits to your Faith, press on and never give up. Find people to pray with, stay in the Word and seek answers from Godly people.

> *"Faith is a sounder guide than reason. Reason can go only so far, but faith has no limits."*[20]   -Blaise Pascal

To be effective in the gift of Faith you need to:

STOP relying on your own power.
LOOK for where the Holy Spirit is working.

LISTEN to what God would have you do or more importantly not to do.

BE WHAT GOD CREATED YOU TO BE and follow Him without any doubt or hesitation.

> *"Fear imprisons, faith liberates; fear paralyzes, faith empowers; fear disheartens, faith encourages; fear sickens, faith heals; fear makes useless, faith makes serviceable."*[21]
>
> -Harry Emerson Fosdick

GIVING:

"…if it is giving, then give generously"
Romans 12:8

Most of us have met a generous person who would give the shirt off their back to help others. They are some of the kindest people on Earth and they genuinely love helping other people. They have an extraordinary way of knowing a person's exact financial and physical needs at just the right time in their lives. They lovingly give from their heart out of the gratitude for what Christ has done for them. They give freely and have no strings or conditions attached to their gifts.

> *"Each of you should give what you have decided in your heart to give, not reluctantly or under compulsion, for God loves a cheerful giver."*   2 Corinthians 9:7

The people with the spiritual gift of Giving are some of the most cheerful people you will ever meet. My friend with this gift, who has passed away now, was the most humble and kindest person I have ever known in my life. He never met a stranger and was always upbeat no matter what he was going through in his life. His funeral was full of people from every walk of life who adored him. His church greatly appreciated not only his generosity but his genuine love of other people. He not only helped financially but he invested his time into other people's lives.

"If I give all I possess to the poor and give over my body to hardship that I may boast, but do not have love, I gain nothing."   1 Corinthians 13:3

My friend loved and cared for everyone he met. It was as if he was constantly seeking to help people every day of his life. I watched him during a time when his income hit a slump and it was hard on him. It wasn't the lack of money for himself that he was worried about, he had Faith he and his family would be fine. He was worried that he wouldn't be able to give to others like he was used to doing in the past. I miss my friend deeply and he left a huge hole in this world that is difficult to fill. He shared Christ's love continuously in his life through his giving and loving on others. The person with the gift of Giving looks at their ability to give as a blessing. They are the happiest and full of joy while they are blessing others. They never want to be put in the lime-light or show off their gifts. Many times they will give without people knowing who made the donation.

"The most obvious lesson in Christ's teaching is that there is no happiness in having or getting anything, but only in giving."[22]
-Henry Drummond

Keep in mind that the person with this gift does not always have to give of their money. Their time is also very valuable especially when it is used to save people and the church money and time. They are generally thrifty, good with finances and they try to stay out of debt. They can easily find ways to decrease costs and wasted time. Their knowledge is a tremendous asset for the church in order to accomplish goals and projects. They even have the ability to find other people willing to help with projects at reduced costs or even for free.

"For the love of money is a root of all kinds of evil. Some people, eager for money, have wandered from the faith and pierced themselves with many griefs."
1 Timothy 6:10

The spiritual gift of Giving realizes money is a tool that God allows us to use. A person may not be called to travel the world to do missions work but they may be able to pay for the people who are going. If you are striving for a job with a greater income you need to have the goal of having greater giving, not just the accumulation of money and things. If God has blessed you then be a blessing to others. The giver knows money is a tool to expand God's Kingdom so let it be used to let people know Jesus Christ is their Savior.

> *"Give, and it will be given to you. A good measure, pressed down, shaken together and running over, will be poured into your lap. For with the measure you use, it will be measured to you."* Luke 6:38

To be effective in the gift of Giving you need to:

STOP worrying about getting burned from giving.
LOOK for those in need of money, resources, materials or financial education.
LISTEN to God for the timing of what should be given.
BE WHAT GOD CREATED YOU TO BE, and be a blessing to others to help them in their moment of need to let them know they are loved by God.

> *"You have not lived today until you have done something for someone who can never repay you."*[23] -John Bunyan

HEALING:

Have you ever had the wonderful experience of being miraculously healed? I have! I've had three specific healings as an adult and one as a child. As a small child I reached up and put my fingers on the eye of a stove set on high. My Great Grandmother was a local healer and she blew on my fingers, said a Scripture and the pain stopped. She called it "blowing out the fire." To this day I have no finger prints on the fingers I burned.

My Mom told me stories of how my Great Grandmother, who she called Momma, would be called on at all times of the night to help with babies suffering from Thrush. Families would wake her up in the middle of the night with a crying baby. She would rub a leaf in the baby's mouth then blow in it and would seal the deal with a Bible verse. The parents were so excited to tell her what a great job she had done they would come over early the next morning and wake her up again to show her the happy and healthy baby.

I was healed of depression, glaucoma and sores on my arm as an adult. I was adjusting a local Faith healer, yes they can have back issues, and I asked him to pray for my arms. I had over a dozen sores on both arms that were driving me crazy. A pimple would come up and when it popped it turned into an itchy sore that causing scars on my arms. After his prayer I felt the Holy Spirit tell me to treat the sores differently. When I would go to pick at the sore I stopped and asked Jesus to heal my arm. I would follow that with a prayer for the Faith healer's health and his ministry. To this day I have neither sores nor scars on my arms.

My Faith Healer friend was one of the most humble men you would ever meet. You would look at him and think of him as just a good ole country boy. He had a slower approach to life than others. I feel it gave him a better ability to listen to the Holy Spirit. This trait helped me nickname him the Holy Sloth. When he was working in the Spirit he focused on the task at hand and really tries to please God with his Faith.

He had a huge compassion for the sick and would frequently go past his own physical strength to help others. He was also very much against taking money to heal. He just asked for expenses when he traveled to churches for healing services. He told me how upset he became when a preacher once said to him he would be a millionaire in a few months if he had his gift. Even though the preacher tried to have him return he never went back to that church!

The spiritual gifts of Healings are powerful gifts for the Kingdom of God. They allow people to see and experience the power of God on Earth. They can help a non-believer come to a relationship with Christ or grow the Faith of a believer. The person using these gifts is using a powerful weapon against Satan and it requires a great deal of obedience to use the gifts.

Scripture uses the plural of gifts meaning there are many different kinds of spiritual gifts of Healing. Some using the gifts seem to be better at asking for healing of certain kinds of diseases. Others are able to listen to the Holy Spirit and relay specific messages to the sick for the actions required which will lead to a cure. There is also the demonic element of disease and some do better with spiritual warfare to heal the sick. There are so many aspects of Healings but one of the most common elements is Faith. Faith and healing are like peanut butter and jelly, they just belong together. Faith appears to be the most important condition of healing throughout Scriptures.

> *"Very truly I tell you, whoever believes in me will do the works I have been doing, and they will do even greater things than these, because I am going to the Father. And I will do whatever you ask in my name, so that the Father may be glorified in the Son. You may ask me for anything in my name, and I will do it."*   John 14:12-14

Faith in God is simply trusting and believing in His promises. This Scripture states that we, *"whoever believes in me,"* will not only do the miraculous works that Jesus did but we will do even greater things than He did. The majority of time when the word "Faith" is used in the 4 Gospels it describes healings. The catch is we do not need to have Faith in our own Faith; we need to have Faith in God's faithfulness.

"Lord my God, I called to you for help, and you healed me."
Psalm 30:2

We must realize all miracles of healing are from God and are never from the individual using the spiritual gifts of Healing. Studies of many healing ministries show how they crashed and burned when the focus was taken off God's power and placed on the individual. Practicing with humility is the most important thing for a healing ministry to last.

"...they will place their hands on sick people, and they will get well.' "   Mark 16:18

Scripture states clearly that believers have been given some pretty incredible things to do while here on Earth. We are supposed to love God, love our neighbors and tell them about Jesus. But we are also given abilities, through our spiritual gifts, to not only teach and serve others but to actually perform miracles in their lives.

"Is anyone among you in trouble? Let them pray. Is anyone happy? Let them sing songs of praise. Is anyone among you sick? Let them call the elders of the church to pray over them and anoint them with oil in the name of the Lord. And the prayer offered in faith will make the sick person well; the Lord will raise them up. If they have sinned, they will be forgiven. Therefore confess your sins to each other and pray for each other so that you may be healed. The prayer of a righteous person is powerful and effective."
James 5:13-16

Healing involves specific acts of obedience. It can take prayer, fasting, anointing, specific instructions, confession of sins, and most of all Faith. If you are sick, seek out believers that have an abundance of Faith and ask them to pray for you. Confess your sins in a safe place and repent of those sins. Be prepared to be given a Word of Knowledge about your condition and prayerfully be ready for what the Holy Spirit may ask you to do.

The last sentence of this Scripture instructs those who have been helped through emotional, spiritual and physical hurts to throw a rescue rope of prayer to those going through the same thing they experienced. If you have experienced the healing then your prayers for those in need will be *"powerful and effective."*

> *"She (my mother) became a warrior far superior to any epic hero. She became a giant on her knees. With a sword in one hand she battled the enemies of death and disease, and with her other hand stretched toward heaven she kept beseeching God's help and His mercy."[24]*   -Bishop T.D. Jakes

Healing can happen in places like the mind, the body and the spirit. The mind is the front line battle ground with Satan. By entertaining sinful thoughts they can eventually become actions which create excessive stresses on the body. The sins of the flesh may afflict the body with disease and create spiritual darkness and anxieties. Eventually the spirit is attacked because the enemy has now invaded our mind and body. It can make us question our relationship with God and eventually cause us to drift further away from Him.

The gifts of Healing have the ability to align the body, mind and human spirit with the Holy Spirit to produce wholeness in a person. This can result in an instantaneous healing or it may require a process. Be patient, be obedient and remember that God loves you and wants the best for you. God deeply wants a relationship with you but it is a two way street. Study His Word, pray, and listen. He is waiting patiently on you.

To be effective in the gifts of Healing you need to:

STOP fearing the world and its anxieties and let God handle those battles.

LOOK at Jesus and do not take your eyes off of Him.

LISTEN carefully to His instructions, they will be specific.

BE WHAT GOD CREATED YOU TO BE, and help bring healing and wholeness to the Body of Christ.

> *"How sweet the name of Jesus sounds, in a believer's ear! It soothes his sorrows, heals his wounds, and drives away his fear."*[25]
>
> -John Newton

HELPS:

> *"No one is useless in this world who lightens the burdens of another."*[26]　　　　-Charles Dickens

I had a friend with the spiritual gift of Helps who has passed. He was a very humble man who worked behind the scenes and never wanted any attention for his works. He had an amazing ability to measure up the needs of others and would work diligently to meet those needs. He was described by his peers as a man with a "servant's heart" who would put down his own priorities to go and bless others. He was very much a difference maker through his humble behind-the-scenes actions.

> *"Therefore if you have any encouragement from being united with Christ, if any comfort from his love, if any common sharing in the Spirit, if any tenderness and compassion, then make my joy complete by being like-minded, having the same love, being one in spirit and of one mind. Do nothing out of selfish ambition or vain conceit. Rather, in humility value others above yourselves, not looking to your own interests but each of you to the interests of the others."*
>
> Philippians 2:1-4

This is not only the gift of Helps verse it was my grandmother's verse. She had a servant's heart and used it whenever she could. She especially loved people who others did not care about and helped them with their needs. She was always putting her own projects aside and going out of her way to help others. She loved supplying her famous corn bread dressing and gravy at church pot lucks and never wanted the spot light for her works. She was the quiet behind-the-scenes worker and rarely asked for help with her own projects. She gained joy from the sense of accomplishing what God gave her to do as a true servant of God.

> *"In everything I [Paul] did, I showed you that by this kind of hard work we must help the weak, remembering the words the Lord Jesus himself said: 'It is more blessed to give than to receive.'"*   Acts 20:35

The person with the spiritual gift of Helps receives a deep joy in helping others; especially the ones that cannot help themselves. They understand being blessed by serving others. They can spot the practical needs of others and are very loyal to stay until the project is completed. They are not interested in leading others; they want to work with others or just be given a project to complete on their own. They are good listeners who are hardworking and full of compassion. They are quick to say "yes" to God.

> *"The greatest among you will be your servant. For those who exalt themselves will be humbled, and those who humble themselves will be exalted."*   Matthew 23:11-12

Those practicing this gift are surely some of the *"greatest among you."* They are truly the hands of the Body of Christ. They come by when everyone is gone and mow the grass, empty the trash and clean toilets at church. They find the jobs others do not want to do and they do the job with the joy of Christ in their heart.

"And whatever you do, whether in word or deed, do it all in the name of the Lord Jesus, giving thanks to God the Father through him." Colossians 3:17

To be effective in the gift of Helps you need to:

STOP waiting and move on with the projects God gives you to do.
LOOK for those with practical needs and help them to the best of your ability.
LISTEN carefully for God to give you a message to deliver to those you serve.
BE WHAT GOD CREATED YOU TO BE, a humble servant providing Christ's hands and feet through acts of selfless service for those in need.

"I would never want to reach out someday with a soft, uncallused hand-a hand never dirtied by serving-and shake the nail-pierced hand of Jesus."[27] -Bill Hybels

LEADERSHIP:

Do you have one of those friends that act like they're right all the time and it's frustrating because they usually are? They'll ask you for advice and do something completely different from your suggestion. They're usually organized and efficient and if their heart is with God, they have great motives for the directions they choose. They constantly prepare for the future and if you ask them where they plan to be in 5, 10 or 30 years they will give you a well thought out answer.

A Leader is similar to Administration but is focused on people and relationships rather than tasks and things. They're passionate and desire to have lifelong friends. They focus on the "who" of goals. They can see the problem and put together a clear vision and direction for those involved. Scripture tells them to carry out their work with "diligence" meaning they need to proceed with a careful urgency to accomplish the goal. These people are orderly, responsible, decisive, loyal and determined but they do not like wasted time, money, talents, resources and energy.

> *"The authority by which the Christian leader leads is not power but love, not force but example, not coercion but reasoned persuasion. Leaders have power, but power is safe only in the hands of those who humble themselves to serve."*[28]   -John Stott

Leaders care deeply for God's people and recognize the hidden potential in each person. They are very persuasive and can motivate others to grow in their potential. The Greek root word for Leader is "to make to stand" which fits perfectly since they are excellent at delegating jobs to others.

They have an uncanny ability to make a person stand and do a job, even if the person thinks they're not qualified. Taking a risk on others abilities can bring out spiritual gifts by showing them they are qualified in God's eyes. Leaders thrive on a job well done but they delight in the success of building up people who thought they were of no value.

Many times leaders will take a leadership role when there is no one stepping up to fill the position. They lead well in a crisis because they can stay focused on the task at hand during turbulent times. They are not the behind the scene administrator and they do not care much for long committee and planning meetings. They are very much the "up front' and "take charge" person in the public eye. They take a strong stand in the truth and it can be hard to change their mind. They themselves need a strong Leader to believe in. They will follow a good leader and be loyal for a lifetime and they expect the same loyalty from others. Christian leaders should look to Jesus as the ultimate leader.

The most important qualities of a Leader should be humility and obedience to God. You need to recognize when others are suffering under your leadership and do something about the situation. Your main purpose as a Leader is to make more Leaders as humbly and efficiently as possible to build up God's kingdom.

> *"To the elders among you, I appeal as a fellow elder and a witness of Christ's sufferings who also will share in the glory to be revealed: Be shepherds of God's flock that is under your care, watching over them—not because you must, but because you are willing, as God wants you to be; not pursuing dishonest gain, but eager to serve; not lording it over those entrusted to you, but being examples to the flock. And when the Chief Shepherd appears, you will receive the crown of glory that will never fade away. In the same way, you who are younger, submit yourselves to your elders. All of you, clothe yourselves with humility toward one another, because, 'God opposes the proud but shows favor to the humble.' Humble yourselves, therefore, under God's mighty hand, that he may lift you up in due time."*
>
> 1 Peter 5:1-6

To be effective in the gift of Leadership you need to:

STOP being prideful and let God use you to build His Kingdom.
LOOK for ways to accomplish goals to bring others closer to Christ
LISTEN for God's safest and most efficient direction to the goal.
BE WHAT GOD CREATED YOU TO BE; a humble servant being used of God to build up other Leaders who guide other people to heaven!

> *"According to Scripture, virtually everything that truly qualifies a person for leadership is directly related to character. It's not about style, status, personal charisma, clout, or worldly measurements of success. Integrity is the main issue that makes the difference between a good leader and a bad one."*[29]
>
> -John MacArthur

MERCY:

The people with the spiritual gift of Mercy are the "Lovers of the Lost." They are sensitive to those hurting and are drawn to those who are unloved and rejected. They enjoy helping the elderly, the disabled, the mentally ill, the outcasts, the lonely, the rebellious, the grieving and the under privileged.

> *"Rejoice with those who rejoice; mourn with those who mourn."*   Romans 12:15

They are more than just sympathetic to other's needs; they are empathetic and can feel the pain of others. They will stay with you and comfort you through the storms of life. They rejoice in a life regained for the Kingdom of God and they understand the value of people even if they think they have failed.

> *"Therefore, there is now no condemnation for those who are in Christ Jesus"*   Romans 8:1

Those with the spiritual gift of Mercy live out this verse. They are kind and gentle and their walk is all about God's love for others. They will love you where you are and show you Christ's love through their actions. They supernaturally sense how others are feeling and will give emotional aid at just the right moments in people's lives. My friend with this gift is a "Love Sponge!" She will absorb love and multiply it back to others. She is a joy to be around and always seems to care about every part of your life and genuinely cares about you and your family.

> *"...if it is to show mercy, do it cheerfully."*   Romans 12:8

The Scriptures tell us to use the spiritual gift of Mercy *"cheerfully."* My friend is the poster child of cheerful. She is always smiling and looking to pass on God's love to someone; cheerful is her middle name.

"A cheerful heart is good medicine..."

Proverbs 17:22

Scripture tells us cheerfulness is good medicine. Those with the spiritual gift of Mercy actually give their *"good medicine"* to the broken down and poor in spirit which can promote healings in their mind, body and spirit. They have the heart of God and they show His love through action.

"Praise be to the God and Father of our Lord Jesus Christ, the Father of compassion and the God of all comfort, who comforts us in all our troubles, so that we can comfort those in any trouble with the comfort we ourselves receive from God."

2 Corinthians 1:3-4

Many people ask what God's Will is for their life. Those with the spiritual gift of Mercy know the first thing is to *"comfort those in any trouble with the comfort we ourselves receive from God."* They truly turn their own hurts and pains of life into comfort for others because they understand the unconditional love of God. They have a direct line for God to give them directions on how a person needs to be loved. God also gives them powerful prayers for those in need of God's mercy and love. They are exceptional prayer warriors for the Body of Christ.

To be effective in the gift of Mercy you need to:

STOP feeling ashamed and unworthy to do God's work.
LOOK for those who need their cup refilled with the Holy Spirit's love.
LISTEN for God's instructions on how to show them His love.
BE WHAT GOD CREATED YOU TO BE, and be a Love Sponge for God. Absorb Jesus' love and squeeze it out cheerfully to others.

"God uses ordinary Christians to change lives - one conversation at a time, one meal at a time, one act of mercy at a time."[30]

-Tony Merida

MINISTRY or Service:

"Harmony is produced in ministry when everyone seeks to be a servant."[31]   -Elizabeth George

The word Ministry means serving, aiding, or relieving and literally means to wait tables. There are many people in the Body of Christ with the spiritual gift of Ministry who are never fully appreciated for all they do in the background of the church. They volunteer willingly for some of the most difficult jobs and keep the church body in motion. They do this because they know they are building God's Kingdom by gathering people together for the sake of Christ.

"And let us consider how we may spur one another on toward love and good deeds, not giving up meeting together, as some are in the habit of doing, but encouraging one another— and all the more as you see the Day approaching."
Hebrews 10:24-25

This spiritual gift has a strong desire to gather groups of people together and help them feel warm and welcome for a purpose. They know they are seed planters, milk providers and meat servers. They build the body through Outreach, Special Events, Children and Youth ministries, Missions and Relief ministries. They spiritually feed believers through Worship ministries, Discipleship, and Counseling. They also give Christians areas to exercise their Faith through Visitation, Service areas, Volunteer Events, Camps and Retreats.

Those with the gift of Ministry literally build up Christians from the womb and provide opportunities for them to learn and trust God to do good works until they are placed in the grave. Whew, it's exhausting just going over all the things these people handle in a given day. But they know their work opens the door for others spiritual gifts to grow and be put into action.

> *"I have set you an example that you should do as I have done for you. Very truly I tell you, no servant is greater than his master, nor is a messenger greater than the one who sent him. Now that you know these things, you will be blessed if you do them."*   John 13:15-17

People with the spiritual gift of Ministry are true servants who bless others. They truly want Christ's example to be shown to everyone and are willing to go to great lengths to obtain the goal. Most of us never give a second thought to the tables, chairs, food, plates, and utensils set up for us at Wednesday night supper or special events. Ministry does. Have you ever considered the planning involved with all the Sunday school classes from the newborns to the elderly? Ministry does. Ever wonder how church counseling organizations for marriage, substance abuse, family and financial problems are handled? Ministry does. What about when you sit in a Sunday morning service, do you ponder the time spent to make sure the seating, lighting, sound, stage set-up, and bulletins are ready for worship and learning about our Father God? Ministry does. I cannot praise this group of men and women enough for all they do. I call them the backbone of the Body of Christ because of the load they carry.

> *"However, I consider my life worth nothing to me; my only aim is to finish the race and complete the task the Lord Jesus has given me—the task of testifying to the good news of God's grace."*   Acts 20:24

Those using the spiritual gift of Ministry truly understand this passage of Scripture. My wife falls into this gift category as a behind the scenes doer of Christ. She thinks of the little things that bless others. She always puts great thought into purchases for others and loves to send encouraging Facebook posts to those having birthdays and anniversaries. She truly has a heart for helping others feel blessed and enjoys simple functions like serving tables or decorating at retreats.

My wife does not like the lime light and was panicked when she was chosen to be the head of a women's ministry some years ago. She spent endless hours planning for her weekend and even changed a major portion of the weekend schedule. She wanted to go over her personal testimony early so the women going through the weekend could feel more comfortable closer to the beginning of the weekend. She wanted them to relax into the arms of Jesus and gain all He had to offer on their weekend. God created her to help people feel warm and welcome for a purpose.

"Ministry's not an option for a Christian; it's a privilege."[32]
-Lori Hatcher

To be effective in the gift of Ministry you need to:

STOP getting hung up on every detail in ministry and do your best with what you have to work with.
LOOK for people to help you with the ministries and delegate responsibilities to them to avoid burn-out.
LISTEN for God's creative ideas to share with others and be a blessing to them.
BE WHAT GOD CREATED YOU TO BE, and help people feel warm and welcome for the purpose of knowing Christ!

"Personal ministry is not about always knowing what to say. It is not about fixing everything in sight that is broken. Personal ministry is about connecting people with Christ so that they are able to think as he would have them think, desire what he says is best, and do what he calls them to do even if their circumstances never get "fixed." It involves exposing hurt, lost, and confused people to God's glory, so that they give up their pursuit of their own glory and live for his."[33]   -Paul David Tripp

MIRACLES:

Miracles, Working or Effecting of:

"I believe miracles are to be prayed for, not wished for."[34]
                                    -Wanda E. Brunstetter

"...and to another the effecting of miracles, and to another prophecy, and to another the distinguishing of spirits, to another various kinds of tongues, and to another the interpretation of tongues."   1 Corinthians 12:10 NASB

The word *"miracles"* mean force, power or strength. It is where we get the word dynamite. The word *"effecting"* means operation, working or energizing and is where we get the word energy. The spiritual gift of Effecting of Miracles is the supernatural ability for the Holy Spirit to show the power of God by acts of obedience that requires our energy.

It is rare to find miracles just happening in Scripture, they usually require someone obediently working to carry out God's power or proclaim them to be happening. An example of obedience is when Moses had to hold his hands up for the Israelites to beat the Amalekites. When he became tired Aaron and Hur lifted his arms until the battle was won. Most all Miracles seem to require some specific form of obedience.

TYPES OF MIRACLES

The spiritual gifts of the Working of Miracles is another gift described in a plural form meaning there are many types of miracles:

MIRACLES OVER CREATION require a change in nature like parting the Red Sea, Manna from heaven, the Star of Bethlehem or Jericho's walls falling down. They can include supernatural changes in the environment like Jesus calming the sea, prophesying the destruction of the Temple in Jerusalem and telling the fishermen to cast their net on the other side of the boat to catch a net full of fish.

MIRACLES OVER CIRCUMSTANCES require a change of the mind. Ester could have been killed when she confronted the King but his mind was changed by her obedience. This eventually led to saving the entire Jewish race.

MIRACLES OVER THE BODY require a change in health that heals people of mental, emotional and physical issues. There are so many Scriptures about physical healing. Think about the people you know who turned their lives over to Jesus and were instantly freed by grace from addictions of drugs, alcohol and pornography. It may not be walking on water but it is a real miracle for those people in bondage to sin. I personally have been on the receiving end of being freed from alcohol and have enjoyed several physical healings.

MIRACLES OVER THE SPIRITS are a change in possession. This is where demons are cast out of people to free them from bondage and receive spiritual healing. There are many examples of these in Scripture like Jesus casting out demons and sending them into the pigs.

MIRACLES OF THE MATERIAL require a change in provisions like the widow with no food. Elijah blessed her jar and jug to never run out of flour and oil. It also includes Jesus feeding thousands and turning water into wine. This can also be a provision of money like when Jesus told the disciples to catch a fish and it had money in it to pay taxes.

MIRACLES OF SALVATION are changes in the heart. For those thinking miracles have stopped, this is the biggest reason to be excited about miracles. Miracles can go beyond the natural order of the universe into the supernatural like Jesus walking on water. But it goes even further too individually place us into an eternity in heaven with God. I find it ironic when those who do not believe miracles are still happening will turn around and ask you to give your life to Jesus and be in Heaven for eternity. Eternity in Heaven is the biggest and most important miracle of all.

> *"After the Lord Jesus had spoken to them, he was taken up into heaven and he sat at the right hand of God. Then the disciples went out and preached everywhere, and the Lord worked with them and confirmed his word by the signs that accompanied it."*   Mark 16:19-20

Henry Blackaby mentioned Miracles of Circumstances in his book Experiencing God. He would pray for an amount of money needed for missions and a check for the exact amount would show up at just the right time. I love how God arranged the amount to be the same just to show He was involved. It gave confirmation to the project being funded as being the will of God.

This brings up Signs and Wonders because they tend to be similar to miracles. From large to small, all miracles have a purpose and it's to glorify God. They can provide a Sign such as just the right amount of money needed which gives confirmation that God is involved with the miracle. On the other hand a Wonder tends to be a miraculous effect to gain the attention of others, even to the point of terror. It basically grabs people's attention to back up God's Word and deliver an important message. It can be a really good message about upcoming events or it can be a really bad message of impending doom.

> *"Jesus said to them, 'A prophet is not without honor except in his own town, among his relatives and in his own home.' He could not do any miracles there, except lay his hands on a few sick people and heal them. He was amazed at their lack of faith."*   Mark 6:4-6

This person with the spiritual gift of Miracles may be limited by the Faith of others around them. Jesus could do no miracles in his hometown other than heal a few sick due to the lack of Faith by the people there. Find out where God is working and get involved so miracles can happen.

> **"Then Jesus began to denounce the towns in which most of his miracles had been performed, because they did not repent."**
> Matthew 11:20

When miracles are performed it does not necessarily mean people will be saved. Jesus was disappointed with the cities where he did the most miracles because they did not repent and turn to God. Miracles can provide verification that God is involved but there will always be those who continue in their disbelief. Sometimes people are just there for the show.

> *"If you want miracles to happen in your life, then stop trying to work out your situation by yourself and obey God. He is a miracle working God!"*[35]   -Jacqueline (Jackie) McCullough

To be effective in the gift of Miracles you need to:

STOP having Faith in your own Faith.
LOOK to God's faithfulness.
LISTEN to Him and be obedient down to the exact letter of His request.
BE WHAT GOD CREATED YOU TO BE, and do *"greater works than these"* and be a blessing to others while giving glory to God.

> *"I believe in miracles, but I trust in Jesus. If you believe the Bible, you know that God is a miracle-working God. And God is not limited in any degree nor any respect. He is totally sovereign. Do you believe that? I hope you do. Believe in miracles, but don't put your faith in miracles. Put your faith and your trust in the Lord Jesus Christ."*[36]   -Adrian Pierce Rogers

PASTOR:

"God has entrusted us with his most precious treasure - people. He asks us to shepherd and mold them into strong disciples, with brave faith and good character."[37]   -John Ortberg

The word used for "Pastor" is used 18 times in the New Testament but is translated "shepherd" 17 out of those 18 times. The one time it is used as "Pastor" is when it is described as a spiritual gift in Ephesians 4:11. For a better understanding of this gift we can compare the spiritual gift of Pastoring to the work of a shepherd.

> **"The gatekeeper opens the gate for him, and the sheep listen to his voice. He calls his own sheep by name and leads them out. When he has brought out all his own, he goes on ahead of them, and his sheep follow him because they know his voice. But they will never follow a stranger; in fact, they will run away from him because they do not recognize a stranger's voice."**   John 10:3-5

Notice how Jesus describes going out ahead of the sheep so they can follow Him. Sheep cannot be driven from behind, they must follow their shepherd and the shepherd needs to know the right direction to take his flock.

I know many people with the spiritual gift of Pastoring and they tend to be very gentle people with a genuine desire to help people grow in Christ. They are very protective of the people they know and especially the underdogs. They are full of truth and they tend to be more focused on "who" the church helps more than "how" the church runs its day to day operations. They tend to lean more toward serving the needs for the Body of Christ.

Jesus used this chapter of John to describe a good shepherd's (Pastor's) abilities. The voice of the Shepherd is obviously important because the sheep learn their voice and follow them. There are many reasons this is important such as having them follow the shepherd to green pastures and for protection from strangers.

A shepherd is responsible for their flock to be fed good teachings just as a shepherd leads their flock to green pastures. A person with the spiritual gift of Pastoring is divinely created to speak truth into people's lives and find good teachers for their flock. Shepherds also protect the flock by keeping them away from poisonous plants just as a Pastor is to keep their flock away from false teachings that could poison their mind. The more the flock hears good and sound teachings, the better they will be at recognizing the false ones and stay away from them.

"I am the good shepherd. The good shepherd lays down his life for the sheep. The hired hand is not the shepherd and does not own the sheep. So when he sees the wolf coming, he abandons the sheep and runs away. Then the wolf attacks the flock and scatters it. The man runs away because he is a hired hand and cares nothing for the sheep."
John 10:11-13

A pretty serious call of the shepherd is to protect the flock from predators even unto death. Think about laying down one's entire life for others. Not just their death but all the years of their life as a servant. The spiritual gift of Pastoring is a long-term lifelong commitment to the Body of Christ as a servant. It requires giving up of one's time to supply needs to others and requires ongoing care for those in need. It is not a quick fix to problems. Fortunately those with this gift are uniquely created to handle this kind of service to others. It is no wonder why so many of them end up in professions like the military, EMTs, police and firefighters.

I once told a patient that had the spiritual gift of Pastoring that he did not have to run a church. I even reassured him that his gift was not that of an organized administrator that runs the entire church. His gift was about relating with people and helping them in their walk with

Christ. I shared with him that he had a unique ability to go after the lost sheep like the person who leaves the church. I explained that many people attend a church for many years and when they leave no one even checked on them to find out what happened. I said he could go to that person or couple and because of the way God created him, he could sit with them and discuss what happened. It may bring them back but if it doesn't at least it may stop the spirit of offense that could keep them out of another church in the future.

> *Then Jesus told them this parable: "Suppose one of you has a hundred sheep and loses one of them. Doesn't he leave the ninety-nine in the open country and go after the lost sheep until he finds it? And when he finds it, he joyfully puts it on his shoulders and goes home. Then he calls his friends and neighbors together and says, 'Rejoice with me; I have found my lost sheep.' I tell you that in the same way there will be more rejoicing in heaven over one sinner who repents than over ninety-nine righteous persons who do not need to repent."*   Luke 15:3-7

The spiritual gift of Pastoring is all about tending to the Body of Christ. It is helping them learn about Christ so they can get to know Him and learn to trust Him and become what they were created to be. It is also about going after the sheep that strays off from the flock and gets lost or hurt. Pastors have a very important call on their lives to give opportunities to others to become the best version of what God made them to be.

To be effective in the gift of Pastoring you need to:

STOP wondering if you were called to help people.
LOOK around at the rows of hurting Christians in the church pews.
LISTEN to God for their needs and help lead them to a deeper relationship with Christ.

BE WHAT GOD CREATED YOU TO BE and pour out the truth of Christ while serving the needs and protecting God's children.

"God has not abandoned us any more than he abandoned Job. He never abandons anyone on whom he has set his love; nor does Christ, the good shepherd, ever lose track of his sheep."[38]

-J. I. Packer

PROPHECY:

The word "prophet" has been battered around by Satan over the years. When you hear the word you feel as if you are about to be served poisoned Kool-Aid or have all your possessions taken from you and be forced to live in a commune. When you hear people saying Jesus is coming back on this date and He never does, it puts a bad light on the ones actually trying to bring Biblical messages to those who need it. Satan obviously enjoys messing with God's children by destroying the reputation of the ones responsible for pointing others to God's Word.

Prophet can mean a foreteller; one who predicts a future. It can also be a forth teller; one who is divinely-empowered that speaks the mind of God. Simply put, the person using the spiritual gift of Prophecy is a messenger of God's Word. Their job today is not revealing new truths about God; it is to point people back to the Word of God. Their words are generally corrective in nature and call for repentance of sins. To some they appear to be the party pooper taking away all the "fun" of their sin. When this gift is used correctly it can lead others to a healthy relationship with their Creator and build up the Body of Christ.

Those using this gift can spot fake and phony people quickly and cannot stand hypocrisy. They have a supernatural ability to say the right thing at the right time that cuts deep into the heart of the matter at hand. They are very comfortable with Scripture and sees God's Word as an absolute authority for life. They are very logical and are not easily swayed by emotions and they live by, "If it is truthful and right then do it."

They tend to be more of a kick-in-the-butt quick fix rather than staying with people for the long haul. They are like the meatball surgeons in the TV series M*A*S*H who stopped the bleeding and sent the patient on to others for long term recovery. Those with this gift often see the brokenness of this world like potholes, dents in cars, and houses that need painting. It makes them good at detailed jobs but God gave them these lenses to look through because they need to find broken people to give them the right message at the right time.

> *"But in your hearts revere Christ as Lord. Always be prepared to give an answer to everyone who asks you to give the reason for the hope that you have. But do this with gentleness and respect, keeping a clear conscience, so that those who speak maliciously against your good behavior in Christ may be ashamed of their slander."*
>
> 1 Peter 3:15-16

Those with the spiritual gift of Prophecy should always *"be prepared to give an answer"* for *"the hope that you have"* in Jesus. This is usually not a problem because of their love of Scripture and the jewels they dig up from intense study. They are always ready to give an answer but need to be careful about correcting people who are not ready to receive correction. Do not blurt out your opinion to others not asking you for it. They will not receive it well. Scripture says to wait for *"everyone who asks you"* for advice. This is very important because of the dominos God is lining up in a person's life. They need to be ready and willing to hear a message of correction.

Scripture goes on to say the messages should be delivered with *"gentleness and respect."* There is a tendency for the one's using the spiritual gift of Prophecy to appear harsh because they are very black and white in their thinking with no gray zones and no compromise. Things are either right or wrong. When revealing a person's shortcomings the Prophet should always remember the grace that was given them for their sins as they point out the sins of others.

> *"Follow the way of love and eagerly desire gifts of the Spirit, especially prophecy. For anyone who speaks in a tongue does not speak to people but to God. Indeed, no one understands them; they utter mysteries by the Spirit. But the one who prophesies speaks to people for their strengthening, encouraging and comfort."*   1 Corinthians 14:1-3

Here are some very important remarks about the spiritual gift of Prophecy. It tells us to *"follow the way of love"* and *"eagerly"* desire spiritual gifts, *"especially prophecy."* The word for eagerly reminds me of how crazy in love a football fan can be for their team. What if we could be that in love with Jesus and be that fired up for Him? What if we were able to strengthen, encourage and comfort those around us with just our words because you were obedient to be what God created us to be?

> *"If I have the gift of prophecy and can fathom all mysteries and all knowledge, and if I have a faith that can move mountains, but do not have love, I am nothing."*
> 1 Corinthians 13:2

We all need to *"follow the way of love"* because without love we are *"nothing."* God says of Faith, hope and love He chooses love as the greatest. The idea of love cannot be covered in a few sentences so for now we just need to understand that love is a very important part of all spiritual gifts especially Prophecy.

"A new command I give you: Love one another. As I have loved you, so you must love one another. By this everyone will know that you are my disciples, if you love one another."
John 13:34-35

"When God speaks, he does not give new revelation about himself that contradicts what he has already revealed in Scripture. Rather, God speaks to give application of his Word to the specific circumstances in your life. When God speaks to you, he is not writing a new book of Scripture; rather, he is applying to your life what he has already said in his Word."[39]

-Henry T. Blackaby, Hearing God's Voice

To be effective in the gift of Prophecy you need to:

STOP being a "but God" and be obedient to His call no matter how odd it may seem.

LOOK for those that are broken and need a Word from God.

LISTEN for the truthful messages He wishes for you to deliver to others.

BE WHAT GOD CREATED YOU TO BE, an obedient Mail-person delivering God's Word on time; no matter the conditions.

TEACHING:

"Tell me and I forget. Teach me and I remember. Involve me and I learn."[40]   -Benjamin Franklin

Most of us can remember a teacher who inspired us when we were young. My High School art teacher was excited about her subject and she poured herself into her students. She offered many ways for her students to express themselves and grow in their art skills. She constantly encouraged her students to stretch themselves at every opportunity. Over our lifetime only a few teachers stand out and sadly we do not remember the majority of those teachers. Every teacher should strive to be the one their students remember and is the one that made a difference in their life. The spiritual gift of Teaching has some tough hills to climb but the rewards are eternal.

> *"In everything set them an example by doing what is good. In your teaching show integrity, seriousness and soundness of speech that cannot be condemned, so that those who oppose you may be ashamed because they have nothing bad to say about us."*   Titus 2:7-8

Biblical teaching of God's Word is held to a very high standard of **"integrity, seriousness, and soundness of speech"** because of the eternal impact it has on people. Biblical teaching is calling to spread the good news of Christ. The teacher needs to know the audience they are teaching. They are building up the church by teaching young and old prophets, pastors, evangelists, exhorters, leaders, administrators, other teachers and those in ministry. The spiritual gift of Teaching should communicate God's Word clearly with truth and accuracy.

> *"Not many of you should become teachers, my fellow believers, because you know that we who teach will be judged more strictly. We all stumble in many ways. Anyone who is never at fault in what they say is perfect, able to keep their whole body in check."*   James 3:1-2

Teacher's words and their walk with Christ are held accountable to a higher standard. It has been said, "What you do speaks so loudly that others can't hear what you say!" Teachers' mouths should be free of cussing and ranting because Scripture says a spring does not produce both fresh water and salt water. The life of a teacher should teach others more than just words.

> *"Don't fall into the trap of studying the Bible without doing what it says."*[41]   -Francis Chan

Those using the spiritual gift of Teaching enjoy reading, research and study to prepare for their lessons. They love sharing thoughts and insights from a variety of sources and are able to take large amounts of information and put it into smaller digestible bites. They are usually very confident in the information they have prepared due to the many hours they have put into their study time. They also enjoy presenting their information in different formats like charts, pictures, cartoons, graphics and bullet points to clearly communicate their ideas.

Teachers can reach all types of audiences through their words but also through dramas, song-writing, and artistic interpretations of Biblical stories. A true and dedicated teacher is a special gift to the church. They take every moment as an opportunity to spread the good news about our Lord and Savior Jesus Christ.

> *"For everything God created is good, and nothing is to be rejected if it is received with thanksgiving, because it is consecrated by the word of God and prayer. If you point these things out to the brothers and sisters, you will be a good minister of Christ Jesus, nourished on the truths of the faith and of the good teaching that you have followed."*
> 1 Timothy 4:4-6

True Biblical Teachers know the Word of God and share it with their brothers and sisters. They know interpretations of God's Word are serious and eternal and they help others be *"nourished on the truths of the faith."* Lives are changed through the speaking of God's Word and it ultimately brings people into God's Kingdom.

> *"The Spirit gives life; the flesh counts for nothing. The words I have spoken to you—they are full of the Spirit and life."*
> John 6:63

True Biblical Teachers know the Holy Spirit is what brings the Scriptures to life! Teachers bring life to others by bringing them the Word of God!

Biblical Teachers also know it is a priority to teach children Biblical truths in order to help guide their future lives. I love the hearts of those who teach children about God. They are so dedicated to plant the seed of God's Word and pass the children along to those who can water the seeds. They may not see all their seeds sprout and grow but when they do they experience a heavenly joy for a job well done for the Lord.

"If we don't teach our children to follow Christ, the world will teach them not to."   -Anonymous

"All Scripture is God-breathed and is useful for teaching, rebuking, correcting and training in righteousness, so that the servant of God may be thoroughly equipped for every good work."   2 Timothy 3:16-17

To be effective in the gift of Teaching you need to:

STOP being a bad example. Follow God's truth and be an example of truth to others.
LOOK for God's Words to share the truth to others, no matter their age or status.
LISTEN for creative ways to share God's truth no matter where you are.
BE WHAT GOD CREATED YOU TO BE, and teach others God's truth so they can do good works and grow in Christ.

"The Word of God I think of as a straight edge, which shows up our own crookedness. We can't really tell how crooked our thinking is until we line it up with the straight edge of Scripture."[42]
                    -Elisabeth Elliot

TONGUES:
Diverse and Interpretations

"Groanings which cannot be uttered are often prayers which cannot be refused."[43]   -Charles Spurgeon

When Scriptures mention Diverse Tongues it is like saying tongues have many children. There are several different types of tongues but all are from the same Father. But as any good child, they need to follow His rules.

> *"All of them were filled with the Holy Spirit and began to speak in other tongues as the Spirit enabled them. Now there were staying in Jerusalem God-fearing Jews from every nation under heaven. When they heard this sound, a crowd came together in bewilderment, because each one heard their own language being spoken."*
>
> Acts 2:4-6

In the New Testament the first use of the spiritual gift of Diverse Tongues was to supernaturally speak a language that was understood by different nationalities. The ones using the spiritual gift of Tongues were clearly speaking the languages of different people groups.

> *"'...we hear them declaring the wonders of God in our own tongues!' Amazed and perplexed, they asked one another, 'What does this mean?' Some, however, made fun of them and said, 'They have had too much wine.'"*
>
> Acts 2:11-13

Many were amazed and 3000 people were baptized and added to the Faith because of hearing the *"wonders of God"* being spoken in their own language. Unfortunately signs and miracles will always have unbelievers who cast doubt like the ones claiming *"they have had too much wine."*

"Everything must be done so that the church may be built up. If anyone speaks in a tongue, two—or at the most three— should speak, one at a time, and someone must interpret."
1 Corinthians 14:26-27

The second use of the spiritual gift of Diverse Tongues is the ability to speak an unknown language. Scripture has several rules for this use of this gift and *"someone must interpret"* in order *"that the church may be built up."* Most of the time this is an encouraging Word for the church. Paul goes on to say that prophecy, if there is no interpretation of tongues, is better because people need to understand what is said. Tongues are not only for believers but they can be a sign to unbelievers as well. There needs to be an interpreter of this type of tongue in order for the congregation to understand what God is trying to tell them.

"So if the whole church comes together and everyone speaks in tongues, and inquirers or unbelievers come in, will they not say that you are out of your mind?"
1 Corinthians 14:23

If there is no interpretation the congregation may look out of their mind or look drunk to unbelievers. Those with the gifts of prophecy, discerning spirits and others are called to verify whether the words spoken in tongues are real or fake. Scripture is clear on tongues in public places; there must be an interpretation unless the message is for the individual. It is not good to create a disruption in the church service. Individuals can stop their tongue according to Scripture.

"If there is no interpreter, the speaker should keep quiet in the church and speak to himself and to God."
1 Corinthians 14:28

The third use of the spiritual gift of Diverse Tongues is a type of prayer language given to an individual for building them up privately. I have friends that describe this as the Holy Spirit stepping in to pray for them when they do not know what to pray.

> *"In the same way, the Spirit helps us in our weakness. We do not know what we ought to pray for, but the Spirit himself intercedes for us through wordless groans."*
>
> Romans 8:26

This prayer is described as being very peaceful. It's a "prayer closet" private conversation with God. We've all been in a place in our lives where we had no idea what to pray, this type of Tongue allows the Holy Spirit to pray for us.

Unfortunately the spiritual gift of Diverse Tongues is currently a dividing issue among denominations and individuals. I'm a Southern Baptist who believes all of the gifts of the Holy Spirit are still working. Even though I believe in all the gifts I do not speak in tongues nor do I have all the spiritual gifts.

> *"Therefore, my brothers and sisters, be eager to prophesy, and do not forbid speaking in tongues."*
>
> 1 Corinthians 14:39

It is interesting that one of the most controversial spiritual gifts is Tongues, yet God tells us not to *"forbid speaking in tongues."* God knew there would be controversy over tongues when He had this verse written. Obviously it is not forbidding someone from speaking in a current foreign language they had never learned? That could be very useful in a foreign country so it seems this Scripture is dealing with the unknown tongue. There are rules for the use of Tongues so it can unify and not divide the church.

By witnessing the speaking and singing of tongues in several settings and I've seen both the fake ones and the real ones that brought the peace of the Holy Spirit. I even once felt like I interpreted a tongue as the word "peace" while friends were quietly praying for a brother in need. There are real and fake versions of the spiritual gifts. We need to know and trust God better so we can rightly divide the good ones from the bad ones.

Years ago I was the head of a Tres Dias Men's retreat and it was two weeks before the main weekend. These weekends are very multi-denominational and during a team meeting two of my friends got into a public argument about tongues. I had already made it clear that I do not speak in Tongues but I did not mind men quietly praying in Tongues during the weekend. I also made it clear this weekend was not the place to call down for the Baptism of the Holy Spirit. One of my friends said there are absolutely no Tongues on the weekend and another said there would be Tongues. Neither man was in a position of authority over the weekend and had no business stirring up this conflict and division.

Over the next few days several men became offended and were dropping out of serving on the weekend. I was battling a depression at the time and this divisiveness was devastating to me as the weekend spiraled out of control. God got one word to me and it was, "Fast!" I drank only water for four and a half days and God gave me instructions for the next meeting. I took off my shirt in a sign of humility as I washed those men's feet in front of the team. I also had a list of Scriptures that God gave me read over the two friends. My friends and the team were healed of division and the weekend was a success.

The healing of the team followed my obedience to God but fortunately it was not the only healing. After washing their feet I sat down with a sandwich to break my fast. After my first bite I realized my six-month depression was completely gone. Even though Satan tried to divide the team with the gift of Tongues God meant it for good. Ironically my friend who said absolutely no tongues on the weekend has a saying to this day, "If God wants me to be purple I'll be purple." I hope he gets his wish and is turned purple for God one day.

During the same men's weekend we were having another foot washing. I stood there watching some brothers praying over another brother and he began to speak in tongues for the first time. The men were not calling down for the "Baptism of the Holy Spirit," they were simply laying hands on and praying for this man who was of a non-tongue speaking denomination.

After witnessing this I asked God, "If you want me to speak in tongues, I'll do it." The volume of the music and praying in the room seemed to drop in half and I clearly heard, "I am training you in Prophecy." I actually turned around to see who said those words to me and there was no one.

After the message I concentrated my efforts on learning more about Prophecy. Obviously the weekend was a personal mile marker in my life. I was chosen to be a leader by my peers, I was obedient to God and carried out my leadership role and was personally healed of my depression. It was an amazing mountaintop experience for me even through the depression and divisiveness.

> **"Do all have gifts of healing? Do all speak in tongues? Do all interpret?"**   1 Corinthians 12:30

Paul was going through a laundry list of gifts explaining that everyone doesn't have all the gifts. My story has a point; everyone does not speak in Tongues just like everyone does not have a gift of Healing or Prophecy. Speaking in Tongues is not the only evidence of the Holy Spirit being inside of us. There are many spiritual gifts that show up through our obedience that indicates the Holy Spirit is within us.

"And these signs will accompany those who believe: In my name they will drive out demons; they will speak in new tongues; they will pick up snakes with their hands; and when they drink deadly poison, it will not hurt them at all; they will place their hands on sick people, and they will get well."

Mark 16:17-18

If you are a *"who believe"* person you have been given great power through the Holy Spirit to accomplish the perfection of God through the imperfections of others. But please follow the rules; they were put there for a reason.

To be effective in the gift of Tongues you need to:

STOP breaking the rules for your own selfish gratification.
LOOK for ways to unify the church and not divide it when using Tongues.
LISTEN carefully to what God's message is for the people and interpret the message when necessary.
BE WHAT GOD CREATED YOU TO BE and carefully deliver God's encouragement to both believers and non-believers to build up the church.

"God has given us two ears, but one tongue, to show that we should be swift to hear, but slow to speak. God has set a double fence before the tongue, the teeth and the lips, to teach us to be wary that we offend not with our tongue."[44]   -Thomas Watson

WORD OF KNOWLEDGE:

"Knowledge is but folly unless it is guided by grace."[45]

-George Herbert

"My goal is that they may be encouraged in heart and united in love, so that they may have the full riches of complete understanding, in order that they may know the mystery of God, namely, Christ, in whom are hidden all the treasures of wisdom and knowledge."   Colossians 2:2-3

Have you ever encountered a person that you did not know but when they spoke to you they knew something personal about you? When used correctly a person using the spiritual gift of the Word of Knowledge can receive supernatural messages about people or circumstances. Keep in mind these messages can be very sensitive as they expose the person receiving them and need to be held in strict privacy.

These messages are very dependent upon the timing and obedience of the user of the gift because they are generally information for a situation going on at that moment. This information can be from the past, present or future. It may also come from a personal experience, a word, Scripture, insight, dream, or vision from the Holy Spirit. The person using the spiritual gift of the Word of Knowledge is not necessarily smarter than other people; they are just willing to be a vessel used of God to deliver a timely message. It doesn't take a PHD in Theology to receive a Word of Knowledge.

"We tend to be a generation of Christians who major on minor matters but do not seem to possess the true measure of the gospel in the knowledge of God. We do not really know God. At best we know about Him."[46]   -Sinclair B. Ferguson

These messages are designed to build up and encourage an individual or the Body of Christ even if it's a warning. Because this type of message is usually very specific it verifies the person giving the word as a deliverer of a message from God. This opens a door to give a Word of Wisdom to the recipient of the message to help them change their lives. Wisdom is Knowledge in action so Knowledge is only as good as the actions used from it. Knowledge without Wisdom can be very dangerous so this gift should be used with humility and grace.

Any Christian with any education level can receive the spiritual gift of the Word of Knowledge. Many are students of Scripture who look for information that can help people in their day to day lives. They love sharing information and ideas with others which lead them to a better understanding of their relationship with Christ. They are created to receive the Word of Knowledge and mix it with God's Word to deliver it to those who need to hear it as a Word of Wisdom.

> *"Do your best to present yourself to God as one approved, a worker who does not need to be ashamed and who correctly handles the word of truth."*   2 Timothy 2:15

We should all strive to be the unashamed, approved worker *"who correctly handles the truth"* and be the best person God intended us to be. The better our walk the more effective we can be in building up God's Kingdom through His Word. I was blessed with a correction in my walk over a decade ago at a Men's retreat. During the weekend two men, at different times, came to me with a gentle corrective word. They both told me I sometimes come off sarcastic when I was making jokes and I could be hurting people's feelings. I agreed and made changes in my jokes. We should all take proper criticism as God's way of helping us to become better people.

> *"Brothers and sisters, if someone is caught in a sin, you who live by the Spirit should restore that person gently. But watch yourselves, or you also may be tempted."*
> Galatians 6:1

Those using Words of Knowledge need to be gentle as they correct others. Just because they have the answer does not mean they are above temptation. Been there and done that! I am very careful when people ask my advice because I have had to eat my own words many times and do the very thing I told others to do. Sometimes the person using the spiritual gift of the Word of Knowledge is receiving a message for themselves!

I try to always tell those seeking advice from me to look for confirmation from other sources about what I've told them. It may be the first time they're hearing about their situation or somewhere in the middle or I may be the last message they will receive.

GRAND JURY

Early in practice I was called to be on Jury Duty. I tried desperately to get out of serving because I was the only source of income for my family. If I didn't work there was no income and it cost over a $1000 a week in expenses to keep my office doors open. I had just paid out a large amount of taxes and we were very low on money at the time. The only offer from the courts was to postpone the date. The judge was determined to make an example out of a doctor even though I was the sole provider.

God gave me a Word of Knowledge to go to Jury Duty as scheduled and not to postpone. I argued with God saying it was horrible timing and they were picking a Grand Jury which guaranteed a week at the court house. I finally agreed with God. I went to the court house with my Bible in hand hoping they would think I was a crazy religious guy and let me go home.

I watched the Judge choose a "random" amount of people for the Grand Jury out of the cards with our names on them. He took a chunk right out of the middle of the fanned out cards in his hand. As he pulled out the middle of the alphabetized cards, I knew I was going to be on the Grand Jury because my last name starts with an "M". I asked the man next to me what his last name started with and he said, "L." I told him he was going to be on the Grand Jury with me and then they called his name. He looked at me and then my Bible and slowly walked away. He then did a double take as they called my name and I walked into the room behind him.

The District Attorney came into our room and had a strange look on his face as he described our duties as Grand Jurors. He said that the secretary who usually puts everything together for the week of Grand Jury was out with Rocky Mountain spotted fever. He said we would be finished by Wednesday at lunch time. My Word of Knowledge was paying off but I knew I was there to deliver a message to someone. After the last session of the last day of Grand Jury I spoke with an attorney who prosecutes child molestation cases. I asked her if there was a problem with getting rid of one predator and another one attacks the same child later. She agreed it was a problem.

I shared with her that the spiritual gift of Discerning Spirits is a prime target of Satan from an early age because they can recognize the enemy. Satan loves to send predators to these children to mess them up early in life so no one believes in their gifts later. I challenged her to ask the child, off the official record, if they can see or feel when evil or demons are around. She received the information well and I did exactly what God asked me to do. Ironically the amount of patients I saw that week was my exact average number for patients per week for the year. I know God did that just to show He was involved and cared about me!

"The first step towards knowledge is to know that we are ignorant."[47]   -Richard Cecil

To be effective in the gift of Word of Knowledge you need to:

STOP finding excuses to avoid delivering God's messages to others.
LOOK for those who need to hear from God.
LISTEN to God for the message you need to deliver so it can change their life.
BE WHAT GOD CREATED YOU TO BE, a divine messenger for God.

"Too many Christians are fighting graduate school sins with a grammar school knowledge of God."[48] -John Piper

WORD OF WISDOM:

"Now to each one the manifestation of the Spirit is given for the common good. To one there is given through the Spirit a message of wisdom, to another a message of knowledge by means of the same Spirit." 1 Corinthians 12:7-8

The person using the spiritual gift of the Word of Wisdom takes a Word of Knowledge to the next level by solving problems with the information they have been given. Knowledge and Wisdom are for the **"common good"** and is needed when ordinary common sense comes up short. When there seems to be no answer, wisdom shines in the darkness. Those using this gift seem to be "old souls" ready with a wealth of information for just about every situation. They seem to know just what to say to calm an argument or solve a problem.

"But the wisdom that comes from heaven is first of all pure; then peace-loving, considerate, submissive, full of mercy and good fruit, impartial and sincere."
James 3:17

Those using the spiritual gift of Wisdom should strive to deliver their messages with God's examples from James. God's wisdom is perfect and pure, be obedient not to mess it up. His wisdom should be delivered in a loving, peaceful, fair and compassionate way that does not divide the Body of Christ but unifies it.

"True wisdom consists in two things: Knowledge of God and Knowledge of Self."[49] -John Calvin

Those using Wisdom tend to deeply study Scriptures along with a variety of information but mostly they study people and their habits and reactions. This allows Godly messages to flow from them to speak life into others. These messages are usually done with great understanding and come from a righteous perspective. They not only solve the problem, they build up the church and the individual at the same time. True use of this gift points people to Jesus, not themselves.

> *"If any of you lacks wisdom, you should ask God, who gives generously to all without finding fault, and it will be given to you. But when you ask, you must believe and not doubt, because the one who doubts is like a wave of the sea, blown and tossed by the wind. That person should not expect to receive anything from the Lord."* James 1:5-7

James, as usual, is very blunt with his words. If you need wisdom just ask God! But, even if you do not like what you hear, you need to believe this is the best information for changing your life's direction. Unfortunately many do not heed God's direction for their lives. The daughter of a friend of mine saved herself for marriage and unfortunately her husband began an adulterous affair a few months into their married. It was devastating for this Godly family. God put a strong conviction on me to call her new husband. I barely knew the man and I really did not want to make the call.

I finally made the call and asked if I could share some things God laid on my heart for him. He was willing to listen so I explained to him that God had given him a Godly family to help with the past problems of his dead beat dad and broken family. I told him God wanted to restore him but he had a very small window of time to fix his problem through repentance. I said the road would be very long and hard for gaining the families trust back.

I gave him the flip side of his life if he continued his own way. I gently told him he would become like his dad and would lose everything to drinking and poor life choices. He took the conversation well but did not listen to the wisdom I was offering. Within a short period of time I learned he moved in with a woman responsible for tearing another family apart and soon lost everything to alcohol. His very bad choices of "friends" stole what few possessions he owned. Many years later I asked my friend about him and he has no idea what has become of him to this day.

> *"Furthermore, just as they did not think it worthwhile to retain the knowledge of God, so God gave them over to a depraved mind, so that they do what ought not to be done."*
> Romans 1:28

Sadly this man did not think the message was worthwhile, so God gave him over to a depraved mind. The word depraved means "failing to pass the test." It's sad how many of us have failed to pass the tests when we were told a better way from someone willing to speak life into us. An unfortunate part of using this gift is when people do not listen to the Word. I hold on to a glimmer of hope for this man. I hope he remembers what God tried to do for him and he will run back to Him just as the prodigal son ran back to his father.

When using the spiritual gift of the Word of Wisdom we need to understand that some people plant the seeds of God's Word and some water them but it is God's job to grow them. Do not let times like these discourage the delivery of the message; some changes take a lifetime to grow.

To be effective in the gift of Word of Wisdom you need to:

STOP gaining knowledge and never use it to build God's Kingdom.
LOOK for people who need help in life's struggles and are searching for God's way out.
LISTEN for God to give you a helpful and truth filled Words to share at the right time for the right person.

BE WHAT GOD CREATED YOU TO BE, an interactive librarian with an encyclopedia of information who takes in knowledge and passes out wisdom to others.

> *"Wisdom is the right use of knowledge. To know is not to be wise. Many men know a great deal, and are all the greater fools for it. There is no fool so great a fool as a knowing fool. But to know how to use knowledge is to have wisdom."*[50]
>
> -Charles Spurgeon

Those were the 20 Spiritual gifts listed in Scripture. You are created to have several of them and use them in various ways and in various levels. God has intertwined your DNA and His gifts to make you a unique creation. You have the ability to grow God's Kingdom whether it is behind the scenes on the front lines or somewhere in between. Joyfully receive your gift, feed it, grow it and use it. God wants to use you to build up the church and help others to experience an eternity in heaven with Him. You are part of the greatest miracle when your spiritual gift is used to bring the lost to Christ. Let God flow through you and show His love to others.

TALENTS AND THEIR SPIRITUAL GIFTS

Don't worry if you didn't see your spiritual gift listed in the 20 Biblical spiritual gifts. There are many talents that God has given us that are not directly listed as the gifts in Scripture. They simply fall under one of the 20 Biblical spiritual gifts. Here are some examples of those talents or actions and their gifts:

<u>Acting/Drama:</u> Strong in Teaching & Ministry; can be in all gifts.

<u>Artistic Skills:</u> Strong in Ministry & Helps; can be in all gifts.

<u>Celibacy:</u> A type of fasting to bring you close to God.

<u>Carpentry:</u> Strong in Helps; can be in all gifts.

<u>Church Attendance:</u> Expected in all gifts.

<u>Communication:</u> Leaders, Prophecy, Teaching, Pastoral & Evangelism; can be in all gifts.

<u>Compassion:</u> Strong in Mercy & Encouragement; should be in all gifts.

<u>Craftsmanship:</u> Strong in Helps; can be in all gifts.

<u>Creativity:</u> Strong in Ministry; can be in all gifts.

<u>Dreams:</u> Strong in Discerning Spirits; can be in all gifts.

<u>Exhortation:</u> Same as Encouragement

<u>Exorcism:</u> Strong in Discerning Spirits, Healing, Miracles, Prophecy and Tongues.

<u>Fasting:</u> Can be used in all gifts to draw close to God.

<u>Financial Management:</u> Strong in Administration, Teachers, Prophecy, Leaders & Givers; can be in all gifts.

<u>Governments:</u> Same as Administration & Guidance.

<u>Guidance:</u> Same as Administration & Governments.

<u>Happiness:</u> Not a listed gift but we find joy in serving the LORD through our spiritual gifts!

<u>Helping Others:</u> Same as Helps

<u>Hospitality:</u> Making people feel warm and welcome for a purpose is Ministry.

Intercessory Prayer: Strong in Discerning Spirits, Tongues, Mercy, & Encouragement

Listening: Strong in Mercy & Encouragement; can be in all gifts.

Love: A fruit of the Spirit and should be used in all the gifts.

Martyrdom: Strong in Evangelism & Apostleship but can happen in any gift.

Mechanical Abilities: Strong in Helps; can be in all gifts.

Missionary: Strong in Apostleship, Evangelism & Ministry; can be in all gifts.

Music Talent: Strong in Ministry; can be in all the gifts.

Patience: Strong in Faith but needs to be used with all gifts.

Prayer: A requirement for all spiritual gifts.

Preaching: Strong in Evangelism, Pastor, Teacher, Prophecy, Word of Knowledge & Word of Wisdom.

Premonitions: Strong in Discerning Spirits; can be in all gifts.

Ruling: Same as Leadership

Sense of Humor: Can be found in all gifts.

Serving: Same as Ministry

Service: Same as Ministry

Shepherd: Same as Pastor

Singing: Strong in Teaching and Ministry; can be in all gifts.

Song writing: Strong in Teaching, Ministry, Encouragement; can be in all gifts.

Speaking: Strong in Leaders, Prophecy & Teaching; All are called to share their testimony to glorify God.

Visions: Strong in Discerning Spirits, Leaders, Apostleship & Prophecy; can be in all gifts.

Voluntary Poverty: A type of fast from material things to bring you closer to God.

Witnessing: Strong in Apostleship & Evangelism; everyone should share Christ with others.

Writing: Teaching, Prophecy, Pastor, Word of Knowledge / Wisdom, in all gifts

"It is not great gifts that God blesses so much as it is great likeness to Christ."[51]   -Robert Murray McCheyne

STOP ignoring the fact God gave you spiritual gifts, plural!
LOOK for ways to grow and strengthen your spiritual gifts.
LISTEN to Godly advice about how to use your spiritual gifts.
BE WHAT GOD CREATED YOU TO BE, a joy-filled Christian using their spiritual gifts to follow God's Will and builds God's Kingdom.

"God has given a spiritual gift to the church in you, and you dare not keep it to yourself."[52]   -Aaron Niequist

PONDERING POINTS

Which spiritual gifts sound the most like you?

Do you recognize spiritual gifts in people you know?

Are all spiritual gifts from the same Spirit?

Are some Spiritual Gifts more important than others?

What are some spiritual gifts that are more in the limelight?

What are some spiritual gifts that are more in the background?

What are some spiritual gifts that seem more educational?

What are some spiritual gifts that seem more creative?

What are some spiritual gifts that seem more loving?

What are some spiritual gifts that seem more business like?

What are some spiritual gifts that seem more organizational?

Why is there so much confusion about spiritual gifts?

What would help to solve this confusion?

What fears are keeping you from using your spiritual gifts?

CHAPTER SEVEN

HOW THE ARMOR OF GOD RELATES TO SPIRITUAL GIFTS

"Prepare your shields, both large and small, and march out for battle! Harness the horses, mount the steeds! Take your positions with helmets on! Polish your spears, put on your armor!" Jeremiah 46:3-4

HOW STRONG IS MY ARMOR

Scripture speaks of times when we need to Armor up and fight battles for ourselves and others. Anytime we go into battle we need to be well-prepared. Gathering an army, developing good battle plans and having proper supplies are basic needs for the battle. High of the list of supplies for battle is the Armor because it protects us from the enemy's weapons. Another important item is utilizing people in their area of expertise to accomplish needed goals. We have an enemy and we need an army to stand firm against him.

"Finally, be strong in the Lord and in his mighty power. Put on the full armor of God, so that you can take your stand against the devil's schemes. For our struggle is not against flesh and blood, but against the rulers, against the authorities, against the powers of this dark world and against the spiritual forces of evil in the heavenly realms." Ephesians 6:10-12

Imagine if an army put the best Armor they had on a group of weak and untrained soldiers. These soldiers would be defeated easily in battle.

In the same way a Christian soldier should be well trained and *"strong in the Lord"* to complete mighty deeds for Him. The same Christian should strive to have the absolute power to overcome the immediate resistance of Satan through *"His mighty power."*

As Christians our struggles are *"not against flesh and blood"* they are with *"the powers of this dark world."* Our true enemy is Satan and his well-organized forces who are trying to take people to Hell every day. Satan is a defeated foe but he still causes a great deal of misery in the world. He has a threefold agenda of killing, stealing and destroying anything of God. He would love to destroy us but if he can't he will do his best to kill the spiritual gifts God gave us. He knows these are the weapons God gave us to defeat him. These gifts pose a great threat to him and his plans especially when we have unity in the Body of Christ while using the gifts. All Christians need basic training to understand who provides their strength.

> *"I can do all this through him who gives me strength."*
> Philippians 4:13

You need to allow God's power to flow through you to grow your Faith. Every time you win a battle you get a notch in your belt for a job well done. These wins build on each other for a firm foundation in your trust for God. Never let defeats along the way discourage you, this happens to every Christian. Satan loves to make you feel defeated so you will give up. In the famous battle cry of *Galaxy Quest* the movie, "Never Give Up, Never Surrender!" Stand back up, dust yourself off, learn more about God and your enemy and follow your orders from God.

> *"Oh that we would hunger to be filled with the Word of God; for there is no greater armor, no greater strength, no greater assurance that He is with us, and in us, when we go forth in battle equipped and nourished by His instruction and determined to stand firm on His promises."*[53]
> -Billy Graham

ARMOR UP

The next few chapters are about the five pieces of the Armor of God and the Sword of the Spirit described in Ephesians to learn what God has in store for your future with Him. Hopefully you've become familiar with the description of your Biblical spiritual gifts after taking the spiritual gift test and read about their positive qualities in chapter 6. In the following chapters you will learn how to use your spiritual gifts along with the Armor of God to *"stand against the devil's schemes"* and defeat the enemy.

> *"Therefore put on the full armor of God, so that when the day of evil comes, you may be able to stand your ground, and after you have done everything, to stand. Stand firm then, with the belt of truth buckled around your waist, with the breastplate of righteousness in place, and with your feet fitted with the readiness that comes from the gospel of peace. In addition to all this, take up the shield of faith, with which you can extinguish all the flaming arrows of the evil one. Take the helmet of salvation and the sword of the Spirit, which is the word of God."* Ephesians 6:13-17

The Armor of God is made up of a Helmet, Breastplate, Belt, Shoes and a Shield. The weapon you've been given is the Sword of the Spirit which is the Word of God. You are told to put on the *"full armor of God"* to *"stand firm"* against Satan and his army of demons. Scripture points out the spiritual warfare happening all around you and Ephesians 6 is the battle cry to alert you of the danger of Satan's attacks on your life.

> *"For though we live in the world, we do not wage war as the world does. The weapons we fight with are not the weapons of the world. On the contrary, they have divine power to demolish strongholds. We demolish arguments and every pretension that sets itself up against the knowledge of God, and we take captive every thought to make it obedient to Christ."*
> 2 Corinthians 10:3-5

We've been given *"divine power to demolish strongholds!"* The weapons we have come from obediently using the spiritual gifts and the Armor of God. Every Army has Special Forces to accomplish specific assignments and this is the same with the Christian Army. This is where the spiritual gifts become essential to fight our enemy. The Body of Christ has a multitude of Special Forces using their gifts to carry out missions for God.

The Armor of God helps protect those gifts as they advance the Kingdom. Each piece of Armor is specifically designed to protect their group of spiritual gifts. The Shield of Faith gives the first layer of protection over all The Armor pieces and their gifts.

THE GOOD, BAD AND THE UGLY OF THE SPIRITUAL GIFTS

God gives us spiritual gifts to build up the church and to be ready for battle. Many years ago God showed me how the Armor of God is related to the spiritual gifts. As a hobby, I studied personalities and I began to see patterns in the way Satan attacks what I thought were personality types. It took many years of studying God's Word and hearing hundreds of testimonies over 25 years at Tres Dias to finally connect the dots. The patterns I saw were not so much personalities; it was the spiritual gifts being attacked.

I observed people with the same spiritual gifts having the same personal problems and attacks in their lives. I asked God to give me Satan's battle plans for how he attacks us based on our spiritual gifts. God blessed me with the knowledge of the Gift-Killers and how we are attacked by Satan. I noticed certain groups of gifts have similar strengths and weaknesses. I connected the Armor of God with the spiritual gifts by grouping specific sets of gifts with specific pieces of the Armor of God.

Over the next few chapters you will learn which spiritual gifts are related to specific pieces of the Armor of God. You'll also learn how Satan tries to kill your gifts and how you can stand firm against those attacks. You'll see the Good, the Bad and the Ugly of each of the spiritual gifts and learn how their weaknesses can lure them into Satan's traps.

THE GOOD
(Going Forward)

"In the same way, let your light shine before others, that they may see your good deeds and glorify your Father in heaven."
Matthew 5:16

The Good represents the positive actions of people as they properly use their spiritual gifts for building up God's kingdom. It describes how God intended His spiritual gifts to be used. This was covered to some extent in the chapter 6 definitions of the gifts. The characteristics of the gifts will be covered in more detail in the next few chapters.

THE BAD
(Going Backward)

The Bad is when the Christian is weakened and shows signs of distress with their spiritual gift. They are beginning to drift away from Godly people and God Himself. I call this the "idiot light" on the dash telling you to check the engine. This is not necessarily sin but it will lead to sin if not taken care of soon.

"But they did not listen or pay attention; instead, they followed the stubborn inclinations of their evil hearts. They went backward and not forward." Jeremiah 7:24

When this happens they begin to stumble *"backward and not forward"* and become twisted by the static of the world and interference from Satan. It may come from stress, exhaustion and burn out but they stop listening to God and begin to go after the *"stubborn inclinations of their evil hearts."* They start shutting others out of their life and begin the slippery slope into the ugly sinful side of their gifts.

THE UGLY
(Going Sin-Ward)

> *"Do not love the world or anything in the world. If anyone loves the world, love for the Father is not in them. For everything in the world—the lust of the flesh, the lust of the eyes, and the pride of life—comes not from the Father but from the world. The world and its desires pass away, but whoever does the will of God lives forever."*
>
> 1 John 2:15-17

Unfortunately when someone *"loves the world"* Satan sets a snare for their weaknesses. Their love shifts direction from God to the World and they can fall into the Ugly sinful use of the gifts. This use of God-given talents for evil represents a fallen Christian. It also represents the "Anti-Gift" type of talent used by non-believers that goes against the will of God.

The sins of the Ugly side fall into three categories. These three areas of sin are what happen to us when our love for our Father grows cold and we seek after our own desires. They are *"Lust of the Flesh,"* *"Lust of the Eyes,"* and the *"Pride of Life."*

LUST OF THE FLESH
(Internal Cravings)

> *"When the woman saw that the fruit of the tree was good for food and pleasing to the eye, and also desirable for gaining wisdom, she took some and ate it."* Genesis 3:6

The original sin of Adam and Eve begins with the three areas of sin. Eve first saw the fruit as *"good for food"* yet she was forbidden to eat of this tree. She was tempted by the fleshly desire to take the fruit so *"Lust of the Flesh"* was committed with the body through gluttony and selfish desire. It seemed so innocent at first. How could taking a bite of a beautiful fruit be evil? But disobedience to God always ends with bad results which lead to sin and then death.

> *"There is a way that appears to be right, but in the end it leads to death."*   Proverbs 14:12

It may not be an immediate death but Satan picks at your weakened flesh and makes weak spots. These weak spots put small holes in your Armor which eventually tear open and allows the floodgates of sin to pour into your life. *"Lust of the flesh"* is characterized by all sorts of sexual immorality and addictions like food, alcohol and legal or illegal drugs. It is the "Internal Cravings" of worldly pleasures.

LUST OF THE EYES
(External Cravings)

Next Eve noticed the fruit to be *"pleasing to the eye"* so *"Lust of the Eyes"* crept in and added to her disobedience. This sin begins by thinking what can be wrong with taking a quick glance at something beautiful; it's only a little eye candy?

> *"The eye is the lamp of the body. If your eyes are healthy, your whole body will be full of light. But if your eyes are unhealthy, your whole body will be full of darkness..."*
> Matthew 6:22-23

The problem with a glance is it can become a stare and then a thought followed by an action. We see better clothes, better cars, better homes, better possessions and even what we think are better spouses. We begin to desire those possessions to the point of doing anything to obtain them. This is idol worship and coveting. We become jealous and envy what others have which leads to becoming dissatisfied with what we have. We desire the "External Cravings" of the world and become ungrateful.

These "External Cravings" eventually take over your entire thought process and then your actions. Your next step is always gaining the next possession to get more happiness. Unfortunately the happiness is short lived when it is not seeking more of God. These sins can lead us into crippling debt causing us to work more to pay the bills rather than spend time building God's Kingdom. It also steals time from our family. Most of us can simply look at our bank account to see where we store up our treasures and most of them are not of God.

Even entertainment can fall into *"Lust of the Eyes"* when we see the glitz and glamour of Hollywood. As we view what they produce we allow more and more sin to creep into the things we watch. We may even say it was a good show except for the cussing, the sexual immorality, the godlessness, etc. What Satan puts before our eyes is well-designed to break down our barriers to sin. Even commercials are designed to lure you into believing a simple product will bring you happiness and fulfillment in your life.

PRIDE OF LIFE
(Mental Cravings)

Lastly Eve saw the fruit as *"desirable for gaining wisdom"* so the *"Pride of Life"* has now entered her heart. This is when someone cares more for themselves than others. Eve was tempted by the serpent telling her she could be like God if she ate of the fruit. Adam and Eve's love for each other was like no other humans on Earth because God made them for each other. The only thing Adam loved more than Eve was God. Eve thought if she could be like God then Adam would love her as much or more than he loved God.

This arrogant selfish ambition of the *"Pride of Life"* seeks "Mental Cravings" and desires to be worshiped and loved more by others. Pride takes credit for and boasts of achievements so they are held in high esteem by those around them. The prideful do not mind gossiping about others to tear them down in order to build themselves up. They love to "one up" the ones around them in order to have a higher value of themselves. Their love has grown cold for others so they use their knowledge and talents to step up the ladder of life all the while stepping on others on the way up. They will eventually destroy anyone in their way to reach their self-centered goals.

These three areas of sin show the journey of drifting away from a God-centered life to a self-centered life of sin. Many of us have stumbled into these areas in our own lives and prayerfully do not wish to go back to those dark times. We all are tempted by sin and all of us have fallen victim to sin. We are in a world filled with the opportunity to choose sin but we are more than overcomers. God gave us the ability to choose to do His Will for our lives and avoid sin. Generally if we are in God's Will and being obedient it will be an uphill climb but it's better than a destructive life of sin.

> *"For though we live in the world, we do not wage war as the world does. The weapons we fight with are not the weapons of the world. On the contrary, they have divine power to demolish strongholds. We demolish arguments and every pretension that sets itself up against the knowledge of God, and we take captive every thought to make it obedient to Christ."*
>
> 2 Corinthians 10:3-5

Each of the three areas of sin starts by arguing with God's Word. Satan, the serpent, asked Eve if she would surely die if she ate of the fruit. He questioned God's Word. It is necessary to *"take captive every thought to make it obedient to Christ"* to avoid the things that tempt your flesh. Stop looking at worldly possessions with lust and focus on God more than yourself so you can tear down the strongholds in your life.

Take the thoughts and arguments from the enemy and sentence them to death.

The following chapters will show you ways to grow your individual spiritual gifts by maturing in Christ. You'll receive practical advice on using your gifts to build God's Kingdom. You'll learn Satan's battle plan for destroying your life so you can recognize the early warning signs of his attacks. This will be valuable information to stop those attacks in your personal life.

For years I've kidded about my book been saying, "I'm 20 months pregnant with quadruplets and if I do not hurry up and write the thing Jesus will come back and no one will want to read it." I've covered up a lot of the bad things that happened to me in my life with humor. I say it's better to laugh about it rather than cry about it. Even though the journey of writing this book has brought many tears; God is good and faithful. I have learned so much and I realize the trials are for the pattern of good and will bring about Godly changes in people's lives. I knew I would be attacked by Satan for writing this book; I mean I'm giving out his battle plan for goodness sake!

PART OF MY TESTIMONY

Here is a bit of my journey getting this information to you. As I wrote my book Satan began relentless attacks on my family and me. The worst of this was my Mom developing Alzheimer's. I'm an only child and my Dad left my Mom and me when I was 9 years old. Mom never remarried so I became fully responsible for my Mom.

At 68 years old my Mom was $100,000 in debt and she had 7 rental properties that were $20,000 behind on their payments. The renters were tearing up the properties and to top it off Mom hoarded at her clinic and her large lake home. She was "asset rich and cash poor" but sadly she had everything invested in real estate in the worst economic times for property values.

There was so much anger in me as I tried to process the mess my Mom left me. It felt so unfair and it should not have been my problem. I am a very practical person who can see the long term numbers required to fix problems. My internal calculator broke! I saw endless years of fixing her problems and cleaning up her hoarding.

The worst of the worst times fell during my son's senior year and the beginning of his college years. It was a nightmare for our family! I had to get non-paying renters out and sell the properties they were destroying. I desperately needed money to pay off her debt. Teresa and I even remodeled one of her rental houses to move my Mom into so we could clean her hoarded home. Thank you to my friends who helped with painting that home.

In the second year of my Mom's problems I started a Daniel fast because I was drowning in responsibilities and desperately needed answers from God. The Daniel fast is simply eating fruit, vegetables, nuts, grains and drinking water for 21 days. Fasting can help a person get closer to God when they are seeking answers to their problems.

During those 21 days I had a nasty virus, broke my ankle, aggravated a severe tendonitis in my thumb, and cracked a tooth that became my first crown. Two of my personal vehicles needed costly repairs and my Mom's home and her vehicles were hit by a tornado that did $5000 of damage to her home and cars. By the way, Mom had dropped all of her insurance in her declining mental state.

To be honest I was using the Fast as a tool to manipulate God into doing good things for me. I discovered a very different turn of events as I realized God is not the Mob. No matter what you pay Him or do for Him, He does not promise to keep us safe from everything in this broken world. He simply promises to be there with us through all the good and the bad. I could not twist God's arm to make Him give me a good life!

It took almost 3 years to clean out my Mom's lake home to put it on the market. Money was bleeding out quickly and there seemed no way out. Satan struck me down at the exact moment I was going to reveal his battle plans through this book. My writing was completely shut down except for one chapter I wrote during those dark times. God said, "No" to that chapter because it was like my life, rushed! God did not want my hurried-up-bullet-pointed lessons. He wanted conversational chapters as if I were talking directly with you and not at you. So Satan won the battle and shut down my writing for over 6 years.

But God! I love when I hear "But God" because something good is about to happen! But God got a message to me in the fall of the third year of the worst three years of my life. He told me it would be better after February. I stopped when I heard this and told God I would wrestle Him till my hip broke for this promise. I was so deep in the weeds and the future looked so bleak. I desperately needed this message to be true. Little did I know what the next 6 months was going to be like?

During the next 6 months my Mom had major car repairs, roof leaks and continued severe mental deterioration. She drove off the Sunday morning of my family's Christmas get-together and became a missing person while it rained several inches that day. Thank God the police found her the next morning driving around in downtown Birmingham over an hour and a half from her home. Her car was completely fogged up inside because she did not know how to work the defroster. She was using an old blanket to wipe the inside of her windows to see. It was a miracle she did not kill herself or others that day. The next day we got a call from our real estate agent telling us her lake home contract fell through and the buyer backed out.

We were running out of money and needed the sale of that home to pay for my Mom to be in a Memory Care unit. A few days later I was anonymously turned over to the Department of Human Resources for being a "bad" son. I realized I was turned in by a family down the road that had a car that looked like my Mom's sister's car. My Mom walked into their house by mistake a few times because she had missed the turn into her sister's neighborhood. I spent over an hour describing all the things I was doing for my Mom to DHR. They quickly dropped the investigation, especially after I told them they could gladly take over her care from me.

In January I put my Mom in a home because of the pressure around me even though I only had enough money to keep her there for less than 3 months. I found it strange how everyone had the answer, "Put her in a home" but no one offered to pay for the home. Others said, "Move her in with you" but my wife and I work in our clinic together so we could not care for her during the day. We did not have the money to hire sitters for her while we worked and no one offered to stay with her or pay the sitters either.

I balled up in a fetal position and cried most nights trying to make sense of the madness surrounding me. I barely had the energy to work at my own clinic after working tirelessly on her problems. I had to take off so much time to help with my Mom's affairs and I lost tens of thousands in income all while my son was entering college.

My stress levels were unbearable. The only reason I was barely holding on was because of God's message I had received 6 months earlier! But God did show up! In mid-February we sold her lake home securing the nearly $4000 a month for Mom's Memory Care Home. At the end of February we sold the house we remodeled for Mom and it was not even on the market. It even sold with the contents so we did not have to move her furniture again. Her two vehicles sold weeks later and as promised, "It was better after February." We eventually sold all of her properties and paid off her debt. God kept His promise to me and I am hugely grateful. Mom perked up a little in her new settings but she continued to deteriorate mentally.

A couple of years later Mom could not control her bodily functions. God encouraged me to Fast. Keep in mind I cannot do a Fast on my own. If I said I am going to Fast today my stomach would try to eat itself in the next 15 minutes. I'm also the type to never miss a meal. A couple of days into Fasting on just water I was called and told I had to move my Mom into a skilled nursing facility and I had 30 days to move her.

That news meant I would have to spend over $2000 more a month for her care. I was now scared to do any more Fasts after the news. As I began to run out of her money for her care, I would be forced to put her on Medicaid and award her to the state if she lived much longer. While my life was being stolen from me I began to understand the "why" of the entire situation. I was supposed to go through this to show you how Satan attacks us and how we can stand firm against those attacks. My Mom passed away in the early months of COVID and she had an Insurance Policy for $60,000 she left for me.

2020 was Hades on Earth for me and my family as my Mom and Dad died weeks apart. Both of them were suffering from Alzheimer's but died of COVID. A hurricane hit our trailer near the beach causing over $10,000 of uninsured damages, we had to pay to have a roof on our home, and I had a large deductible to pay from my 5 days in the hospital with COVID pneumonia. There were so many unexpected bills that year, but God! The total cost of the unexpected bills was almost exactly $60,000!

God saw me through the worst times of my life. The years of putting this book together has grown my Faith and helped me way beyond my expectations. In 1990 I actually asked for more Faith a couple of months before my Mom's dementia began. I had no idea what lay ahead of me but I knew the purpose of this book was to encourage Christians to grow their Faith.

God took the worst trial of my life and used it to grow my Faith. I realized when God called me to a Fast He did it in order to draw me close to Him during the hardest of the hard times. Mom was going to get Alzheimer's disease, I was going to crack my tooth, break my ankle and be covered up with problems with or without Fasting. The Fast was not the problem; it was the answer. God drew me close in those times so I could get through the trials with His help.

I write this not to have you feel pity for me but to celebrate how much God cares about us and our problems. If you buy a self-help book on marriage you want the author to be successfully married. You want them to have counseled couples and had many success stories or at least suffered trials of their own and overcome those trials. The same applies to this book. If I plan to suggest for you ask God to grow your Faith, then there should be a time in my own life where I did the same. I should be able to show you a way to navigate through the process. I should also be able to write success stories of helping others with their spiritual gifts but most of all I should be successful with my own gift and my own Faith.

Much of my Mom's problems prepared me for this book. I feel as if I had been near the edge of Hades and ready to give up but God kept His promise and stood there beside me through everything. There were so many divine moments during those years which showed He cared about me and my problems. There is even more to my story of writing this book and God's faithfulness to come in future chapters.

> *"Be strong and courageous. Do not be afraid or terrified because of them, for the Lord your God goes with you; he will never leave you nor forsake you."*
> Deuteronomy 31:6

There were times that I thought God forgot about me and those times tested my Faith. Fortunately He never left me. By sharing my own experiences and those of my patients and friends I hope to help you get through the trials of your life. I pray you find your true purpose and fight back when you get knocked down. I hope you use your spiritual gifts to their full potential to protect yourself and to help others who are in battles of their own.

The first part of this book was necessary to discover "Why Am I Here?" You're not a collection of the bad things that happened to you. You are a uniquely designed creation of God designed for a purpose. You have a design and a purpose from God and you need to study and understand the spiritual gifts He gave you. You are in a battle for not only your life but the lives around you. Put on the full Armor of God! Protect yourself with the Shield of Faith and stand firm with the Sword of the Spirit! Pray for God to pour out His guidance for you through the next few chapters. This is where each piece of armor and the gifts represented by them will be covered in great detail.

I've shared individual pieces of this information with hundreds of people over many years with great results in their lives. Now it has all come together to help countless people stand firm and fight the good fight and become "well done" servants of the Lord! Pray that God reveals to you how to use this information to protect you and become a more effective Christian so you can build up the church with your spiritual gifts.

> *"When you put on the full Armor of God, you're telling the Devil that he has to go through Jesus to get to you!"*
>
> -Anonymous

STOP fighting your battles without the Armor of God and other believers.
LOOK closely at your Sword, the Word of God, and keep it sharpened.
LISTEN closely to the battle plans and always be ready for battle.
BE WHAT GOD CREATED YOU TO BE, a righteous well-armored warrior for Christ.

PONDERING POINTS:

Why do we all need to put on the Armor of God?

Who is our enemy?

What are the 5 pieces of the Armor of God?

What does the Sword of the Spirit represent?

How should you use the Sword of the Spirit?

Can you give some good examples of spiritual gifts in action?

What are some ways we stumble in our Faith?

What can drive us to the ugly sins of life?

What are some examples of Lust of the Flesh?

What are some examples of Lust of the Eyes?

What are some examples of Pride of Life?

Can you think of reasons for those who fell from the Faith?

How do we fight falling from the Faith?

What do you do with thoughts that are unpleasing to God?

Have you ever felt God left you alone?

When will God leave you?

Do you fear using your spiritual gifts and Armor of God to go up against Satan?

CHAPTER EIGHT

THE HELMET OF SALVATION

"Stand firm then, with the belt of truth buckled around your waist, with the breastplate of righteousness in place, and with your feet fitted with the readiness that comes from the gospel of peace. In addition to all this, take up the shield of faith, with which you can extinguish all the flaming arrows of the evil one. Take the helmet of salvation and the sword of the Spirit, which is the word of God."

Ephesians 6:14-17

The Roman helmet was very important in battle with swords and battle axes swinging at every turn. By protecting the brain, the body's command center, it allows one to "keep their head" during battle. The helmet was tightly fitted on the head in order to not slip off or spin around and prevent seeing clearly in battle. The brow ridge protected the eyes yet still allowed one to see the coming attacks and the battle in front of them. The helmet also represents the ranks in the army to let others know who's in charge.

SPIRITUAL GIFTS REPRESENTED BY THE HELMET OF SALVATION

Administration
Leadership
Apostleship

These are the three main spiritual gifts related to the Helmet of Salvation. They are similar in their leadership qualities but they differ individually in their actions. Administration governs over things while Leadership rules over people. The spiritual gift of Apostleship has vision and gives the church new missions. Together these gifts work out the plans and goals to spread the good news of Jesus Christ. The gifts related to the helmet are well-suited for moving Christians and supplies to build up the Body of Christ.

If an army has no leadership in battle, the odds of winning would be about zero! When battling with Satan and his forces, we need leadership to equip us with battle plans, weapons, food, and supplies along with information like the strengths and weaknesses of the enemy. The Helmet of Salvation encircles our head with the truth of the saving grace of Jesus Christ. Because of this, Godly leadership seeks God's Will and plans accordingly. They relay this information to others in the Body of Christ to prepare everyone and everything for the battle. The requirements of Leadership are heavy with responsibilities to not only win the battle but to do it with the least amount of damage as possible.

WE ALL HAVE SPIRITUAL GIFTS PLURAL

Our spiritual gifts may not be as strong as others but aren't we all called to Lead our family, especially by example? It may seem like a small task but preparing ways for your children to be taught about the love of Jesus and planning family life around church is a small version of Administration. All families should have a vision and direction to become more like Christ!

There are those specially equipped for leadership but every Christian is called into some form of leading others. We need to be a leader to our family, friends and co-workers. It does not mean taking charge and forcing others to do our will, it means humbly following God's Will. We need to carry His example into our homes, offices and our neighborhoods and not be afraid to mention Jesus to those around us. We all have a testimony of how Jesus saved us and we all need to tell others about Him. Most of all we need to lead by example so others will listen.

THE GOAL OF
THE HELMET OF SALVATION
"The Goal is the Goal"

"In their hearts humans plan their course, but the Lord establishes their steps." Proverbs 16:9

The goal is the goal of building up the Kingdom of God and those using the gifts represented by the Helmet are extremely goal-oriented. They have a vision and a plan to achieve a desired outcome. If they are close to the Lord they will allow Him to *"establish their steps"* toward the goal. Being close to God is of the most importance while leading others.

"Commit to the Lord whatever you do, and he will establish your plans." Proverbs 16:3

With a strong commitment to God, those using these gifts can establish plans that bring about Godly goals for the Body of Christ. These goals should always be about building up the Church and God's Kingdom with truth, humility, and love.

"Many are the plans in a person's heart, but it is the Lord's purpose that prevails." Proverbs 19:21

THE PURPOSE OF
THE HELMET OF SALVATION
"To give directions to spread the Word of God"

"But the plans of the Lord stand firm forever, the purposes of his heart through all generations." Psalm 33:11

Knowing the direction gives purpose to the Leader and they are experts about direction. They work tirelessly on ways to lead people and move things in the right direction in the most efficient way possible. They also plan who serves where and what goes where as they carry out the goal. Godly leadership, humbly hearing from God, can give direction and purpose to the Church to accomplish a goal of building up God's Kingdom.

> *"I know that you can do all things; no purpose of yours can be thwarted."*   Job 42:2

Leadership can rightly know God's direction's by keeping their mind carefully guarded. God's truth is the main weapon in the battle with Satan. We need to constantly renew our mind with His Word so our first response is of God and not of our flesh. To have victorious battles in our lives we need to know the enemy and his plans against us. Through the study of God's truth we will understand our enemy and be prepared for his attacks.

> *"I will instruct you and teach you in the way you should go; I will counsel you with my loving eye on you."*
> Psalm 32:8

The Helmet of Salvation protects the primary battle ground, our mind. Satan starts his attack by placing unwanted thoughts in our head. If we entertain those thoughts and begin to believe his lies we begin the slide off the slippery slope into sin. Satan will continue the temptations as long as you keep taking the bait. We may be called to be fishers of men but Satan has some powerful bait and does some fishing of his own. He has been tempting mankind for thousands of years but remember…

> *"No temptation has seized you except what is common to man. And God is faithful; he will not let you be tempted beyond what you can bear. But when you are tempted, he will also provide a way out so that you can stand up under it."*
> 1 Corinthians 10:13

God gives us a way out of temptation. The lies from Satan have no power unless you give in to them and feed the lies. The protection from the Helmet of Salvation is the first defense of the *"way out"* of those temptations. A firm foundation of God's Word firmly planted in our minds, leads to Godly thoughts which produce Godly actions. Truth chokes out the weeds of temptation and allows Christ to grow in us. By growing our Faith and becoming more like Christ we will hear God and understand His Will for our lives. The helmet provides direction for our life in Christ.

"Therefore, holy brothers, who share in the heavenly calling, fix your thoughts on Jesus, the apostle and high priest whom we confess."   Hebrews 3:1

THE STRENGTH OF
THE HELMET OF SALVATION
"Hearing God's plan and leading people to the completion of the plan"

"We must pay the most careful attention, therefore, to what we have heard, so that we do not drift away."
Hebrews 2:1

The spiritual gifts represented by the Helmet of Salvation need to be obedient to the Spirit of God and pay *"careful attention"* when hearing from Him. They may have different jobs in the Body of Christ but they fall under an organizational "head" that prayerfully listens to God and gathers needed information. This information should lead to spreading the good news of Jesus Christ, meeting the needs of others, identifying the enemy, using the Armor as protection and helping mature Christians by building up their spiritual gifts. Not listening to God and listening to themselves can cause them to *"drift away"* from God. This will allow the Static and Interference to take them off course.

"The mind governed by the flesh is death, but the mind governed by the Spirit is life and peace."
Romans 8:6

When leadership stays humble and close to God they have a clear vision necessary to gather believers for a purpose and expand the kingdom of God! When leadership is *"governed by the Spirit"* they can help lead others to find their life purpose and find peace along the way. When they are governed by their own flesh they will fail.

"We have different gifts, according to the grace given to each of us... if it is to lead, do it diligently..."
Romans 12:6-8

The spiritual gifts represented by the Helmet are very diligent and will see the plan through to completion. Not only are they called to be Godly they are called to be diligent which means to be careful but work as fast as possible. This is about God's timing. When we listen to God He will give us the best possible plan to accomplish His Will with His timing. Leaders need to stay in tune to God's voice and listen carefully for the best plan to reach the goal in His timing.

THE GOOD OF
THE HELMET OF SALVATION
(Going Forward)
"Hearing God's Goals and Direction"

"For I know the plans I have for you," declares the Lord, "plans to prosper you and not to harm you, plans to give you hope and a future. Then you will call on me and come and pray to me, and I will listen to you. You will seek me and find me when you seek me with all your heart."
Jeremiah 29:11-13

Great leadership will humbly *"call on"* God to receive the best direction for the best goal. Then they give those directions to those who follow them in order for everyone to reach the goal together. Being well-equipped with a plan for the future will inspire their followers with the hope God has given them to accomplish great things for the Kingdom.

> *"Here is a trustworthy saying: Whoever aspires to be an overseer desires a noble task. Now the overseer is to be above reproach, faithful to his wife, temperate, self-controlled, respectable, hospitable, able to teach, not given to drunkenness, not violent but gentle, not quarrelsome, not a lover of money. He must manage his own family well and see that his children obey him, and he must do so in a manner worthy of full respect. (If anyone does not know how to manage his own family, how can he take care of God's church?) He must not be a recent convert, or he may become conceited and fall under the same judgment as the devil. He must also have a good reputation with outsiders, so that he will not fall into disgrace and into the devil's trap."*
>
> 1 Timothy 3:1-7

Fortunately there are those with the spiritual gifts of Leadership, Administration and Apostleship who build up the Body of Christ. They live the Godly lives outlined in Scripture and lead the Church Body. They prayerfully listen to God's direction and follow the examples of other good Christian leaders. They love and protect those who follow them and seek to produce more leaders along the way. They step up in times of need and use their lives to build up God's church. They are disciplined and live a life of integrity.

I've known leaders of the church who had great passion to build their church. They gathered information and gathered workers to formulate plans for the church's goals. Their passion overflowed to the members of the church and motivated them with the excitement of future plans. They were professional, organized and efficient with the direction they set into place. Through an extreme work ethic these leaders confidently carried out their plans to completion. In addition to being a good leader of the church they were a good leader of their family and were a good example to those around him.

> *"A leader is one who knows the way, goes the way, and shows the way."*[54]   -John C. Maxwell

These good leaders follow the examples of Jesus Christ. They humbly love their families and plan for their futures. They are trusted by their families because they put God first in their lives and everything flows out of that relationship. They make time with their spouse and children a priority and show them they have value. They make time to serve others in need to show their thankfulness to God for all He has done in their lives. They take time to share Jesus with family, friends, and workers along with anyone who will listen. They truly show the qualities Jesus asked for in a leader.

> **"...whoever wants to become great among you must be your servant"**   Matthew 20:26

THE BAD OF
THE HELMET OF SALVATION
(Going Backward)
"Loving the Goal More Than the People"

The Bad actions of these spiritual gifts are not necessarily sin. They start to slip away from God due to stresses, overwork, and burnout. They can take on to many projects and spread themselves thin. This produces more and more stress, lack of sleep, and attitude changes. The "Bad" is like the check engine light on the dash of a car. It can be a warning of slipping into the "Ugly" sins of these gifts as they drift from God.

Since the goal is the goal to leadership, they can tend to focus only on the goal and overlook the people responsible for accomplishing the goal. Every goal has a bridge to get you from where you are to where you need to go. If they focus only on the goal and never pay attention to the strength of the bridge the bridge may collapse. Faulty bridge work comes from leaders who forget the people building the bridge because they only want to cross the bridge. They forget to share how important the bridge is for the safety of those crossing and rarely praise bridge workers for a job well done.

I watched a Leader of a Mega-Church focus so much on a "purpose" for the church they neglected the core members of the church. He aimed the church at recruiting new members who were thirty-something with children and previously unchurched. They received a boat load of them at a critical time for the church. The church was relocating which meant large amounts of money were needed for the move. The new members did not understand the giving of their time and money and they wanted the best for their children.

The leader hired a firm to constantly talk about the money needs of the church. He preached on the money needs from the pulpit and even had a corporate Sunday school lessons about the need for money over many months. The core of the church, even though they voted 94% to relocate the church, got tired of the constant push for money. The core began to drain out of the church and money became very tight. Programs that fed the core members and made the church great began to be cut due to money problems. More of the core drained out. Eventually the church was barely afloat and full of unchurched, thirty-somethings with kids. Now adrift they had very little leadership to mentor them and grow them in Christ. Unfortunately the Leader left the not so mega-church in financial and spiritual debt.

Many leaders see only the goal and demand perfection from others to the point of bullying and even abandonment. Leaders focus only on the negatives by micro-managing individuals and this causes stressful work conditions. They crush people's spirit by not listening to them and dismissing their ideas.

Have you ever had a boss constantly look over your shoulder and never trust you? Did your work performance improve? No, it probably got worse due to the anxiety of someone just waiting to pounce on your mistakes. This can bring a Leader's goal to a complete stop. Workers will tire from the confusion and demands along with the lack of any form of praise for a job well done. We are all human but being "right" in order to win every battle every time will not win the war if you lose your army.

A leader once said to me he wanted to have a lot of children because he wanted lots of grandchildren to fill his lap in his retirement years. Unfortunately he overworked himself and lost precious time with his children. Some of them strayed into parental nightmares causing extreme relationship problems. Having a goal of grandchildren is a fine goal but if you forget to build a bridge between you and your children you may not have a bridge to enjoy your grandchildren. Many leaders get the cart ahead of the horse with their goals. Make sure you feed the horse and take care of it. Being right to the point of everyone avoiding you will leave you in a dark lonely house at the end of your life.

Leaders can also develop a "Messiah Complex" and believe they are the only one hearing from God and they listen less and less to those around them. I was at a church service where a missionary couple was telling about their mission overseas. Their stories were exciting as they spoke about how God told them to go here and do a specific thing and how God was glorified by their obedience. I heard later that the leader of the church asked them not to say they heard God speak in the second service. They were asked to say something like God laid it on their heart.

My heart broke for those missionaries who, I truly believe, were hearing God's voice based on the tremendous fruit they were producing from their obedience. Leaders... please do not crush the spirit of those around you. Give them purpose, direction and the pat on the back they deserve. This is not just at your job or church, it is also in your home!

The warning sign of leaders beginning to fall is a self-centered arrogance that takes no criticism or opinions from others. They lose their compassion and show no grace for those they lead, even their family. They begin to rule with a dictator-like iron fist demanding perfection in every minor detail. They begin to think they are above the rules and the rules do not apply to themselves. Eventually their leading becomes less Godly and more of the world as they lead their followers into dangerous areas.

They can come on very strong and change everything to fit their agenda. They delegate every job to others and do not offer their own services because their ego says they are above minor jobs. Sadly they generally have a track record of not staying long at churches that do not meet their expectations and demands. They leave one church only to start the cycle over again at a different church and eventually leave that church.

> *Jesus said "...Leave them; they are blind guides. If the blind lead the blind, both will fall into a pit."*
> Matthew 15:14

If the leadership continues leading blindly they will eventually fall into a pit with those they lead. This is the slippery slope into the "Ugly" side of the fallen Christians using the spiritual gifts related to the Helmet of Salvation.

STOP overlooking the people for the purpose.
LOOK at the needs of those helping you achieve God's goal.
LISTEN to and care for the ones carrying the load.
BE WHAT GOD CREATED YOU TO BE, a Godly leader who builds up more Godly leaders with love and humility.

THE MAIN GIFT-KILLING WEAKNESS OF
THE HELMET OF SALVATION
"Pride"

Unfortunately we are all human and we all have weaknesses. Satan targets these weaknesses in the form of Gift-Killers. The main Gift-Killer of the spiritual gifts represented by the Helmet of Salvation is the lack of humility; Pride!

> *"When pride comes, then comes disgrace, but with humility comes wisdom."*   Proverbs 11:2

When leadership becomes self-seeking and not God-seeking they will eventually crash and burn. Do not ever underestimate pride because it brought Satan down! Those using the spiritual gifts of the Helmet need to always remember humble leaders are wise leaders.

> *"Do you see a person wise in their own eyes? There is more hope for a fool than for them."*   Proverbs 26:12

Sadly I have witnessed pride take down many great leaders over the years. It creeps in on leaders and eventually turns into so much arrogance they believe they can get away with anything. They openly sin and fall quickly.

> *"He must become greater; I must become less."*
>   John 3:30

> *"It was pride that changed angels into devils; it is humility that makes men as angels."*[55]   Augustine

THE UGLY OF
THE HELMET OF SALVATION
(Going Sin-Ward)
"Looking to the World for Direction"

The ugly use of the spiritual gifts is when a believer chooses to disobey God and use their God-given talent for evil. God gives us the choice to follow Him or not. He also gives us the choice to use our talents for good or bad and when they are used to sin they become Anti-Gifts. Here is the ugly side of wrongly used talents represented by the Helmet of Salvation. They have been broken down into the three areas of sin discussed in chapter 6:

LUST of the FLESH:
Gift-Killers from Sins of the Body

"Those who live according to the flesh have their minds set on what the flesh desires; but those who live in accordance with the Spirit have their minds set on what the Spirit desires. The mind governed by the flesh is death, but the mind governed by the Spirit is life and peace. The mind governed by the flesh is hostile to God; it does not submit to God's law, nor can it do so. Those who are in the realm of the flesh cannot please God." Romans 8:5-8

Ugly Leadership sets their mind to the fleeting desires of the flesh and will use their talent to manipulate people, especially the opposite sex. They feel ownership of people like property and act as if they are the King and everyone else is pawns. They can also use their own looks to take advantage of others if needed to accomplish a goal.

Poverty in childhood can cause leadership to get whatever they want by whatever means it takes to get it. They can become a sociopath, now called the Antisocial Personality Disorder, which controls other people to get their way. Due to their arrogance they feel nothing can harm them. A controlling type spirit can overtake them and manipulate others around them through blackmail or sex, like Delilah did to Samson. We've seen several Church Leaders lose their ministries to prostitutes or affairs with church secretaries. Leadership should be well aware of the predators seeking to destroy anything Godly and they are not above being targeted for such destruction.

Many in leadership have put rules into place to protect themselves. A good example is having another person join a meeting if their meeting is with the opposite sex. They also never allow themselves to be in a car alone with the opposite sex. Recently this came under fire by women activists as unfair to women. Keep in mind this was around the same time many false allegations against men were coming out. Safe rules like these need to be put into practice to protect both parties involved.

Let's not forget other addictions that seem pleasing to the flesh. Leadership gifts tend to lean more toward legal drugs, alcohol and gambling as they fall from God. As they become addicted to substances, their entire ministry of followers fall apart as their sin grows out of their control.

I had high hopes for a man I met at a Christian retreat that had the spiritual gift of Apostleship. He is one of only a very few I have met with this gift. I watched him and his wife grow in Christ as he spoke at Men's retreats and actively served in a downtown ministry he was building from the ground up. In a flash he fell hard. His Facebook was blowing up with photos of him and his mistress going on a cross country adultery spree. I was shocked at his nerve, posting such disheartening pictures and comments. I'm sure his wife was devastated!

I may have been one of the last contacts he had with brothers that could help him. I texted him a vision I had for him where he was wearing an iron suit similar to the original Iron Man. He was severely beaten up and was lying on his back on the ground. I said I saw a faint glow of life in him as he barely got back up. He slowly walked back to the city he was trying to save while dragging a huge metal sledge hammer sparking

THE HELMET OF SALVATION 195

as it rubbed against the road. He and I texted back and forth a few times and he eventually stopped. The only thing I heard later was he became very sick and was near death and his mistress left him.

This man had so much potential for the Kingdom of God. During one of his spiritual talks at a Christian retreat he spoke of a man begging him for 50 cents at the grocery store. He literally ran to his car to get away from the man. The beggar chased him for a good distance screaming it's only 50 cents. The begging for 50 cents grated against his nerves because of his own poor financial situation even though the beggar was having a much worse time in his life. Eventually he had so much guilt about how he acted about such a small amount of money he went back to give the man some money.

I watched him turn that spiritual talk into hundreds of dollars as men were moved to give him money for his needs and he never asked them for a dime. Ironically most of that money was given to him in the form of 50 cents at a time. Sadly he became spiritually bankrupt through his own disobedience.

> *"...but each person is tempted when they are dragged away by their own evil desire and enticed. Then, after desire has conceived, it gives birth to sin; and sin, when it is full-grown, gives birth to death."*   James 1:14-15

I have prayed for this man not knowing if he is dead or still alive. I pray that he became broken enough to return to God and become what he was created to be, a mighty visionary for God!

STOP chasing pleasures of the flesh that lead to destruction.
LOOK at what God has done for you that can be destroyed by your bad decisions.
LISTEN to God's Word and good advice from others and follow God's Will for your life.
BE WHAT GOD CREATED YOU TO BE, a leader who finds their way through temptation in order to accomplish great things with God.

"Temptation usually comes through a door that has been deliberately left open."   -Anonymous

LUST of the EYES:
Gift-Killers from Idol Worship or Coveting

"You shall not covet your neighbor's house. You shall not covet your neighbor's wife, or his male or female servant, his ox or donkey, or anything that belongs to your neighbor."
Exodus 20:17

When seeking goals, Ugly Leadership can stray from God's Will and focus on worldly methods and not Godly methods. They idolize other worldly leaders who are not grounded in the truth. Just because a leader is charming and exciting does not mean they are a good Christian leader to be followed. Worldly charm can be like a light to a moth that only gets burned in the end.

I once told a friend he was more of a worldly leader than a Godly leader. Unfortunately I was not in a good state of mind at the time and I did not do it in love and it caused great harm to our friendship. If not for the actions of another leader mending us back together we would not be friends to this day. Years later he admitted my statement was correct but he was not in a state of mind to receive the message at that time in his life. Recently I texted him and told him he was more of a Godly leader than a Worldly leader. Over the decades our friendship has proven to be a prime example of iron sharpening iron. There have been many sparks along the way and it has been quite the show.

"Those who want to get rich fall into temptation and a trap and into many foolish and harmful desires that plunge people into ruin and destruction. For the love of money is a root of all kinds of evil. Some people, eager for money, have wandered from the faith and pierced themselves with many griefs."   1 Timothy 6:9-10

When Ugly Leadership fixes their eyes on things of the world, they lose focus on God. They envy what others have and want quick fixes to obtain those desires. An administrator at my son's Christian School stole quite a bit of money from the school's funds. I'm sure they did not start with the intention of stealing from children. Most likely they had some bills to pay and they did not have the money to cover them at the time so they "borrowed" some from the school to avoid late penalties and interest. They may have even paid the money back but another situation may have demanded more money.

At some point they did not pay back the money and probably thought, "That was easy, no one caught me." They may have justified their theft by thinking they deserved the extra money for all the hard work they did for the school. Eventually the point of no return hits and Satan's trap worked perfectly. The person's theft is discovered and their identity is revealed to the public as a legal case is brought against them. Sadly the school shut down a few years later due to financial issues.

Using the spiritual gifts God gave someone to steal from children obviously shows a person *"wandering from their faith and piercing themselves with many griefs."* Stay close to God and His Word to avoid the snares Satan is setting out to entrap us.

> *"You shall not steal."*　　　　　Exodus 20:15

STOP looking to the world for contentment.
LOOK to Jesus and be grateful for what He has done for you.
LISTEN to God when He says, "NO!"
BE WHAT GOD CREATED YOU TO BE, a leader who cares deeply about their family, co-workers and everyone around them.

> *"The desire to love is to give. The desire to Lust is to get."*
> 　　　　　　　　　　　　　-Anonymous

PRIDE of LIFE:
Gift-Killers from Selfish Ambition

"In his pride the wicked man does not seek him; in all his thoughts there is no room for God."

Psalm 10:4

Ugly Leadership gets frustrated "working their way up the ladder" which leads to shortcuts that can destroy people on their way to the top. One shortcut is overlooking sins in a person doing a "good job" to reach the leaders goal. This acceptance of lack of integrity from others opens the door to sin within a group of followers that will grow out of control. It will lead to bigger problems which will eventually be used by Satan to bring down a ministry.

Instead of making their life and ministry better they blame others for their own short comings. Competition becomes rivals, and they seek to destroy them through slander and gossip. They can use their power to destroy those in opposition as they ridicule anyone who differs from their point of view. They are very sensitive to any form of criticism which comes from a deep hidden insecurity from within. They usually react badly to the criticism and will permanently cut off people and family that go against them in any way.

The desire for perfect followers and friends can lead to becoming lonely as they cut off relationships with those that do not meet their expectations. When a person pushes Godly people away from themselves they are a victim of Satan's scheme to destroy them. It is an effective divide-and-conquer plan that has been used for thousands of years.

Ugly Leadership demands "their way or the highway." Prestige and fame causes a higher demand of honor and loyalty from followers and family. This unreal desire of perfection and worship from followers and family is destructive. It can cause those around them leave since they will never be good enough to meet the leader's expectations. If leaders are broken inside they may not have the ability to love others more than something they see can be used for their own needs. They don't see others, they don't hear others and they don't feel others pain. They are not looking for partners in life they are looking for obedient servants.

They may have been a bully in school, especially if they came from a bad home life, and they can continue this into their adult life. A bully seeks some form of self-worship by being the strongest and meanest leader of them all. False gods demand worship, sacrifice and works but they can never get enough to satisfy their appetite. The bully has little to no remorse for the ones they are torturing, they only feel the self-satisfaction for being at the top.

Leadership's information gathering abilities can turn into gossip or blackmail as they work their way to the top. They think nothing of snooping in someone's room, going through texts and emails along with listening in on conversations. Fear becomes a tool as they threaten to expose damaging information they gathered from others. This causes people to build up defenses because they fear their dirty laundry being aired in public. Workers and family literally shut down any personal communication with them and become robotic with little sense of purpose.

As the leader gathers information on others they eventually see only the bad in others and believe they are the only one who is right. This lets them think they can use anyone for their purpose since it is the only right way. They expect complete obedience from everyone and will sacrifice people for results. Ugly Leadership demands unreal expectations and perfection from workers and forces people into questionable practices resulting in sin to reach the goal.

Eventually Ugly Leadership feels as if nothing can touch them as they openly sin. This leads to public shame and destruction of their lives and leadership. I watched a friend I admired for their ability to lead others fall terribly into sin. His ministry was listening to your problems and giving back so much comfort and good advice. He spoke great lessons on Christ and worked hard to accomplish his goals. Sadly I also watched as this man's pride and arrogance brought him to a point where he thought he could get away with anything.

His caring approach brought women closer to him and he fell deeply into multiple adulterous situations. His ministry imploded and he left a canyon of destruction in the Church Body in multiple states. His entire family shunned him and will have nothing to do with him now.

I met with him a few times afterward not to approve of his actions but to show the love of Christ to him even in his sin. I returned the favor he did for me during some hard times in my life. The organization we serve represents 1000's of people and they preach God's grace above all things, yet only a handful of them reached out to this man after what he had done. Practically everyone abandoned him because his sin was among those people. His family even abandoned him. He still serves in some prison ministries but I could tell he was lonely.

> *"But when his heart became arrogant and hardened with pride, he was deposed from his royal throne and stripped of his glory."*   Daniel 5:20

God told me to give a message to a Spiritual Leader who was even closer to this man than I was. The top of the folded paper asked, "How big is grace?" He opened the folded paper and it said this man's name. I told him not to be mad at me for the message. I did not want to deliver it but God really wanted him to know how big His grace is for all of us.

This Spiritual Leader is one of the best preachers on grace I've ever heard but he became very angry. He told me of the damage he was dealing with among the people he knew who were hurt by this man. Keep in mind we will be tested on the very things we preach. I do not yet know the effect of this message on him but I was obedient to deliver the message.

STOP thinking the grass is greener on the other side.
LOOK at the future God has planned for you and not the one Satan is planning for you.
LISTEN to the ways God is giving you to get out of sin.
BE WHAT GOD CREATED YOU TO BE and stay as far away from sin as possible and take better care of the spiritual gift God gave you to build up His Kingdom.

> *"Self-centered indulgence, pride and a lack of shame over sin are now emblems of the American lifestyle."*[56]
>
> -Billy Graham

PROTECTING YOURSELF FROM THE GIFT-KILLERS OF THE HELMET OF SALVATION

LIVING IN HUMILITY

> *"Remember your leaders, who spoke the word of God to you. Consider the outcome of their way of life and imitate their faith."*   Hebrews 13:7

Is your life worth imitating? If people around you were asked if you show the character of Christ would their answer be yes? Would your family feel as if you showed the love of Christ in your home? This may be a tall order but it is asked of all Christians especially leaders. You are a mouthpiece for the direction God wishes to take us but if your actions are not Christ-like then you will have no Godly followers. You can talk the talk and walk the walk but your walk talks louder than your talk talks!

"...Instead, whoever wants to become great among you must be your servant, and whoever wants to be first must be slave of all. For even the Son of Man did not come to be served, but to serve, and to give his life as a ransom for many."
Mark 10:43-45

People are the only thing that matters to God and He does not want any to perish. The only way to lift people up is to be beneath them. Become the servant leader that God uses to lift up those people. Your top leader to follow as an example is Jesus Christ.

"Humble yourselves, therefore, under God's mighty hand, that he may lift you up in due time."
1 Peter 5:6

If you stay the course, God will reward you in *"due time"* to be a leader. The old saying "Rome was not built in a day" is true but it sure fell fast. Humility is the best foundation of a great leader. Work diligently on creating a foundation of imitating Christ that will not be shaken during tough times and Satan's attacks.

Jesus said, "From everyone who has been given much, much will be demanded; and from the one who has been entrusted with much, much more will be asked."
Luke 12:48b

Start small and build on your life's goals. By building a foundation on the truth and humility of Christ, leaders will prove themselves to be worthy of more responsibility. Keep focused on God and His Will to accomplish goals and build up your experience and reputation. Do not get in a hurry; do the small tasks with the same amount of excitement, excellence and focus as the large tasks God asks you to complete. Never start with a poor foundation; your accomplishments will not stand the test of time.

"But to you who are listening I say: Love your enemies, do good to those who hate you, bless those who curse you, pray for those who mistreat you. If someone slaps you on one cheek, turn to them the other also. If someone takes your coat, do not withhold your shirt from them. Give to everyone who asks you, and if anyone takes what belongs to you, do not demand it back. Do to others as you would have them do to you." Luke 6:27-31

This is a tall order from Christ for those in leadership. This goes against the very nature of the world but isn't that what Christ calls all of us to do. Without Christ we have no way out from the cravings of our fleshly desires. We need to mature our Christ-likeness with truth and humility.

The hardest part of any job can be starting the job. So please start building up the spiritual gifts God has given you to help build His Kingdom. Those with the spiritual gifts represented by the Helmet of Salvation need to read John Maxwell and George Barna books on Christian leadership. Take Christian management courses and leadership seminars. Get your hands dirty by volunteering for small projects that build your skills before tackling large projects. Build yourself up by doing tasks others avoid to appreciate your workers. Learn to develop leadership skills to properly lead a team to accomplish a goal with great efficiency. When you learn how things work from the bottom up it enables you to properly lead through your experiences.

Consider interning or being mentored by others with leadership skills. Most of all surround yourself with people grounded in the truth that will hold you accountable. Since a trait of leadership is building lifelong friends, choose those friends carefully. Staying in the truth and being surrounded by those who value the truth produces great leaders.

STOP wasting time and get started maturing your spiritual gift.
LOOK for ways to grow your spiritual gift through Scripture.
LISTEN to Christ and Godly Christian leaders who can mentor your spiritual gift.

BE WHAT GOD CREATED YOU TO BE and do well with the small things of God so you can accomplish bigger things with God.

> *"There is no such thing as a self-made spiritual leader. A true leader influences others spiritually only because the Spirit works in and through him to a greater degree than in those he leads."*[57]
>
> -J. Oswald Sanders

MAMAW'S LEADERSHIP

> *"Who is wise and understanding among you? Let him show it by his good life, by deeds done in the humility that comes from wisdom."*   James 3:13

If you desire to be a great leader then you need to be a humble leader. Even though my Mamaw had a different set of spiritual gifts than leadership she was called to be the leader in her home. My Granddaddy was not the best of husbands and tended to drink a lot. One day the police called my Mamaw to pick up my Granddaddy because they thought he was drunk again. They did not realize he was having a stroke and almost died. Following the stroke he was in a wheel chair for over two decades and my Mamaw stuck with him and became the leader of the home.

My Mamaw had a great effect on my son and me because of her servant's heart and her humility. She not only taught me carpentry, plumbing and roofing, she showed me what it was like to live a life of humility. She was responsible for me giving my heart to Jesus when I was 12 years old by taking me to church every chance she could. She was also the reason my son got baptized. Even though my son knew Jesus was the Son of God he was scared to get water up his nose during his baptism. He loved his Mamaw and knew she was dying of cancer and he wanted her to see him baptized before she died. Her humble heart made her the best leader I have ever encountered in my life.

The day of her death I sat next to her in her home as she took her last breath. My wife Teresa was on her way to pick up our 10 year old son from school. I called Teresa to let her know Mamaw passed away. When she drove up to the school Brody was visibly upset and being hugged by the teachers. As he sat in the car Teresa explained Mamaw had passed away. I'll let my son describe the things that happened next. This is a few paragraphs from a paper he wrote six years later in 10th grade:

"I woke up the next morning like any other and went to school. This time though something went different. During the time we prayed we bowed our heads quietly. In that time that felt like eternity God talked to me. He told me it was her time and at that moment I jumped up and ran to the bathroom almost drowning in tears. As I sat in there with tear stains all on my clothes I remember thinking this can't be. Why would he tell me this? Through that I comforted myself to think it must not be.

Later the clock hit 3 and we left. I walked outside and saw my mom across the parking lot in tears. I walked up and thought it can't be? And yet it was. She told me that on the way over she got a call telling her she left for the kingdom. She sat and wondered why I didn't cry. I was in too much shock that he told me so all I said was, I knew.

We pulled in to the open field with the overgrown garden and the driveway filled with cars. Family sat outside crying at the corpse that used to hold what we held near. As I opened the door the smell blasted me and I knew this may be the last this ever happens. As I walked in the tile had been rubbed to almost colorless from feet and on the cot was the empty shell. I went over and the first thing I knew to do was to hold her hand. I picked it up but it now was cold and lifeless, that's when I broke. The tears fell like rivers and memories fell with them."

God told my son that Mamaw would die that very day. After her body was zipped up in the black plastic bag and carried out of the house I asked Brody about God speaking to him. He told me it happened while he was in chapel at his Christian school. He said during a silent prayer time God told him she was going to pass away that day. I asked him what verse he had been studying in chapel and it was the following:

> *"Do nothing out of selfish ambition or vain conceit, but in humility consider others better than yourselves. Each of you should look not only to your own interests, but also to the interests of others. Your attitude should be the same as that of Christ Jesus."*   Philippians 2:3-5

Humility simply requires that you treat others as if they are better than yourself and this was my Mamaw. She would always put her things aside to help others. I always loved how she was taking food to the "old folks" when she was 80 years old. My Mamaw was a great leader simply by being an example of humility.

Just before the funeral my son requested I play *"You Have Been So Good"* by Lenny LeBlanc because he said it reminded him of her. Most 82 year old's funerals around here play old southern hymns but my son was requesting a more modern praise song be played during her funeral. I couldn't just play the song I had to explain the song. My son's request roped me into speaking at my Mamaw's funeral.

I walked in to the funeral to tell about Brody's experience and give the reason for the song I was about to play. Unfortunately I met the weeping eyes of my cousin Jennifer and I could not speak. Within seconds I felt as if two men came along my side and lifted me up under my arms but no one was there, to this day I believe they were angels. I quickly regained myself and began to speak. I was able to tell everyone about my son's experience. I told how goodness followed my Mamaw and why they were about to hear a sweet song that reminded her great grandson of her humility and love and of her goodness.

> *"All of you, clothe yourselves with humility toward one another, because, 'God opposes the proud but gives grace to the humble.'"*   1 Peter 5:5

We should all strive to have our grandchildren and great grandchildren remember us this way. I believe humility is earned at a high price and is not easily learned. It comes through a lifetime of service to others. That lifetime is usually filled with tremendous trials and having to painfully remove the deep shrapnel of pride and hurt from the past. This was my Mamaw.

> *"He has shown you, O mortal, what is good. And what does the LORD require of you? To act justly and to love mercy and to walk humbly with your God."*   Micah 6:8

When leading *"act justly"* by staying close to God so you know His Will for your life. *"Love mercy"* by treating those with respect who are helping you to achieve the goals by complimenting them on a job well done and helping them gently learn from their mistakes. Most of all *"walk humbly with your God"* as you lead others to the goal of building up God's Kingdom.

I write this story about my Mamaw because I cannot teach you to love others more than yourself. For some reason you may have grown up relying on yourself and you learned you could only count on yourself. You became your own best friend and worked hard not to let yourself down. You seek out others with leadership abilities and love learning from them until you feel you have passed their abilities and you move on. Now is your time to seek out the ultimate Leader, Jesus. Follow His example of humble leadership and see what you can really accomplish through obedience to His calling on your life.

STOP letting pride destroy your life and the lives around you.
LOOK at the humble example of Jesus and follow His leadership example for your life.
LISTEN to Jesus for examples of humility, love and mercy.
BE WHAT GOD CREATED YOU TO BE; a humble leader for Christ.

"Humility is not thinking less of yourself, it's thinking of yourself less."[58]
　　　　　　　　　　　　　　　　　　　-Rick Warren

GROWTH IN CHRIST
The Spiritual Gifts Related to
The Helmet of Salvation

UNDERSTAND "WHOSE" YOU ARE

"Your love, Lord, reaches to the heavens, your faithfulness to the skies. Your righteousness is like the highest mountains, your justice like the great deep."　Psalm 36:5-6

Sometimes leaders struggle with love because goals have driven their entire life. Marriage may have been a goal but was it out of love or accomplishment? Now it is time for love to become your goal. Strive to accept God's love and allow yourself to pour out that love to others around you. God loves you and your abilities to help people with His direction for their lives. He wants you to spend an eternity with him and with all the people you helped bring to heaven. Follow the greatest leader the world has ever seen and follow Christ!

CONFESS AND PROGRESS

"Whoever conceals their sins does not prosper, but the one who confesses and renounces them finds mercy."
　　　　　　　　　　　　　　　　　Proverbs 28:13

Leaders are good at hiding their sins and weaknesses. This is like having a bad front end alignment on a car that eventually causes the tires to wear out. Not confessing your sins can lead to making deals with Satan without even knowing you signed the contract. You worry about looking bad if people ever found out about your sins. You begin to think your sins make you unworthy to carry out God's plans and you back off from God's Word and water down the direction you are leading people. Confess your sins in a safe place and be free so you can move forward. Good accountability with someone you trust is freeing and allows growth in Christ

RENEW YOUR MIND

"We demolish arguments and every pretension that sets itself up against the knowledge of God, and we take captive every thought to make it obedient to Christ."

2 Corinthians 10:5

For leaders the renewing of their mind and having the mind of Christ is of upmost importance. Your mind is where you work out the details for accomplishing God's work. Interference from Satan and the static of the world can have destructive effects on those goals. By keeping your mind on Christ you can easily distinguish between good and evil and choose good.

Have you ever wondered if some thoughts are demonic? Angels are described as ministering spirits in Hebrews 1:14 and their name means messenger. Not all angels are good. The chief of all bad angels, Satan, can have his ideas planted in your mind. Examples of this are shown in 1 Chronicles 21:1 when David was incited (seduced, or persuaded) by Satan to do a census. David declared a census to be taken in order to know the strength of his army. The problem was he was not relying on God for strength he was looking to his own army. David was even warned by Joab that this was not of God but David continued with the census. David calculated his army's strength and decided he had enough of an army to win and a battle followed. He lost the battle badly due to his pride of relying on man and not God.

Other examples are when Satan prompted Judas to betray Jesus in John 13:2 and Ananias let Satan "fill" his heart and lie to the Holy Spirit about keeping money from the church in Acts 5:3. Amazing how death and destruction follow when Satan's lies take root in a person. David's disobedience led to the death of much of his army, Judas committed suicide and Ananias along with his wife fell over dead after being confronted about taking the money.

Satan's ministry is to kill, steal and destroy so expect death, plunder and destruction to follow his lies. By entertaining a lie it becomes an action. We are so predictable that Satan keeps on using the same bait like sex, drugs, power, money, and material possessions. The theme is always the same, gratification of self through the eventual destruction of us and others.

> *"Therefore, with minds that are alert and fully sober, set your hope on the grace to be brought to you when Jesus Christ is revealed at his coming."*   1 Peter 1:13

A thought is the easiest thing we can destroy. Take the thought captive and replace it with a Godly thought. If tempted, read your Bible, listen to Christian Music, call a trusted Christian friend, read a devotion or Google "verse of the day" but most of all seek God and let Him fill your thoughts. I had a friend once tell me when he had a memory of an old girlfriend randomly pop up in his head he would pray for them to take his thought captive.

Imagine you're walking down a neighborhood street and there are houses on either side of the street. Jesus is barely visible at the far end of the street and you are trying to get to Him. As you walk, the demons in the houses and yards keep trying to lure you inside their house of sin to keep you from reaching Jesus. The demons would love to have you enter their house and keep you away from Jesus. This makes you less effective for building God's Kingdom and they get to stay on Earth a little longer.

The other problem is stopping to argue with demons. When you do this you take your eyes off Jesus and stop your walk toward Him. Do your best to keep your eyes on Jesus and do not entertain thoughts that will lead you into one of their houses. Keep focused on Jesus, keep walking and keep your thoughts on those things that are pleasing to God.

"The LORD detests the thoughts of the wicked, but those of the pure are pleasing to him."   Proverbs 15:26

"Satan uses a vacant mind as a dumping ground."
                                                    Anonymous

COMMUNICATE WITH GOD

"Whoever has ears, let them hear what the Spirit says to the churches."   Revelation 3:22

Many times leaders look to other leaders for guidance. Unfortunately they can look to the wrong leader if they do not compare them to Christ's leadership. If Jesus was standing over you and looking at all you do would it stand up to His truth or your truth. Always make sure your leadership will stand up to Jesus' approval.

W.W.J.D. (What Would Jesus Do) should be on your wall in your office and your home. Listen carefully to God's Word and His teachings in order to follow Him and lead others. Communicate with God on a regular basis to adjust the course when necessary to stay in His Will.

STOP giving free rent in your head to the bad thoughts from Satan.
LOOK to Jesus and not the temptation.
LISTEN regularly for pure thoughts so you can have the mind of Christ.
BE WHAT GOD CREATED YOU TO BE; a committed follower of Christ with a mind full of His truth, grace, glory, and mercy.

USING THE SPIRITUAL GIFTS REPRESENTED BY THE HELMET OF SALVATION WITH THE FRUITS OF THE SPIRIT

LOVE: Does your leadership promote love among those around you? Would those you lead say you have the love of Christ in you?

JOY: Do the goals you received from God bring joy to both you and those around you when they are accomplished? Do you take time to soak in the joy from a plan well done? Do you celebrate joyfully with those who helped you reach the goal?

PEACE: Is your home and office peaceful when you're around? Do you bring peace or division to your work and home? Are you a gatherer or a scatterer?

PATIENCE: Can you give time for people to grow and mature into leaders? Do you help a person learn from their mistakes or do they fear you when they make a mistake? Is time your enemy or is it an opportunity to encourage others?

KINDNESS: Do people think you reward them for a job well done? Do your words build others up or tear them down?

GOODNESS: Do people think you are a person of integrity? Do people see you doing good things for other people including your family?

FAITHFULNESS: Do you obediently follow God's plan even if it is not your own? Can you always say you prayed for and listened to God for His plan?

GENTLENESS: Do you see others needs as something you strive to do something about? When someone makes a mistake are you gentle or full of anger?

SELF-CONTROL: Can you control your temper when people say bad things about you and work with them for the best solution? Could you hold a raw egg in your closed fist and not break it while you are having an argument with another person?

TAKE THE MIRROR TEST

"But the Lord said to Samuel, 'Do not consider his appearance or his height, for I have rejected him. The Lord does not look at the things people look at. People look at the outward appearance, but the Lord looks at the heart.' "
1 Samuel 16:7

When a leader looks at their self in a mirror they may only see themselves. Only when they allow Christ to fill every crack and broken area of their heart will they begin to look like Christ to themselves and those around them. These broken areas are rarely seen by others and are well-kept secrets. Their fear of exposing weaknesses can keep them from reaching their full potential in Christ. Allow the repairs to begin and pick up the mirror to see the progress. One day you will see Christ smiling back at you!

STOP relying on yourself and allow God to lead your life.
LOOK only to those led of God for leadership role models.
LISTEN to those around you when asking if you show the love of Jesus to others.
BE WHAT GOD CREATED YOU TO BE and show love and mercy to those you lead through humility to build God's Kingdom.

PONDERING POINTS

What are the gifts related to the Helmet of Salvation?
How is the Helmet an important piece of Armor physically?
How is the Helmet an important piece of Armor spiritually?
What is the goal of the gifts of the Helmet?
What is the purpose of the gifts of the Helmet?
What is the strength of the gifts of the Helmet?
What is the gift of Apostleship and why is it confusing?
What are some examples of good and bad Leadership?
What are some examples of good and bad Administration?
What is the main weakness of Leadership and Administration?
What are some examples of bad boss or leader decisions?
How is the leadership in your home, office or church?
What are ways you can improve your leadership skills?
How humble are you on a 1-10 scale?
How prideful are you on a 1-10 scale?
What are ways to be more humble?
What is the best way to avoid temptation?
How can you renew your mind in Godly ways?
How can you stop a thought from becoming an action?
What fears can stop this group of gifts?

"May he give you the desire of your heart and make all your plans succeed."   Psalm 20:4

CHAPTER NINE

THE BREASTPLATE OF RIGHTEOUSNESS

"Stand firm then, with the belt of truth buckled around your waist, with the breastplate of righteousness in place, and with your feet fitted with the readiness that comes from the gospel of peace. In addition to all this, take up the shield of faith, with which you can extinguish all the flaming arrows of the evil one. Take the helmet of salvation and the sword of the Spirit, which is the word of God."

Ephesians 6:14-17

The Breastplate of a Roman soldier was important for protecting his vital organs. It was a secondary protection if his shield was lost or failed to protect him. God protected the most vital part of us through His grace by giving us His righteousness.

"He made Him who knew no sin to be sin for us, that we might become the righteousness of God in Him"

2 Corinthians 5:21

Justification is when God declared you righteous. Imagine being in a court where you are guilty of a crime with a life sentence. The Judge walks in and says there is someone here who is willing to take your place in jail. He pounds his gavel on the bench and declares you blameless even though you were guilty. You did not earn being freed, it was a gift. This type of freedom could neither be bought nor earned through your works. It can only come from believing Jesus, the Son of God, took your life sentence when he died a perfect sacrifice for your sins and made you blameless in God's eyes.

"Wealth is worthless in the day of wrath, but righteousness delivers from death."   Proverb 11:4

SPIRITUAL GIFTS REPRESENTED BY THE BREASTPLATE OF RIGHTEOUSNESS

Discerning Spirits
Encouragement
Evangelism
Healing
Mercy
Miracles
Tongues Diverse
Tongues Interpretation

"Create in me a pure heart, O God, and renew a steadfast spirit within me."   Psalm 51:10

The eight spiritual gifts represented by the Breastplate of Righteousness are the heart of God. He uses these spiritual gifts to show His love to His children by saving them, building them up and healing them. The list may seem to be all over the map but they all have a unique connection. This group requires a regular communication with God in order to function correctly. This connection with God needs a *"pure heart"* in order to avoid the interference of Satan and the static of the world.

If you are using Discerning Spirits you need to know from God which spirits are good and which are bad. Many times it's like distinguishing between a left and a right hand because they look so much alike. If you are encouraging someone you need to know what words God would have you speak to them to bring blessings to their life.

Evangelism needs to know their audience in order to deliver a specific message to bring them to Christ. Healing and Miracles need specific instructions for their gifts like go dip in the Jordan seven times, walk around the city seven times, rub spit and dirt on their eye, and don't whack the rock! Tongues need to allow God to communicate through them and bless those around them with an Interpretation to build up the Body of Christ. Communication with God is the key with this set of spiritual gifts to bless those around them.

The Breastplate of Righteousness protects the vital organs responsible for supplying the entire body with oxygen, blood, and digested nutrients along with filtering and removing the toxins of the body! This is a pretty important list of jobs being done by this area of the body. Discerning Spirits helps identify the toxins attacking the body while Healing rebuilds the damaged cells. The adrenal glands give a Miraculous boost to the body in times of need while Mercy pumps the heart to remove toxins through the kidneys and out of the body. Evangelism supplies the oxygen through the lungs so the body can have life while Encouragement and Tongues build up the body with nutrients to keep it healthy.

Those represented by the Breastplate will stand in the crossroads of people's lives. Their job is to communicate with God and do everything possible and impossible to help others find the path to righteousness through Christ. They will pour out the love of Christ to others through Mercy and Encouragement. They will expose the enemy through Discerning Spirits and lead others to Christ through Evangelism. They can bring Healing to hurting souls and show Miracles, especially the miracle of Salvation. They can also build up others by letting them know God loves and cares about them through Tongues and its Interpretation.

> *"Above all else, guard your heart, for everything you do flows from it."* Proverbs 4:23

The Breastplate protects the heart of the Body of Christ so the love of Christ can flow to others. This group of gifts excels in their ability to give hugs from Jesus!

WE ALL HAVE SPIRITUAL GIFTS PLURAL

Some spiritual gifts may not be as strong as others but aren't we all called to "Love our neighbor?" Shouldn't we all show some of these spiritual gifts though some form of Love, Encouragement and Mercy? Are we not called to tell others about Christ in the Great Commission? We may not go oversees on a mission or speak in front of a church but we can simply share our testimony of how Christ saved us with others. Maybe this could lead to the Miracle of their salvation!

THE GOAL OF
THE BREASTPLATE OF RIGHTEOUSNESS
"To Obediently Build Up the Church"

"And this is love: that we walk in obedience to his commands. As you have heard from the beginning, his command is that you walk in love."   2 John 1:6

The spiritual gifts related to the Breastplate of Righteousness are well-equipped to help build up the church. They lead people to Christ, encourage them, warn them of evil, and take care of their wounds. Without Mercy would we have had a Mother Teresa? Without Evangelism would there have been a Billy Graham? Without the Miracle of salvation where would we go when we die? When tuned into God these gifts can hear the exact needs of others and lovingly supply those needs for their spiritual, mental and physical healing at precisely the right time.

THE PURPOSE OF
THE BREASTPLATE OF RIGHTEOUSNESS
"To Show the Heart of God"

When walking close to God this set of spiritual gifts spreads the Heart of God throughout the world. This group of gifts love, love, loves to share God's love! God wants the best for His children and He deeply cares for our needs. His heart is for everyone to be in heaven with Him forever and that none perish. This group of gifts feels the Heart of God.

Having someone comfort and encourage us at just the right time can rescue us from Satan's traps. This can heal us on many levels. Helping people heal, whether it's a physical, mental or spiritual healing, lets people know God cares about them. These spiritual gifts may have a goal of building up the church but they do it caringly one person and one heart at a time.

"And now these three remain: faith, hope and love. But the greatest of these is love." 1 Corinthians 13:13

THE STRENGTH OF
THE BREASTPLATE OF RIGHTEOUSNESS
"Knowing the Emotional and Spiritual Needs of Others"

Being the heart of God in the Body of Christ allows those using these spiritual gifts to show God's love to others. They have a direct line to God for receiving specific information to build up, comfort, heal and encourage the church. They know exactly what to say or do to bring a non-believer to Jesus or a broken Christian back to the church. Sometimes the big guns of Miracles and Healing are brought out to really show that God's involved. Since there is so much communication with God within these gifts, prayer becomes a powerful tool to accomplish mighty things for the Kingdom of God. This group of gifts has an amazing prayer life. If you are in need of prayer seek out these believers to pray for you, especially in Spiritual Warfare!

"Therefore confess your sins to each other and pray for each other so that you may be healed. The prayer of a righteous person is powerful and effective." James 5:16 NIV

I like how the New King James Version translates this passage.

"Confess your trespasses to one another, and pray for one another, that you may be healed. The effective, fervent prayer of a righteous man avails much."
James 5:16 NKJV

This group of spiritual gifts can have *"effective"* and *"fervent"* prayers due to their nature of communication with God. This type of prayer is powerful like an electrical current energizing a filament in a lightbulb. Their prayers have such a way of encouraging and energizing others to be better and to seek God.

"Therefore encourage one another and build each other up, just as in fact you are doing."   1 Thessalonians 5:11

THE GOOD OF
THE BREASTPLATE OF RIGHTEOUSNESS
(Going Forward)
"Helping Others Know They Are Valued by God"

The spiritual gifts related to the Breastplate of Righteousness are some of the most emotionally driven gifts. They delight in moving people toward becoming Christ-like through interaction, experiences and relationships. They help people feel valuable by showing them they are part of something bigger than themselves. They see the potential in people and love them where they are in their life. They are excellent comforters and counselors in times of need and will stay with you for the long haul if necessary.

They see and hear the needs of others and have perfectly timed words to speak life into them. A patient of mine would take homeless people to her home and let them shower, enjoy a few hot meals and sleep in a comfortable bed for a few nights. She knew how to show them they had value.

> *"Delight yourself also in the Lord, and He shall give you the desires of your heart."*   Psalm 37:4

These spiritual gifts are incredible prayer warriors and delight in seeing Jesus change lives supernaturally. The love of Christ flows from these gifts as they build up the Body of Christ and they genuinely desire to share the love of Christ.

THE BAD OF
THE BREASTPLATE OF RIGHTEOUSNESS
(Going Backward)
"Knowing What is Right and Choosing What is Wrong."

The Bad actions of these spiritual gifts are not necessarily sin. They start to slip away from God due to stresses, overwork, and burnout. Because their lives can become hectic they may begin to look for quick fixes to the problems of others. They begin to spend less time with people in need and give generalized non-personal messages of encouragement and comfort that are not specific for the person they are helping. They may even brush them off by recommending a program that wastes the hurt person's time. They ignore hearing from God for specific messages to help because they are in a hurry in their own life. If they are not properly tuned into God, their frazzled lives cause them to misinterpret or even ignore His messages.

A friend was in a hurry to buy a birthday gift and she bought a set of the stemless wine glasses for another friend. She forgot the friend had alcohol problems in the past. The love was there but they allowed worldly static of their life to scramble the message. Slow down and focus to get the right message in order to bless others.

> *"Do not let any unwholesome talk come out of your mouths, but only what is helpful for building others up according to their needs, that it may benefit those who listen."*
> Ephesians 4:29

This group of gifts can sometimes talk too much to fill "dead air space" and overstep with their words. When encouraging and comforting others you learn a lot of intimate details about people's lives and by talking too much you can slip into gossip. You can destroy a person's walk with God if they learn you told their secrets to others. They distrust you, then the church, then Christianity as a whole. I have a friend that loves to give the full name of a person as he describes the full details of their sins. I frequently have to tell him their names are not needed for prayer to be effective.

Sometimes people guess, with great judgement, what the sins of others may be. I remind them it is all speculation until the truth is revealed. Please do not engage in either speaking or listening to gossip; both are equally bad. One feeds fuel to the fire while the other one burns the victim needing help. Some that fall into this group of gifts have trouble self-regulating their thoughts, speech, behaviors and feelings. Obedience and self-control are of upmost importance when using these gifts.

> *"Show me, Lord, my life's end and the number of my days; let me know how fleeting my life is."*
> Psalm 39:4

Those represented by the spiritual gifts in the Breastplate of Righteousness can easily fall into boundary problems with others trying to suck their time away. Time is short and there are many people needing God's love and encouragement. It's ok to say to the person you're helping, "I will help you with your problem but you need to make baby steps. If you don't make baby steps I'll have to go help someone else." If boundaries are not made up front it can quickly lead to personal burn out. This can eventually lead to not helping anyone at all because of past hurts from time-suckers.

Many of these gifts have such a desire to help others but they neglect their own responsibilities because their time was abused. I've seen friends work on other people's homes while their home was literally rotting. They spread themselves out in a dozen different directions, except for their own home and family. Be careful not to neglect those closest to you when you help others. Ask any church leader about how difficult it can be to balance helping those in the church and making time to love and build up their own family.

> *"See what great love the Father has lavished on us, that we should be called children of God!"* 1 John 3:1

Many in this group of gifts have had a rough past that defines their life. Remember, it is not what happened to you that makes you who you are; it's what God created you to be! Because of their ability to recognize the enemy, Satan sends special predators aimed at destroying their life.

These predators attack children in every horrible way possible at any age to make them unable to use their spiritual gifts in the future. The predators may seem like the best thing since sliced bread but when it is suspected they are being controlling they break out the fangs and claws. These constant attacks leave the future injured adult with their life upside down.

This constant life of being hurt can lead to a person to become controlling themselves in order to get what they want. By becoming a "Mother Hen" they can control others through a false love designed to fill their own needs. They may even enable people to continue in their state of need so they will feel needed themselves. Unfortunately I have seen these situations crumble and the family is left in pieces when the controlling person dies or is unable to function. Another way of controlling others comes from building a wall to keep from being injured again. It doesn't matter what happens to others as long as the one inside the wall never gets hurt again. This can end in a sad and lonely life.

If some in this group of gifts do not get an occasional pat on the back or receive gratitude and encouragement from others, their fuel gauge hits empty. They can take an ounce of "gratitude fuel" and run hundreds of miles to help others. But without occasional fuel they may become angry and resentful when they are not noticed for their good works and can stop helping others. Keep in mind God will use us many times when our tank is empty just to show it was of Him!

Many in this group of gifts can suffer from a low self-esteem making them feel as if they are of no use to God. Do not fall victim to your past, God made you better than your past. If He made you His child and gives you a future with Him, you have value and significance!

> *Jesus said, "Be careful not to do your 'acts of righteousness' before men, to be seen by them. If you do, you will have no reward from your Father in heaven. So when you give to the needy, do not announce it with trumpets, as the hypocrites do in the synagogues and on the streets, to be honored by men. I tell you the truth, they have received their reward in full. But when you give to the needy, do not let your left hand know what your right hand is doing, so that your giving may be in secret. Then your Father, who sees what is done in secret, will reward you."* Matthew 6:1-4

The Jewish culture promotes *"acts of righteousness"* or *"acts of piety"* through three main actions. They were Almsgiving, Prayer and Fasting. Jesus showed the hypocrisy of the Pharisees by explaining more about the when and where of these acts. They were to be done anonymously and cheerfully without the acts being seen by others. Go to your prayer closet to pray and avoid repetitive prayers in public. Do not announce giving to others and when you fast, look good and do not complain about it. Do your good works to be obedient to God, not to look good to others.

> *"The righteous do good and forget about having done it! The unrighteous however, keep a mental record of all the good that they have done."*[59]   -Zac Poonen

STOP making your life so busy you can't use your spiritual gifts.
LOOK for ways of reducing the things in your life that takes away time with God.
LISTEN to God for specific words and actions to help others.
BE WHAT GOD CREATED YOU TO BE and be the heart of God.

THE MAIN GIFT-KILLING WEAKNESS OF THE BREASTPLATE OF RIGHTEOUSNESS "Disobedience"

The Goal of these spiritual gifts is obedience because disobedience is the main problem facing these gifts. Keeping people with these gifts on task... squirrel... can be difficult as they seek more... squirrel... experiences of life. This group reminds me so much of Doug the dog from Disney's movie "UP." He was very loving and eager to help but he had a hard time focusing.

> *"Don't you know that when you offer yourselves to someone to obey him as slaves, you are slaves to the one whom you obey—whether you are slaves to sin, which leads to death, or to obedience, which leads to righteousness?"*
> Romans 6:16

Romans ask if we are *"slaves to sin"* or do we choose *"obedience, which leads to righteousness?"* Obedience within this group of gifts is extremely important in order to get the precise message from God to those in need. Obedience in prayer, obedience in listening to God, obedience in delivering the message and obedience to carrying out the job you were called to do are all vital to accomplishing God's Will.

> *"The Lord is far from the wicked, but he hears the prayer of the righteous."*   Proverbs 15:29

All Christians became righteous in God's eyes when we were obedient to believe Christ died for us on the cross. When the spiritual gifts represented by the Breastplate of Righteousness are being obedient and walking close to God they hear God's messages and can become a powerful force for the church. Many times they just need to slow down and focus to hear from Him. It is hard to get a hug from Jesus when you are running by Him! He loves you dearly, so love Him back!

> *Jesus said, "If you love me, keep my commands."*
> John 14:15

THE UGLY OF
THE BREASTPLATE OF RIGHTEOUSNESS
(Going Sin-Ward)
"Running Away From God"

> *"Since we have these promises, dear friends, let us purify ourselves from everything that contaminates body and spirit, perfecting holiness out of reverence for God."*
> 2 Corinthians 7:1

When the spiritual gifts related to the Breastplate of Righteousness start down the ugly path into sin, they run hard away from God. They will run into a brick wall trying to get away from Him only to get up again and again to run into the same brick wall. There is an overwhelming desire to seek experiences of life and when they are not grounded in the truth these experiences are extremely destructive to themselves and the people around them.

The ugly use of these spiritual gifts is when a believer chooses to disobey God and use their God-given talent for evil. God gives us the choice to follow Him or not. He also gives us the choice to use our talents for good or bad and when they are used to sin they become Anti-Gifts. Here is the ugly side of wrongly used talents represented by the Breastplate of Righteousness. They have been broken down into the three areas of sin discussed in chapter 6:

LUST of the FLESH:
Gift-Killers from Sins of the Body

"What then? Shall we sin because we are not under the law but under grace? By no means!"   Romans 6:15

Unfortunately this group of gifts can fall into many sexual sins as they seek experiences to fulfil their lives. I've seen this happen so many times in my life as previously good people turn to a life of sexual sin. I've seen people with the gifts of Mercy and Encouragement fall for married people as they try to help them. They develop an emotional connection and Satan sets the trap. Keep in mind cheating is not always physically touching, making out or flirting. If you are becoming emotionally connected to another person and find the need to delete text messages and emails so your spouse won't see them you're already there!

Many of us have witnessed famous Evangelists brought down in shame when found with prostitutes. Other church leaders leave the ministry because of affairs with church secretaries and even sinful sexual relations with young teens and children. I personally knew an Evangelist who went down this path and served time in jail for his sins.

Satan delights in his craftsmanship of these situations. It doesn't start with a new preacher walking into a church and saying to themselves, "I think I will have an affair with the secretary today." Satan plans perfect storms to break down defenses on both sides until sin takes over their lives. The experience of desire outweighs the truth and destruction follows. The domino effect of a single experience can last generations. Is it worth the eternal damage for a fleeting desire?

Unfortunately the spiritual gifts related to the Breastplate of Righteousness can have a terrible past. There can be verbal or sexual abuse, molestation and rape at very early ages. Satan sends specially equipped predators to destroy their lives. I see this in several of these gifts but I see it more commonly in Discerning Spirits. Satan hates that God gives some people the ability to recognize him and his demons so he attacks them early in their lives.

These attacks leave the person upside down in the world and they can bounce back and forth mentally with bi-polar disorder. They struggle with their past and their present because they see a spiritual world in constant battle that most of us cannot see.

When I see a tree bending in the wind I see the tree bending but this gift can sometimes see, feel or hear the wind bending the tree. The wind is Satan and his demons, while the tree bending is the effect Satan has on people's lives.

Many times I meet these people that have been attacked early in their lives and they seem so out of reach for help. They are bipolar wanderers that seem to have no direction in their lives. They usually have a universal new age approach to God with no real specific direction. If you are this person please know you are a child of God. It's not what happened to you that makes you who you are; it's what God created you to be.

"Knowing the truth concerning the deep workings of the evil spirit helps the individual not only to overcome sins but to eliminate unnecessary afflictions as well."[60]   -Watchman Nee

I tell those with Discerning Spirits to ask God to give them a friend with a sound-mind and the same spiritual gifts as theirs. This helps tremendously with predators because it's hard for the predators to get under two radars. If the friend says the people you are hanging out with could be dangerous then listen to them closely. They become watchers over each other's lives and help protect each other from the enemy. Many times this "friend" can be your own parent if they have this gift and are of a sound-mind.

> *"I will be a Father to you, and you will be my sons and daughters, says the Lord Almighty."* 2 Corinthians 6:18

Many parents with Discerning Spirits give up their child for adoption. The parent's lives were in such a whirlwind of chaos they could not possibly see themselves raising a child. Try your best not to blame them if you were given up for adoption. They most likely have your same spiritual gift and have been attacked all of their lives. It was not their fault you were attacked, it was Satan. Look to your Father in heaven as your true Papa because truth says we are all adopted as His *"sons and daughters."*

Unfortunately the disobedience of this group of gifts places it on a direct path of destruction. While speaking with a dear friend about his spiritual gifts I shared where I have noticed gifts in the Breastplate of Righteousness are shallow in their study of Scripture. They can read a Scripture hanging on the wall and go six months on one sentence from God. He said this offended him but I was correct about my observation. I asked if I needed to learn a foreign language to talk with him in his "Gift Language" because mine is obvious and to the point. When I talk with people in this group of gifts, the most important message is to Read and study the Word! It will help grow your Faith, which is the only thing that will keep this group sane.

> *"Sanctify them by the truth; your word is truth."*
> John 17:17

My friend and I talked some more and I realized the people with these gifts are experience-seekers and I was a truth-seeker so I asked him, "What is more important, Experiencing God or the Truth of God?" He looked at me not quite knowing what to say and letting him off the hook and I said, "Both!" As a truth-seeker I need more of God's experiences and as an experience-seeker he needed more of God's truth. Most of the problems facing this group of gifts are from seeking experiences for a high in their life while ignoring the truth of God. Another friend took my advice of reading more Scripture and made it a priority in his life. He thanked me later for being up front with him and pointing out his weakness.

Experience seeking without the truth of God can lead to addictions of all types. Not just drugs and alcohol but sex, food and dangerous thrill seeking can be added to the list. Some people in these gifts are the perfect examples of the "Addictive Personality Disorder" craving any high in life. Sadly many mental disorders such as bipolar disorder and depression can be associated with this addictive personality. One of the biggest diagnostic factors is having a close relative with these problems. Unfortunately I have witnessed this frequently when talking with patients about these gifts. Many of them have a parent or grandparent suffering with similar addictions.

STOP seeking worldly experiences that draw you away from God.
LOOK for experiences that draw you close to God.
LISTEN to God and believe Him and grow your Faith in His truth!
BE WHAT GOD CREATED YOU TO BE; a thrill seeker seeking the truth through Godly experiences!

> *"God has defeated Satan through the death and resurrection of the Lord Jesus Christ. Through this overwhelming victory, God has also empowered you to overcome any temptation to sin and has provided sufficient resources for you to respond biblically to any problem of life. By relying on God's power and being obedient to His Word, you can be an overcomer in any situation."*[61]
>
> -John C. Broger

LUST of the EYES:
Gift-Killers from Idol Worship or Coveting

Many of the spiritual gifts related to the Breastplate of Righteousness slip deep into materialism. Having nice things is not a sin; it's why you want them that can lead to sin. Seeking to impress others or gain power over them through possessions is a sin. If your identity is in possessions and you think this will make people like you more or give you superiority over them, you are wrong. The appetite of materialism is never satisfied, it always wants more. They may buy a 2 year old Mercedes over a new Nissan claiming quality but it really can be a status symbol of idol worship in their life.

Eventually they feel less satisfied and less grateful as they gain more and more stuff. This leads to less happiness and becoming less likable because nobody likes a show off. You are left with two options. The first is to die before becoming "happy" because you will never find true joy in the things of this world. The second is discovering your quest for possessions will not bring you the happiness you seek and you find God before you die and discover the joy He has for your life. There is a God-shaped hole in everyone's heart, fill it with God not stuff.

> *"What good is it for someone to gain the whole world, yet forfeit their soul?"*   Mark 8:36

I had someone close to me constantly seek "Get rich quick schemes." They chased money and would try every new pyramid or multi-level program. It would end the same way every time. They would spend so much time and money building up their levels they lost focus on their job and their family and their God.

They spent a great deal of money traveling to conferences to get energized about making their future fortune. The time and money they spent on useless schemes never matched what they could have made if they just focused a little more on their own self-employment business.

The real loss was with the family. The time spent away from their family being "busy" and chasing money could never be made up as their life faded away with a devastating illness.

> *"For where your treasure is, there your heart will be also."*
> Matthew 6:21

Constantly seeking material wealth takes over your heart and becomes your idol. You will either run to your idol or you will run to God. Your sacrifice to the idol is money and the precious time with family and friends. We need to focus on our relationship with Jesus and our personal growth through that relationship. We need to realize that the relationships with family and friends are what we will treasure on our death bed, not the time we spent chasing money and things. Money spent on experiences like family vacations to build memories over obtaining material goods makes much more sense when we leave this earth.

You need to be grateful for what you have and help others through our spiritual gifts. You have been given an unlimited inheritance in heaven and there are days you forget what a blessing it will be. When chasing idols of possessions you can become angry from the lack of things in our life.

> *"Get rid of all bitterness, rage and anger, brawling and slander, along with every form of malice. Be kind and compassionate to one another, forgiving each other, just as in Christ God forgave you."*   Ephesian 4:31-32

I watched a friend get very upset at a restaurant when his food did not come out with the rest of ours. He told the waiter the problem. In a few minutes the waiter brought out some food but it was for another friend who had come in late and ordered. The original friend still did not have his food and he started getting louder about not having his food. When his food finally came he continued to complain about the food and the service to both us and the waiter.

This was during a regular weekly Christian men's lunch and it was very uncomfortable. My friend was in no mood to hear his brothers try to calm him down. I wanted to share what was on my heart but he was in no condition to receive the message.

Scriptures describes a man with a great debt he could not pay back. The King showed mercy and forgave his debt. The debt-free man immediately went out to get money from someone who owed him money. The man could not pay him so he had him put in prison. When the King found out what he had done he put the man he had forgiven in prison. My friend has a past that could never be repaid yet he was forgiven. He held this waiter in a state of un-forgiveness for a minor problem. Sadly our group of "Christian men" must have looked pretty bad in the waiter's eyes.

Sometimes it is difficult to stay calm when we are wronged. We love to go to the "It's not fair" button in our brain. It may not be fair to us and we think we deserve better but the reality is; we are all sinners and we all deserve death. Sadly the waiter may have been going through a hard time in their life at that time. The mistake could have been turned into a "God moment" by asking if he needed prayer for situations in his life.

> *"For we brought nothing into the world, and we can take nothing out of it. But if we have food and clothing, we will be content with that."*   1 Timothy 6:7-8

Some with this group of gifts can become so addicted to shopping they cannot go into a store and leave without purchasing something. They end up with piles of new useless items in their home along with piles of debt. They struggle with finances yet they cannot self-regulate their spending habits.

Satan traps them in the bondage of debt that keeps them from being able to give to the church and help expand the Kingdom of God. This is also an example of the "Addictive Personality Disorder." Craving a high from shopping without self-control can become a problem.

STOP thinking happiness comes from things.
LOOK to God and the joy He provides and be grateful for His forgiveness.
LISTEN to God because he wants you to have joy and peace beyond natural understanding!
BE WHAT GOD CREATED YOU TO BE; a joyful and passionate Christian using exciting experiences to bring people closer to God.

> *"It's not how much we have, but how much we enjoy, that makes happiness."*[62]   -Charles Spurgeon

PRIDE of LIFE:
Gift-Killers from Selfish Ambition

> *"For I tell you that unless your righteousness surpasses that of the Pharisees and the teachers of the law, you will certainly not enter the kingdom of heaven."*
>   Matthew 5:20

No one makes it to heaven by being self-righteous. Fortunately Jesus' sacrifice provided us with a righteousness that allows us to enter heaven with Him. Many seek righteousness through experiences without truth. Their pride makes them think they are safe from any harm and these experiences can take them off course. Pride comes in many forms. It usually starts small and then ends up controlling their life.

> *"Since they did not know the righteousness of God and sought to establish their own, they did not submit to God's righteousness."*
>   Romans 10:3

My Mom was an example of how an experience seeker can fall into the "Pride of Life." Mom could shoot any weapon from rifles, pistols, bows, spear guns to muzzle loaders. She was a scuba diver, pilot, biologist, and a Chiropractor. She also had a Masters in Biology. But her divorce from my Dad broke something in her. She drank a little but was neither an alcoholic nor a drug user but she was always seeking worldly experiences.

My Mom believed Jesus was the Son of God but the Church was not a good place for her. She was a cute, divorced, single, petite redhead. Even though I was in elementary school I could see the single guys hitting on her before and after church services. She could not enjoy a simple church service and began to stay away from the church.

At the same time men were getting promotions over her at work in the hospital's blood bank and she felt powerless. She was a strong Helen Reddy kind of woman but she felt the need for more power in her life. This was the perfect storm to push her into areas to experience without truth that offered her power. My Mom began dabbling in the occult. Even though she would never think she was in the occult she was seeking power from another source other than God.

I remembered some of the things my Mom played with over the years. When I was cleaning her hoarded home I found a Ouija Board she had bought in the 70's. It painfully brought up a list of occult things my Mom brought into our home. Mom practiced with Tarot cards to read our future. She had a fascination with Astrology, Scientology, Voodoo, and Spirit Guides along with hypnosis, ESP and crystal power. She would even seek advice from Palm Readers and would go to Séances for advice from Mediums. She was given a Mantra, to chant to herself, for Transcendental Meditation. Even though she believed Jesus was the Son of God, she sought these worldly experiences to gain power in her own life. My Mom always believed in Jesus and was a good mother and good to the people around her. But like all of us she made mistakes.

Furthermore, just as they did not think it worthwhile to retain the knowledge of God, so God gave them over to a depraved mind, so that they do what ought not to be done."
Romans 1:28

I painfully wrote this as my Mom sat in a skilled nursing facility and did not know her sister or me. She could not even make understandable words yet she was a brilliant woman full of knowledge. But she also had some wrong knowledge. I have read of studies of those involved in the occult and many develop mental issues. Sadly she is gone but I know she is in heaven because I know, without a doubt, she believed Jesus Christ was the Son of God.

"Saul died because he was unfaithful to the Lord; he did not keep the word of the Lord and even consulted a medium for guidance."   1 Chronicles 10:13

Sadly Saul did not seek the Lord for guidance, he sought a medium. This lack of trust in God led to his death. A small part of me cannot help but think my Mom's state of mind might have been due to her wrong choices, I don't know for sure. I prayed many spiritual warfare prayers for my Mom with no visible help. I know she did not think she was using Satan's schemes to build up the power in her life. I think she was fooled into thinking it was harmless fun and just another experience of life! Sadly it took away more from her life than it gave her. Her constant search for more power stole her time and took her away from family.

I've read many statistics about occult growth on the rise in America. Even Agnostics are adopting many ideas of the occult. Wicca, which is witchcraft, is growing at alarming rates. Occult groups usually have an anti-God message claiming the church is a crutch for the weak. If they use Scripture it is warped and distorted for their own personal gain.

I was close to a person who twisted Scripture to justify his bad habits of wife swapping. He said to me, "David had multiple wives and his behavior was ok in God's eyes." I asked him to tell me what happened to David in Scripture. He could not tell me about David because he was not interested in studying Scripture to make his life more Godly. David had access to hundreds of women but committed adultery with another man's wife. David murdered the husband of the woman he had an affair with by sending him to the front lines of battle. Don't justify your sin with Scripture, let God's Word work through you to stop the sin.

"Put to death, therefore, whatever belongs to your earthly nature: sexual immorality, impurity, lust, evil desires and greed, which is idolatry."   Colossians 3:5

I watched a friend, who was a dedicated servant of God, fall victim to his pride. This man was never physically abusive to his wife or kids and he did not cuss or drink. He loved his family dearly and worked hard to provide for them. He woke up one Sunday morning and demanded the family attend a new church with no discussion from his spouse or children. Actions like this scared his spouse and she eventually filed for divorce. She feared he was going to develop Schizophrenia like his father yet he was never diagnosed with the disease.

I watched this friend go down some very dark alleys during his divorce. He pushed for full custody, which is almost impossible to win unless the Mother has severe substance abuse or is in prison. He spent all the money he had and was ordered to mortgage his house to full appraised value and split the equity with his spouse. He was ordered to pay a large amount of child support, about half his income, and he did not have a large income. He also paid out large sums of money to lawyers that gave him bad advice. He was broke and could not pay the entire child support. He was paying half of it while he sat in his home in the dark eating the cheapest of meals with no air-conditioning trying to save a few dollars.

The spouse had a shrewd lawyer that had him thrown in prison for not paying the full child support. This was the final nail in his financial coffin as he lost his customers from his small business because he could not meet their needs while in prison. This happened several times as he would stay in jail a few weeks and be released. He now had no money and they were foreclosing on his house and the system still kept putting him back in prison. He felt he had nowhere to turn and sadly he began cussing and drinking to numb his emotions.

I would visit him in prison and give him money for snacks. He was consumed with so much anger from the oppression in his life. Before the divorce this man was heavily involved in the deliverance ministry. He learned how to free people from the bondage of demonic warfare. He became prideful during his ministry and would tell demons to leave the person and go sit at the foot of Satan and tell him what a liar he was every five seconds. He gained great joy in his power over demons.

> *"He [Jesus] replied, "I saw Satan fall like lightning from heaven. I have given you authority to trample on snakes and scorpions and to overcome all the power of the enemy; nothing will harm you. However, do not rejoice that the spirits submit to you, but rejoice that your names are written in heaven."* Luke 10:18-20

We are not to rejoice when demons submit to us! This man boasted to God to do whatever it takes to get him closer to Him. Even as a serving Christian, my friend was a victim to *"Pride of Life"* and he became obsessed with the experience of his power over the demonic realm. He ignored God's truth about the dangerous waters he was treading into. Coming from an observer of this situation I will tell you to steer clear of this kind of pride, it is extremely destructive.

His pride of being the head of the household did not show the love of Christ to his wife. There may be good reasons to leave the church you're attending but sometimes we may be called to make the church we're in better instead of hopping church to church looking for the perfect one. Unfortunately if you find the perfect church they're not going to let you in!

I counseled this friend to do what most of us would see as outrageous. He had nothing, was losing his home, was eating poorly and could not see his kids. Why not tell the judge to sentence him to jail until his debt to society and his spouse were paid off? He was having success talking to inmates about Jesus in jail and he would have 3 meals a day and a place to live.

Unfortunately he ended up running out of state and I've not heard from him. I pray he reestablished his relationship with his children. He dearly loved his kids and they dearly loved him. I pray he found a ministry where he finds joy in serving others. I also pray he learned from his trial and can trust God with his life!

STOP seeking experiences for power.
LOOK to God to use your weakness for His will.
LISTEN and think on what is noble, right, pure, lovely, admirable, excellent, and praiseworthy. Think Godly thoughts not worldly thoughts.
BE WHAT GOD CREATED YOU TO BE and be a powerful tool God uses to build up His Kingdom.

"Many have passed the rocks of gross sins - who have suffered shipwreck upon the sands of self-righteousness."[63]

-William Secker

PROTECTING YOURSELF FROM THE GIFT-KILLERS OF THE BREASTPLATE OF RIGHTEOUSNESS

LIVING IN OBEDIENCE

"Therefore, since we are surrounded by such a great cloud of witnesses, let us throw off everything that hinders and the sin that so easily entangles. And let us run with perseverance the race marked out for us, fixing our eyes on Jesus, the pioneer and perfecter of faith. For the joy set before him he endured the cross, scorning its shame, and sat down at the right hand of the throne of God. Consider him who endured such opposition from sinners, so that you will not grow weary and lose heart."   Hebrews 12:1-3

This group of gifts is so full of the experiences of Christ that they literally *"run with perseverance the race marked out"* for them. They are the Heart of God and can bring joy to others and their selves when they are grounded in God's truth. They use their excitement of experiences to include others and bless them.

I have friends that have a small group of Christian men that shoot guns a couple of times a month and have a Bible study. I have other friends who ride mountain bikes and another group who paddle kayaks together. There are endless possibilities for you to mature yourself with God's Word with other people through fun experiences. Through *"fixing our eyes on Jesus."* and bringing others closer to Christ through awesome experiences you will find joy in a job well done for God. You are wonderfully equipped to come along side others and grow together in Christ on life's journey!

If you are a part of this group of gifts do not *"grow weary and lose heart"* because of poor choices in your past. Jesus *"endured the cross"* so you would be free of your past and be able to have a future with God.

"Finally, brothers and sisters, whatever is true, whatever is noble, whatever is right, whatever is pure, whatever is lovely, whatever is admirable—if anything is excellent or praiseworthy—think about such things. Whatever you have learned or received or heard from me, or seen in me— put it into practice. And the God of peace will be with you."
Philippians 4:8-9

Many with this group of gifts naturally think about seeking an experience to have a high of life. They rarely couple that experience with *"true... noble... right... pure... admirable... or praiseworthy."* They tend to pick out *"Whatever is lovely"* and *"whatever is excellent"* and dive in head first without the rest of God's truth. They leave truth out and wonder why their experiences take them down rabbit trails and eventually off a cliff! Experience without God's truth can be very dangerous.

The Roman Armor buckles the Breastplate and Belt together. If you plan to dodge a spear you don't want the breastplate slipping out of place. This is the same with the spiritual gifts. The gifts associated with the Breastplate need to be buckled to the Word of God from those with the gifts of the Belt of Truth. This keeps them safe while they experience the things of God. It is also for the "stuffed shirts" and those who believe the awesome things of God have passed to experience them in a way they never expected. Go grab someone from the Belt of Truth and show them how God feels!

"Jesus replied, "Anyone who loves me will obey my teaching. My Father will love them, and we will come to them and make our home with them. Anyone who does not love me will not obey my teaching..."   John 14:23-24

Here is a strong message from Jesus to be obedient to His teachings. If you do not follow Jesus' teachings you are showing you are not "all in" on the first commandment, loving God. Jesus wants to make a home with us. Could He sit in your living room and watch TV with you? Would He approve of how you treat your family? Is He ok hanging around with you when no one else is home? Could He watch you on the internet?

> **"You have been set free from sin and have become slaves to righteousness."** Romans 6:18

Unfortunately some words of Scripture have negative effects on those with the spiritual gifts related to the Breastplate of Righteousness. The word obey, servant, and slave can bring up less than positive images in their head. These words often feel restrictive and binding. They may need to choose other words in order to soften what they see as harsh words.

Think of the word slave and think of being in love with someone so much you are willing to do anything to please them. If you are in love with your spouse you should try to do what pleases them and do what they ask of you; this is serving them. If you intend on staying with them for a lifetime, you have agreed to become bonded to each other through the covenant of marriage. Hopefully you share in the burdens of life and help each other with the things neither wants to do. The grass needs mowing, the trash needs taking out, the repairs and cleaning needs to be done. These less than pleasant activities are generally looked upon as slave or servant work but the vast majority of us share in these chores, especially as couples, because of our love for each other.

Find words of equal importance to help you follow Jesus out of your love for Him. If obey bothers you then follow. If servant or slave seems harsh, then think of the love Jesus has for you and all He did for you and He even adopted you into his family forever. You are not supposed to be a slave to your family but you are supposed to be a helpful supportive part of your family. Everyone takes part in the chores and projects that need to be done. They are done out of the love and respect of family. If the words obey, servant and slave bother you then follow, respect and love Jesus with all your body, mind and soul!

> *"Come to me, all you who are weary and burdened, and I will give you rest. Take my yoke upon you and learn from me, for I am gentle and humble in heart, and you will find rest for your souls. For my yoke is easy and my burden is light."*
>
> Matthew 11:28-30

When we are at our worst Jesus wants us to come to Him and rest physically, emotionally and spiritually. He wants what's best for us and He knows how to help run our life. The vast majority of us, let's say all of us, did not do the best job of running our own lives. We are fortunate Jesus forgives foolish people like ourselves and allows us to come back to Him no matter how far we've strayed from Him. Start now and seek Him, find Him, then follow, respect and love Him!

GROWTH IN CHRIST
The Spiritual Gifts Related to
The Breastplate of Righteousness

UNDERSTAND "WHOSE" YOU ARE

> *"Follow God's example, therefore, as dearly loved children and walk in the way of love, just as Christ loved us and gave himself up for us as a fragrant offering and sacrifice to God."*
>
> Ephesians 5:1-2

Sometimes we feel as if we are unlovable for all the bad things we've done in our life. Even through all of our sins we are still *"dearly loved children"* of Christ who died for our sins so we are saved from death. Relax and accept His love for you and show God our love for Him when we *"walk in the way of love"* to bless others who feel unlovable. This group of spiritual gifts is well equipped, as the heart of God, to show love to others and let them know how much God cares for them.

CONFESS AND PROGRESS

As obedient children, do not conform to the evil desires you
had when you lived in ignorance. But just as he who called
you is holy, so be holy in all you do; for it is written: "Be
holy, because I am holy."   1 Peter 1:14-16

Your previous life was a string of satanic attacks designed to keep you
from using your spiritual gifts and being what God created you to be.
You have fallen short and screwed up your life and those around you.
God is good to forgive you of all of those sins and shortcomings and
allow you to get back up and keep moving. Stop seeking evil experiences
that are not pleasing to God and do not seek experiences without truth.
He has called you to be holy so you need to be what he called you to be
and move forward because of His love for you.

Only one experience made you holy and righteous; that was when
Christ, the perfect sacrifice, died on the cross for you. Because of this,
believers can enjoy Godly experiences because He is in them. I've
experienced times of worship at Promise Keepers with thousands of
men where I felt the presence of the Holy Spirit pour over the crowd.
I've felt this on an intimate level many times at Tres Dias and while
listening to praise music at home, in my truck or at church.

Experiencing the Holy Spirit comes in many forms and levels of intensity.
It is difficult to fully describe the feeling of being in the presence of the
Holy Spirit to someone who has not experienced it. The best one word
description I can give is "peace." Now I crave this wonderful experience
of being in His presence. I crave His peace in my life! Confess your sins
and get right with God so you can move on to maturity in Christ. Seek
experiences that are buckled to God's truth and enjoy it when the Holy
Spirit pours His peace over you. It is unmatched by anything of this
world. Go and experience the love of God!

RENEW YOUR MIND

"Submit yourselves, then, to God. Resist the devil, and he will flee from you. Come near to God and he will come near to you. Wash your hands, you sinners, and purify your hearts, you double-minded." James 4:7-8

The only way to *"resist the Devil"* is to know the difference between good and evil. The only way to know the difference between good and evil is to know God's Word and have a relationship with Him. The bully never bothered you when you had a friend bigger than he was. God is a BIG friend! Your Faith in Him will help keeps you in a sound-mind. Faith will keep you from going off the deep end so do everything you can to trust God in all circumstances.

COMMUNICATE WITH GOD

"This is the confidence we have in approaching God: that if we ask anything according to his will, he hears us. And if we know that he hears us—whatever we ask—we know that we have what we asked of him." 1 John 5:14-15

This group of gifts depends on constant communication with God in order to use their spiritual gifts. God wants to give experiences beyond your imagination but He needs to communicate with you for you to join in on those experiences. The best way to communicate with God is by knowing him and His Word better. Stay in the Word, pray, listen to God, go to church and find a small group to live life with. This will help you gain confirmation of God's Will for your life as you get confirming messages from different sources. Fellowship allows you to experience the unity Jesus prayed for because He knows all of the parts of the body are needed to build each other up. Each part offers the strengths of direction, love, truth and action.

Prayer allows us to experience communication with God. Why does a preacher, who does not believe in miracles or healing, ask their congregation to pray to God? If God is not going to do anything to help in our lives, praying to Him seems useless. So why pray? Because God's gifts are still working today! He answers prayers and is still in the miracle and healing business! Pray! Pray! Pray to communicate with your Creator because He loves to hear from you. But when He speaks, listen and do what He tells you to do. Remember you have direct access to the One who created you and the universe!

USING THE SPIRITUAL GIFTS REPRESENTED BY THE BREASTPLATE OF RIGHTEOUSNESS WITH THE FRUITS OF THE SPIRIT

LOVE: Do you show the love of God or do you show a perverted love based on seeking worldly experiences? Do you know that God's love will not leave you in a dark cloud of guilt and shame? Do you know that proper love covers a multitude of sins?

JOY: Is your happiness a momentary flash followed by a long-term downer? Have you experienced the joy of being used of God to help build up others with a well-placed word at just the right time?

PEACE: Does your life show peace or are you running hard and late everywhere you go? Are you able to say "no" to some experiences to do the ones God is clearly calling you to do?

PATIENCE: Are you able to acknowledge your own short comings and forgive others for theirs as you go about life? Your debt was wiped clean, maybe the person aggravating you is destined to Hell so do you think you should show a little Christlikeness to them?

KINDNESS: Is your attitude toward others that of how Christ feels about His children? Are you kind when others make mistakes that cost you time and money?

GOODNESS: Do you expect others to do for you when you do for them? Are you seeking approval from your Father in heaven or from people? When you finish a project for others do you expect nothing in return?

FAITHFULNESS: Can you put your trust in Jesus or do you feel you need everyone else in the world to focus on you and your problems? Are you casting your anxieties on Him and seeking to know Him better through His Word? Are you listening to His advice and sharing His love?

GENTLENESS: Are you in such a frenzy that you cannot slow down to be gentle to others and show Christ's love to them? Have you ever thought your gentle moment of Mercy and Encouragement with a person may be the very thing that keeps them from committing suicide?

SELF-CONTROL: Is it difficult to self-regulate your thoughts, words and actions? Do you have friends that let you vent so you can hear your outside voice? Do you ask Jesus if He approves of your outside voice? Do you let friends vent to you without trying to one-up their bad experiences?

TAKE THE MIRROR TEST

"...Jesus said, "If you hold to my teaching, you are really my disciples. Then you will know the truth, and the truth will set you free." John 8:31-32

When you look in the mirror do you see your heart? Is it in bondage or is it free in Christ? The majority of your bondage is self-made from disobedience. Look closely at Jesus and see how He set the captives free from the bondage of their sins. Look again in the mirror; you are that person and are no longer a slave to sin! Crave the truth of God like water in a desert and experience the living water He graciously gives us. Fill your heart with His love and be free to enjoy His experiences. Live a life pleasing to Him by bringing others to Christ through your actions and experiences. Look once more and see how much the Creator of the Universe loves you!

STOP chasing your desires of worldly and ungodly highs.

LOOK to Jesus for guidance and direction in your experiences.

LISTEN very carefully to God's instructions; they can come in a whisper.

BE WHAT GOD CREATED YOU TO BE; a truth-filled follower of Christ who shows how much they respect and love God through their love to others.

> *"There are only two kinds of men: the righteous who think they are sinners and the sinners who think they are righteous."*[64]
>
> -Blaise Pascal

PONDERING POINTS

What are the gifts related to the Breastplate of Righteousness?

How is the Breastplate an important piece of Armor physically?

How is the Breastplate an important piece of Armor spiritually?

What is the goal of the gifts of the Breastplate?

What is the purpose of the gifts of the Breastplate?

What is the strength of the gifts of the Breastplate?

Has God ever communicated with you? How?

What are some examples of showing the heart of God?

What is the main weakness of the gifts in the Breastplate?

How do these gifts drift from God?

How can these gifts follow God's Will better?

What are some examples of worldly bad experiences?

Are there experiences you wish you never did?

Why is this group so easily addicted to worldly experiences?

How can Christian accountability help with these gifts?

Can a person have exciting experiences with the truth of God?

What does being obedient to Christ mean to you?

How does your disobedience affect your relationship with God?

What fears can stop you from sharing the heart of God?

"If you know that God loves you, you should never question a directive from Him. It will always be right and best. When He gives you a directive, you are not just to observe it, discuss it, or debate it. You are to obey it."[65]   Henry Blackaby

CHAPTER TEN

THE BELT OF TRUTH

"Stand firm then, with the belt of truth buckled around your waist, with the breastplate of righteousness in place, and with your feet fitted with the readiness that comes from the gospel of peace. In addition to all this, take up the shield of faith, with which you can extinguish all the flaming arrows of the evil one. Take the helmet of salvation and the sword of the Spirit, which is the word of God."

Ephesians 6:14-17

The order to *"Stand firm"* is the time we took the side of Christ and drew a line in the sand. At that moment we declared war against Satan and God gave us His truth to help us stand against him. The Belt of Truth is the first piece of Armor to be placed on the body. The Belt holds the Sword of the Spirit, which is the truth of the Word of God, our only offensive weapon.

Many of us started with the Belt of Truth by holding a children's Bible and learning stories and feeding on spiritual milk. As we matured in Christ we built a firm foundation and grew up in our knowledge, love and trust of Him. Hopefully we put away the children's Bible and sharpened the Sword into an adult Bible by gaining a deeper knowledge of Christ. By growing in the knowledge of God's truth we now have a sword worthy of battle, not a rusty butter knife. This knowledge and love for Christ allows us to grow a greater Faith and learn His Will for our lives.

When an army had to advance quickly the belt was also used for tucking in the tunic so it would not get caught up in the legs when running. If the tunic were to be caught up in the legs it could cause a soldier to stumble and fall. This could allow them to be injured, captured or killed. Truth helps us not to stumble in the world while running the race for Jesus!

In Roman culture the belt also was attached to the bottom of the Breastplate and helped it stay firmly in place. If a soldier was dodging a sword and the breastplate slipped out of place it would leave the body open to attacks. These two pieces of Armor need to work closely together to protect the vital organs of the body.

This is the same with the spiritual gifts. The gifts associated with the Breastplate need to be buckled to the Word of God with the gifts of the Belt of Truth. This keeps them safe while they experience the things of God. It is for those stuck in the "religion" and not the "relationship' of God. Those who believe the miraculous things of God have passed are buckled to a group of gifts that experiences the Heart of God. Learn from them and experience God in a way you never expected and teach them some truth along the way.

Be friends with someone from the Breastplate of Righteousness and discover how God feels! Pharisees argued with Jesus about how they dressed, ate and observed the laws to a "T" yet they missed the experience of Jesus standing right in front of them. It's good to have the knowledge of God but it is better to experience God with Truth!

SPIRITUAL GIFTS REPRESENTED BY THE BELT OF TRUTH

Pastor
Prophecy
Teacher
Word of Knowledge
Word of Wisdom

These are the five main spiritual gifts related to the Belt of Truth. They are primarily the logic of the Body of Christ verses the emotions of the gifts represented by the Breastplate. Pastor, Prophecy and Teacher are very similar but have a few differences. A Pastor is able to stay with you longer to fix a problem than those with Prophecy. Prophecy is usually more of a swift kick in the buttock while the Pastor is much gentler while helping others. The Teacher helps you learn the truth and will generally spend the time to get you there.

Both Word of Knowledge and Word of Wisdom are frequently used by the Pastor, Prophet and Teacher. They are used to let others know God is involved in the conversation and to point them back to His Word. This allows for correction and building up of others. Keep in mind that God can give anyone a Word of Knowledge or Word of Wisdom but they are used more frequently in this group of gifts.

Can you imagine the Body of Christ without this group of gifts? No one to Shepherd the flock of believers, no one to point out dangers of the sins in our lives and no one to teach us God's Word. It can be very hard on this group of gifts as they try to help set people on the right path. Many will not take their advice and let their lives fall into ruin as predicted. This group of gifts already sees so much brokenness in the world and this adds great pain in their lives to see others fall by their own choice.

WE ALL HAVE SPIRITUAL GIFTS PLURAL

We all have spiritual gifts, plural! They may not be as strong as others but we aren't all called to teach our children about Jesus? This would require some amount of study on our part to help them learn the truth about God. Time together with God's Word as a family will become the most important part of the day so the children can begin to trust Him and grow their Faith. If we stay in God's Word we can deliver timely messages based on Scripture to others in their time of need.

THE GOAL OF
THE BELT OF TRUTH
"To Rightly Deliver God's Word in God's Timing"

"But in your hearts revere Christ as Lord. Always be prepared to give an answer to everyone who asks you to give the reason for the hope that you have. But do this with gentleness and respect, keeping a clear conscience, so that those who speak maliciously against your good behavior in Christ may be ashamed of their slander. For it is better, if it is God's will, to suffer for doing good than for doing evil."
1 Peter 3:15-17

This is the life verse for the spiritual gifts related to the Belt of Truth. This is the Biblical delivery manual for giving messages to others. The first instruction is to *"revere Christ as Lord"* and have the humility to put Him way above you when delivering messages. Next it tells you to stay in God's Word so you will be *"prepared to give an answer"* at any time. This is not a license to tell everyone what is wrong with them. This part of the instructions is very important; when delivering messages from God be sure to do it for everyone *"who asks"* you for advice.

This group of gifts needs to avoid telling people how to run their lives when they are not asked for their opinion. They generally will not be willing to accept the advice when they do not ask for it. When someone asks for advice, God has already been at work setting up the dominos in their lives so they can understand and accept the correction. Even then they may still choose the wrong direction.

Keep in mind the dominos being set up represents God's timing. If you knock over the dominos before they've been completely set up, the message is less effective to the person receiving it. Timing is crucial when delivering a message and usually when God gives it to you to deliver, He wants it done immediately. It's always good to tell the person receiving the message to look for God to confirm His messages. This may be the first they have heard of this message or it's the confirmation to what God has already been telling the person. Never forget to give the message with *"gentleness and respect"* in order to soften the impact of what are usually some tough pills to swallow.

The last part of this Scripture speaks about the character of the delivery person. Keep a *"clear conscience"* so when a person says bad things about you others will not believe them because of your good character. This group of gifts is watched by others like a hawk watching their prey. People will look at your life for any signs of bad behavior and hold you to a higher standard than others. Work hard to live a good and honorable life because God reminds us that it is better to suffer for doing good rather than evil. They look for you to fail because it allows them a reason to fail themselves.

> *"To this you were called, because Christ suffered for you, leaving you an example, that you should follow in his steps."*
> 1 Peter 2:21

THE PURPOSE OF
THE BELT OF TRUTH
"Do Things Right and Do the Right Things"

"Whatever you do, work at it with all your heart, as working for the Lord, not for human masters, since you know that you will receive an inheritance from the Lord as a reward. It is the Lord Christ you are serving."
Colossians 3:23-24

When speaking and pointing people back to God's Word, doing it right is a must because you are ***"working for the Lord."*** God's Word can bring supernatural change and abundant life to people; so great is the responsibility of the people using these gifts. The person using the spiritual gift of Pastor usually has the calming voice of reason that the flock knows and follows. The Pastor will go after the injured or stray sheep and gently bring them back to the flock with their words and actions. They are willing to be in relationships for the long haul for the recovery of injuries and building up church members.

The person using the spiritual gift of Teaching is more about giving messages from God's Word to groups in order to build up the Body of Christ. They can be in for the long haul for teaching groups but they can also tutor individuals. The person using the spiritual gift of Prophecy is more of a quick fix to a problem. Remember they are the swift kick to the buttock for someone falling from the Faith or someone stuck in a repeating cycle of sin. They are like a medic trying to stop the bleeding of soldiers injured in battle.

Pastors, Prophets and Teachers usually use the spiritual gifts of Word of Knowledge and Word of Wisdom regularly to communicate God's message to others. The Word of Knowledge gives them a deeper and better understanding of the situation at hand. They can turn a Word of Knowledge into a Word of Wisdom for the person they are working with. When all of these gifts work together in a Godly manner, the one receiving the message is amazed and realize God is involved in their life at that very moment. They are immediately convicted to make changes in their life because they know God cares about them and their future.

This set of spiritual gifts understands Who they work for and Who's the boss. I was once asked by leadership why I try to "One Up" the skits I do on the Men's Tres Dias weekends. They said I was making it harder every time I was in charge of the skits. I asked the leadership a simple question, "So do I understand this right, you want me to be average for Jesus?" I explained that Jesus was my boss on the weekend and I respected the leadership I was under. But if people took three days away from work and family to experience God I was going to use every minute I could to bless them. I would explain to my skit team this was going to be a tough weekend but we will bless many men and we will be blessed ourselves for being *well done good and faithful servants.*

"Refuse to be average. Let your heart soar as high as it will."[66]
-A. W. Tozer

Afterwards I had no more issues with leadership about trying to do better each time I served. The men I worked with gave their all to produce some amazing skits and plays. They were exhausted at the end of the weekend but they were blessed to be a part of helping change people's lives through Christ. The point of this story is to not be average for Jesus! Follow your leaders but do the right thing the right way at the right time.

"All labor that uplifts humanity has dignity and importance and should be undertaken with painstaking excellence."[67]
-Martin Luther King Jr.

THE STRENGTH OF
THE BELT OF TRUTH
"Knowing How to Point People Back to God's Word"

"Whether you turn to the right or to the left, your ears will hear a voice behind you, saying, 'This is the way; walk in it.'"
Isaiah 30:21

The spiritual gifts represented by the Belt of Truth are well-designed to know God's Word. They love to study God's Word and share what they learned. When they live Godly lives they have their radios set to God's channel and they stay close to Him to reduce the amount of static from the world. Satan still attacks with interference and tries to speak over God. But knowing God's voice allows this group of gifts to clearly make out God's messages. This Scripture describes how people hear from God. When the message is clear it literally feels like someone in the backseat of your vehicle spoke to you. It's usually short and to the point and has a great effect.

If someone says they have a Word from God to give you, be careful and be on guard but be open. Is the person speaking to you a good person with good fruits in their life? Do they have a good reputation? Is there confirmation to the message and does it make sense to you? There is usually confirmation, before or after, from other sources making the message more clear. The message will never tell you to do something against what God has said in His Scripture. The message will never add to or take away from the Bible. The message is supposed to point you back to God's Word.

"...Do not be afraid of what they say or be terrified by them, though they are a rebellious people. You must speak my words to them, whether they listen or fail to listen, for they are rebellious. But you, son of man, listen to what I say to you. Do not rebel like that rebellious people; open your mouth and eat what I give you." Ezekiel 2:6-8

This group of gifts tends to deal with rebellious people. They are generally running from God and hitting brick walls. I once had an opportunity to speak with a very lost woman who wandered into a men's meeting at a local church. She sat in the back of the room and looked very out of place. At the end of the meeting a friend of mine, who is strong in Discerning Spirits, went up to her and asked what she was doing there. She said she was homeless and had nothing to her name. My friend gave me a strange look and I was very suspicious.

As we talked I confronted her with being a prostitute and a stripper. She was stunned and denied what I said. My friend stepped away for a moment and she asked me how I knew she was a stripper and a prostitute? I told her that God sometimes gives me a Word of Knowledge about people and He gave me this message about her. She seemed genuinely interested in hearing about God so we fed her and arranged for her to stay the night in a hotel near the church. She was supposed to meet with the preacher the next morning. Unfortunately she was kicked out of the hotel for soliciting herself for prostitution that night.

Sadly she was rebellious and deep in demonic control. She had the opportunity to enjoy a banquet with Jesus but she chose to eat out of the garbage in the alley with Satan. Later my friend told me he felt she had brought down several preachers. There is a calling to help others but there are warnings. Jesus wants none to perish and all to hear His Word but there are some that will drag you down into Satan's pit of sin with them. Be sure to take precautions when sharing with the opposite sex and make sure others are close. I hope something I said to her helped her realize that God was aware of her activities and He is willing to help her but unfortunately that night was not her time.

"But if an unbeliever or an inquirer comes in while everyone is prophesying, they are convicted of sin and are brought under judgment by all, as the secrets of their hearts are laid bare. So they will fall down and worship God, exclaiming, 'God is really among you!'" 1 Corinthians 14:24-25

When this group of gifts speaks of the *"secrets of their hearts"* being laid bare, people may become fearful of their sin being exposed. The forces keeping their sins a secret do not want them brought into the light and they will do anything to keep them hidden. By providing a safe place to talk openly about hidden sins they can be brought out into the light and darkness has to flee. Being accountable to other men has been one of the best things I've done to help grow my Faith and help me on my journey to maturing in Christ.

> *"For everything that was written in the past was written to teach us, so that through the endurance taught in the Scriptures and the encouragement they provide we might have hope."*   Romans 15:4

I look at this group of gifts as the archeologists of God's Word. They dig into Scripture to find hidden treasures from God and they love to share them in museums for all to see. Many people love having others do the archeological work so they can enjoy going and looking at the treasures. Sadly Satan would love nothing less but to hide or destroy the treasures all together. He knows the blessings of uncovered treasure will help many find their purpose in life and help build God's Kingdom. The Gift-Killers Satan throws at this group of gifts are designed to keep them from pointing people back to God's Word.

> *"My son, if you accept my words and store up my commands within you, turning your ear to wisdom and applying your heart to understanding - indeed, if you call out for insight and cry aloud for understanding, and if you look for it as for silver and search for it as for hidden treasure, then you will understand the fear of the Lord and find the knowledge of God."*   Proverbs 2:1-5

Archeology of God's Word can help people greatly when they are at a crossroads in their life. This group of gifts has a unique ability to receive important information about a person by receiving a Word of Knowledge.

When a person is willing to have their inner self laid bare they can receive great spiritual healing. It is similar to a festering wound deep inside a body that needs to be removed so the body can fight off the infection.

I once saw a man kneeling and praying during a very emotional time at a Men's Weekend. I looked at him and was startled when I saw what appeared to be his heart with a round lead ball lodged in it causing a great infection. I went to him and explained the wound I saw and he began weeping. The round lead ball was an old musket ball and it represented an old wound that he had carried for decades. He was able to speak of the old wound he had been carrying around for many years.

If I had not given that Pastor my "vision" he may have carried that old wound for the rest of his life. I stepped out on Faith and believed what I saw was real and somehow I knew revealing it to him would help him. When the people in this group of Gifts grow they only do it by stepping out in Faith. It may seem upside down from this world and supernatural but isn't that the nature of God? Remember the rules for hearing from God? Number one, it's 100% Biblical and number two is 99% of the time you don't want to do it!

THE GOOD OF
THE BELT OF TRUTH
(Going Forward)
"Using God's Word to Let Light Overcome Darkness"

"For you were once darkness, but now you are light in the Lord. Live as children of light (for the fruit of the light consists in all goodness, righteousness and truth) and find out what pleases the Lord. Have nothing to do with the fruitless deeds of darkness, but rather expose them."
Ephesians 5:8-11

The spiritual gifts represented by the Belt of Truth are designed to be the *"children of light"* and expose the *"fruitless deeds of darkness"* so the truth can be easily seen. Their gifts use God's Word to let light overcome the darkness. It has been said that all the darkness in the world cannot put out the light of a single candle.

Their job is to point out sin and offer a way out for those trapped in Satan's snare. They are the very definition of tough love when they treat others sternly. They are looking at the future of the one caught up in sin and see the crossroad in their life. They try to point them in the best direction to follow God's Will for their life.

> *"Those whom I love I rebuke and discipline. So be earnest and repent. Here I am! I stand at the door and knock. If anyone hears my voice and opens the door, I will come in and eat with that person, and they with me."*
> Revelation 3:19-20

God rebukes and disciplines the ones He loves through His Word. How does that Word get to us? Obvious things like church and reading your Bible come to mind but what if a person has given up on church and reading their Bible? This group of gifts is specifically made to shine with the light of God's truth. During the moments with people who are lost or falling away from the Faith they are ready for an answer. They wait for the knock on the door from those who ask for help. When they are welcomed in they speak a Word of Knowledge and a Word of Wisdom to show God cares about them and wants a better life for them.

God wants to be part of your life and He wants to *"come in and eat"* with you. He wants to lovingly correct you so you can have a better life and so you can build up others in the Body of Christ. Listen to His voice then reach out, grab the door and ask for His help! When He helps then turn around and lavish the love He poured on you to others, this is His Will for your life.

"Therefore, as God's chosen people, holy and dearly loved, clothe yourselves with compassion, kindness, humility, gentleness and patience. Bear with each other and forgive one another if any of you has a grievance against someone. Forgive as the Lord forgave you. And over all these virtues put on love, which binds them all together in perfect unity."
Colossians 3:12-14

When this group of gifts is operating with *"compassion, kindness, humility, gentleness, patience"* and they *"forgive one another"* they can powerfully use God's Word to build up the church. They use the Word of God like a ladder to help people out of their pit of despair. They show God's love by carefully pointing out the sins that will destroy them and the people around them. An ounce of prevention by this type of tough love can have everlasting eternal effects. The correction may taste bad but when done with gentleness and respect it's like the saying "a spoonful of sugar helps the medicine go down."

"Greater love has no one than this: to lay down one's life for one's friends." John 15:13

Many people in this group of gifts live out this Scripture in their lives through their jobs. They choose to serve in the ministry, military, police, and firefighting along with many service areas like EMT's, nurses, doctors, and teachers. Many people could say they would die for their family or friends but this Scripture is a little different. *"To lay down one's life"* could also mean spending their whole life serving *"one's friends."* Dying for someone is a tremendous sacrifice but look at someone like Mother Teresa who served her whole life to bless others. That is a major sacrifice of one's entire life!

"No sacrifice should be too great for Him who gave Himself for us."[68]　　　　　　　　　　　　　-Henry Ironside

This group of gifts takes care of others, especially when they are in a crisis in their lives. They can stay calm in stress-filled situations where life and death hang in the balance. They generally have an automatic response to know what to do and when to do it without much thought. It's as if they already knew what to do before they did it. As good as this all sounds those using the gifts have weaknesses.

THE BAD OF
THE BELT OF TRUTH
(Going Backward)
"Giving Up"

The Bad actions of these spiritual gifts are not necessarily sin. They start to slip away from God due to stresses, overwork, and burnout. They can take on to many projects and spread themselves thin. This produces more and more stress, lack of sleep, and attitude changes. The "Bad" is like the check engine light on the dash of a car. It can be a warning of slipping into the "Ugly" sins of these gifts as they drift from God.

> *"Those who consider themselves religious and yet do not keep a tight rein on their tongues deceive themselves, and their religion is worthless."* James 1:26

As people using these gifts go through life seeing all of the endless brokenness in the world, their vocal filters can crumble. Their tongues begin to spew out everything they see wrong with people, places and things. Their words may be right but people do not want to be around such negativity so they stop listening to them. As they become less filtered they become angrier and cuss and attack family members for doing things wrong. Unfortunately by not keeping *"a tight rein on their tongues"* they can drift away from God and stop serving God and *"their religion is worthless."* They simply give up on God and His call on their life.

DOING NOTHING

"And let us not grow weary while doing good, for in due season we shall reap if we do not lose heart."
Galatians 6:9

This group of gifts can begin to see the bad in everything and they *"lose heart."* They become unhappy in their job, in their church and with their family and friends. This group of gifts sees all of the brokenness in the world and they can sink into depression easily. They can spiral down toward a "why even try" attitude.

They can stop serving in ministries they once loved because they may have gotten too close to the top management and saw their flaws. They *"grew weary"* and stopped before their *"due season."* Those using these gifts are designed to be "completionists" who are really good at finishing a task or project. It's sad to watch them give up on life and stop *"doing good."*

Do you think Jesus wants you to stop serving in ministries that build up His Kingdom? Do you think He wants you to be a couch potato for Christ? Get over yourself and graciously help ministries serve better and find others you can help. Stop looking at their flaws and look at their fruits. Does the ministry produce good fruit and build up the Kingdom? Then get involved! Does your couch butt-print produce fruit or fungus? I'm guessing fungus which leads me to the following poem:

> One night I had a wondrous dream,
> One set of footprints there was seen,
> The footprints of my precious Lord,
> But mine were not along the shore.
> But then some stranger prints appeared,
> And I asked the Lord, "What have we here?"
> Those prints are large and round and neat,

"But Lord they are too big for feet."
"My child," He said in somber tones,
"For miles I carried you alone.
I challenged you to walk in faith,
But you refused and made me wait."
"You disobeyed, you would not grow,
The walk of faith, you would not know.
So I got tired, I got fed up,
and there I dropped you on your butt."
"Because in life, there comes a time,
when one must fight, and one must climb.
When one must rise and take a stand,
or leave their butt prints in the sand."
Butt Prints in the Sand
-Author unknown

Sometimes judging others harshly turns back on the person using these gifts and they see themselves as unworthy to share God's Word. They believe Satan when he tells them they are not educated enough or their past is too dirty to be used by God. Many Bible teachers were barely literate. They could not answer philosophical questions yet their childlike Faith carried them in front of many people to share the Word of God. They were obedient to the call of God and asked fear to take a back seat to God's purpose for their lives.

No amount of education will ever match up to God's calling on your life. The Pharisees were some of the most educated of Jesus' time yet they completely missed Him standing right in front of them. Self-judgment produces depression which is common in this group of gifts. It can be hard to meet their own high expectations and they become a letdown to themselves. This is another lie from Satan! God loves you, despite your past!

Sometimes life tries to force you away from God. I personally experienced a form of gluttony and became addicted as I sought food for comfort during my Mom's Alzheimer's. I gained 40 pounds in 2 years due to stress eating. Food became a desire of the flesh and I placed it before God for comfort. It slowed me down and caused my body to hurt with all the extra pounds. With other pressures in my life, Mom's disease and feeling bad all the time, it took its toll on me physically and spiritually. I could not write this book, I did not want to go to church and I was struggling as a Christian. Fortunately I had good men in my life to help me. They made sure to keep me close to God. They would not let me be dragged away by Satan!

Once I realized food was an idol in my life I made a deal with God about my food intake and I was able to lose 60 pounds in a year. Unfortunately much damage was done to my body during those years including the onset of diabetes and neuropathy. I have to keep my sugar under control with diet and medication but I still pray for a miraculous healing. It just goes to show you how giving in a little at a time to what is wrong will have lasting effects on our life.

FIXING EVERYTHING

"He says, 'Be still, and know that I am God; I will be exalted among the nations, I will be exalted in the earth.'"
Psalm 46:10

This group of gifts can go from one extreme to another. They may give up on everything or try to fix everything. They can end up spending too much time on projects, duties, research and serving others, all the while forgetting to serve their own family.

Satan loves for you to leave a vacuum in your family so he can fill it with his lies to slowly destroy them. They can have a hard time being still and can lean toward an obsessive compulsive disorder. There are differences between sitting on your buttock doing nothing and being still to hear God. Focusing on God verses distraction by the World and Satan pretty much make the difference. Are you focused on God while being still?

I felt guilty for doing nothing and I always felt I should be doing projects around the house or serving others for Christ. I could not peacefully watch a movie at home because I felt like I needed to do something. I had to go to theaters to enjoy movies because I could not get up and do chores. As hard as it is for me I have had to learn to take some down time and enjoy being still.

Obsessive-compulsive disorders can creep in and bring your gifts to a halt. Some people cannot get out of their homes because they are so busy cleaning their baseboards with toothbrushes. Some leave for work only to return to check to see if they left the stove on or if they locked the door only to drive down the road and turn around to do it again. God forbid if I open a messy drawer, It has to be organized!

> *"Peace I leave with you; my peace I give you. I do not give to you as the world gives. Do not let your hearts be troubled and do not be afraid."*   John 14:27

I call myself a recovering perfectionist and I plan on being the best recovering perfectionist who ever lived! God allowed me to keep piling things on my to-do list until I could not manage the list. I had so little peace in my life and I was at a breaking point. Around this time I was painting my clinic and I hit the ceiling with the roller leaving a dark brown spot of paint.

God made me leave the spot on my ceiling in my adjusting room where I would see it every work day of my life. He made me leave it there to remind me I cannot fix everything. I argued with Him I could fix the spot but He knew what the spot would come to mean in my office. A spot on the ceiling means nothing in a hundred years but the conversations about the spot would matter. I have shared the reason for the spot with many patients and they can relate the spot to the problems in their own lives.

I use the spot both spiritually and physically. I explain the stresses to patients of how trying to fix everything drags us down physically, mentally and spiritually. Satan uses this busyness in our lives to take away our peace and physically wear out our bodies so we cannot serve the Lord. He also uses it to keep the negativity of the brokenness around us on our mind all of the time to depress us mentally. When the physical and mental problems pile up, it's hard to be spiritual and serve God and Satan wins the battle in your life. Be careful not to take on everything that is broken. Listen to God for what He wants you to fix.

SELFISH OR SELFLESS

"Be careful not to practice your righteousness in front of others to be seen by them. If you do, you will have no reward from your Father in heaven." Matthew 6:1

The motives of this group of gifts can drift from serving others to serving themselves. They begin to crave the lime light and enjoy recognition and praises from other people. I confess this happened to me while serving on Tres Dias Men's weekends. As I served I became better and better at producing and directing skits for the weekend. The Men got excited when they heard I was in charge of the skits and looked forward to seeing them. I personally loved being in the skits for the recognition.

I quickly learned that I could no longer be in the skit and direct them at the same time. If something goes wrong with a skit it's real hard to fix it while it is being performed and you are one of the actors. I needed to direct from the outside of the skit and get more men out of their comfort zone by putting them in front of an audience. I needed to step out of the lime-light and become the director full time.

I still got my pats on the back for jobs well done but I realized I needed to step back even further and work on being a producer. I saw a need to grow both actors and directors to do future skits. I try to help Men fill the role of directors and build leaders who could eventually fill roles when I become no longer able. Fortunately I mentored a few and they have produced and directed some amazing skits.

It's nice to be recognized for a job well done but it's more rewarding to help build up others so they can build up God's Kingdom. If you think your service to the Lord is really important then you need to think about helping train others to do what you do!

> *"I long to see you so that I may impart to you some spiritual gift to make you strong— that is, that you and I may be mutually encouraged by each other's faith."*
> Romans 1:11-12

Are you building up spiritual gifts in others with your own spiritual gifts to increase their Faith? Are you just running through the motions and have given up on inspiring others to better their lives and the lives around them? Think about the teachers that inspired you to be a better person or give you direction for your life. Those may be few but are you one of the few willing to encourage and bring out the spiritual gifts in others?

With the rise of "Black Lives Matter" and "Every Life Matters" I see it more as "Every Heart Matters!" Why are we surprised when people act the way they do if no one has inspired them to be better? Everyone has a God-shaped hole in their heart they are trying to fill. They will try to fill it with anything else but God and never find peace. They will never be satisfied unless they are filled with the love of God so they can love others and discover their identity in Christ. Unfortunately it's hard to fill a person who is already full of their self. God waits for them to empty their self and become ready to be filled with the Holy Spirit.

Are you ready for God to fill the God-shaped hole in your heart? Are you ready for Him to fill your heart with the peace of God? Are you willing to empty yourself and allow Him to fill you with the Holy Spirit? Are you ready to have a heart for God and make a difference in the world?

"And hope does not put us to shame, because God's love has been poured out into our hearts through the Holy Spirit, who has been given to us. You see, at just the right time, when we were still powerless, Christ died for the ungodly."
Romans 5:5-6

STOP worrying about all the bad you see in people, places and things.
LOOK for the broken people needing a message from God.
LISTEN carefully for the right message at the right time for the right person.
BE WHAT GOD CREATED YOU TO BE; the coolest mail person for God on the planet!

"Do not grow overconfident following a few victories. Should you not rely upon the Holy Spirit you will soon be thrown once more into a distressing experience. With holy diligence you must cultivate an attitude of dependency." -Watchman Nee

THE MAIN GIFT-KILLING WEAKNESS OF THE BELT OF TRUTH
"Lacking Grace and Being Judgmental"

"You, therefore, have no excuse, you who pass judgment on someone else, for at whatever point you judge another, you are condemning yourself, because you who pass judgment do the same things."
Romans 2:1

Sadly the spiritual gifts related to the Belt of Truth see all the brokenness in the world. They tire of others making dumb mistakes that could have been avoided. They get aggravated with people who run around in circles and fall in a hole only to get out and run back into the same hole again and again. This eventually leads them to becoming very judgmental and showing little to no grace for others. They start deciding who needs to hear God's Word and who doesn't. This is wrong!

They cannot be like Jonah and Nineveh and refuse to tell people about God. They cannot call people white trash and decide they are not worthy to hear about Jesus. They are to do exactly what God tells them to do and deliver whatever message to whoever God says. It's easier to just do God's Will, just ask Jonah about his 3 night waterfront get way!

> *"Do not withhold good from those to whom it is due, when it is in your power to act. Do not say to your neighbor, 'Come back tomorrow and I'll give it to you'—when you already have it with you."*   Proverbs 3:27-28

This group of gifts delivers life changing information to other people. When they receive God's messages they need to be delivered immediately! Don't wait and end up in a dark slimy place only to be vomited up on a beach. Always have grace for others when delivering messages and remember what grace has done for you!

> *"And if by grace, then it cannot be based on works; if it were, grace would no longer be grace."*
>   Romans 11:6

Grace can cover any sin and allow us to be saved from any condition. God is bigger than murder, adultery, and sexual sins. It allows us freedom from the fear of worrying if we can ever do enough to make it into heaven.

> *"Dear friends, let us love one another, for love comes from God. Everyone who loves has been born of God and knows God. Whoever does not love does not know God, because God is love."*   1 John 4:7-8

When delivering messages from God don't forget where you came from and what Christ has done for you. This will help you to be gentle and respectful as God's mail-person. Remember to plant God's Word in your heart and not your head to show God's love when delivering messages. You want God's message to be well received and find fertile soil to grow and multiply so use love and grace to find a way into their heart!

THE UGLY OF
THE BELT OF TRUTH
(Going Sin-Ward)
"Justifying Legal Sins"

The ugly use of the spiritual gifts is when a believer chooses to disobey God and use their God-given talent for evil. God gives us the choice to follow Him or not. He also gives us the choice to use our talents for good or bad and when they are used to sin they become Anti-Gifts.

This group of gifts lead themselves down "Ugly" paths as they see all the brokenness in the world. They have an inner program that makes them think they need to fix all of the brokenness. This can wear them out because all of it cannot be fixed by themselves. Eventually they feel like they have failed and they beat themselves up over those failures which leads them into a depression. The term "weepy prophet" is very true.

This depression can lead them to choose legal but wrong things to "fix" their problems. Things like abortion, gambling, alcohol, cussing, debt, jealousy, sexual sins, pornography, gambling, prescription drugs, love of money, gluttony and being judgmental are some of the favorite choices which can destroy them. When things are legal they tend to justify their right to engage in the activity. They feel they are above being trapped by something legal, but they are wrong. They will become snared by the sins and drift away from God and those who care about them. As they drift away from God's signal they stop hearing Him. God's Word is the life flow of this group of gifts and when it stops the depression can deepen even to the point of suicide.

Here is the ugly side of wrongly used talents represented by the Belt of Truth. They have been broken down into the three areas of sin discussed in chapter 6:

LUST of the FLESH:
Gift-Killers from Sins of the Body

"Let us behave decently, as in the daytime, not in carousing and drunkenness, not in sexual immorality and debauchery, not in dissension and jealousy. Rather, clothe yourselves with the Lord Jesus Christ, and do not think about how to gratify the desires of the flesh."   Romans 13:13-14

When I was young one of my Mom's old boyfriends said, "Preachers, they eat your fried chicken and sleep with your wife." Unfortunately the statement can ring true; I saw it happen in a church when I was young. This behavior is so publically destructive not only to the families involved but the entire congregation. It can keep unbelievers from coming to Christ when they see the hypocritical actions of Christians.

Is the fleeting desire of the lust of the flesh worth keeping people not only out of church but out of heaven forever? When I saw this happen, it did not change my belief in Jesus but it sure changed my mind on what I thought about churches. I avoided churches like the plague for almost a decade!

"And among the prophets of Jerusalem I have seen something horrible: They commit adultery and live a lie. They strengthen the hands of evildoers, so that not one of them turns from their wickedness. They are all like Sodom to me; the people of Jerusalem are like Gomorrah."   Jeremiah 33:14

Sadly it appears that this problem has been going on for thousands of years. There is no excuse for the people of God to commit such sins.

Yet it happens more often than we would like to admit. Most of us have seen leaders of the church fall at the hands of sexual or addictive sins and create havoc among its members.

> *"Listen, my son, and be wise, and set your heart on the right path: Do not join those who drink too much wine or gorge themselves on meat, for drunkards and gluttons become poor, and drowsiness clothes them in rags."*
>
> Proverbs 23:19-21

Following up on the earlier "fried chicken" statement, gluttony is also a real problem. As a person over-indulges and gains weight, the enemy slowly wins the battle in their life. It is such a slow process that the offender barely recognizes it until they are caught in Satan's trap. By seeking the pleasure of food as comfort and not seeking Jesus as your source of comfort, the food becomes an idol.

By the time they realize things are out of hand they have no energy to serve God because of physical restrictions. Their health deteriorates and they end up with a series of health issues that keep them from reaching their maximum potential in Christ. Many of us, including myself, have suffered the results from the actions of this scripture. Seek the LORD for comfort and answers; not the world.

> *"Gluttony is an emotional escape, a sign something is eating us."*[69]
> -Peter De Vries

STOP letting Satan's voice override the voice of God.

LOOK at your own desires, do they reflect those of Christ?

LISTEN carefully To God because Satan's messages can come disguised as light. Stay close to God's Word in order to tell them apart!

BE WHAT GOD CREATED YOU TO BE; a messenger of God giving directions to those who are wandering off God's path for their lives. Point them back to His Word!

LUST of the EYES:
Gift-Killers from Idol Worship or Coveting

"No one can serve two masters. Either you will hate the one and love the other, or you will be devoted to the one and despise the other. You cannot serve both God and money. The Pharisees, who loved money, heard all this and were sneering at Jesus."   Luke 16:13-14

There was a teacher I admired very much that taught Creation vs. Evolution. He was funny and shared information you could easily understand. His ministry was growing but he did not report his love offerings to the IRS. They eventually discovered his "love of money" and put him in jail for tax evasion. Sadly this kind of activity can not only shut down a ministry but it can damage the Faith of those following the teacher.

"How much better to get wisdom than gold, to get insight rather than silver!"   Proverbs 16:16

Jesus was clear about giving Caesar what was Caesars. He knows Satan is lurking closely to find any way he can bring a ministry down. It's sad to watch preachers give such good nourishment for growing a Christian's Faith as they teach on the accuracy of Scripture yet they do not follow it. This group of gifts is held to high standards as they deliver the Word of God. They are watched carefully to see if they will do as they speak. People need people who are good examples of Christianity. Be that example even with your finances!

THE IDOLS OF FALSE TEACHINGS

"Jesus answered, 'I am the way and the truth and the life. No one comes to the Father except through me.'"
                               John 14:6

Some people believe you can live any way you want to as long as you are good because there are multiple paths to heaven. They obviously completely ignore this verse because it has no authority in their life. They believe if you do good and don't hurt others you will make the cut into heaven.

Not hurting others is difficult when you are living anyway you desire. Alcohol and drugs can lead to hurting so many people through accidents and abuse. Getting other people to partake of those substances can lead them to overdosing and death. Is it worth your temporary moment of pleasure to keep others out of heaven?

Pornography is also not victimless. Those are someone's children and grandchildren in the films. There is great substance abuse and sexual abuse in those industries. The desire for more and more pornography can lead to the desires of prostitution and sex trafficking of minors.

Even with these obvious dangers, Philosophers love to debate Christianity with our young people in college. They ask why Christianity is so exclusive and believe they are the only ones going to heaven. They will give an example of an elephant representing religion being felt by three blindfolded men. The first man is feeling the trunk and says his religion is like a snake. The second man is feeling the legs of the elephant and says his religion is like a trunk of a tree. The third blind man is feeling the tail and says his religion is like a rope. The philosopher says the men are all feeling the same thing but they have different ways of describing it, thus all religions are the same.

I've found that many philosophers have trouble answering their own questions. The philosopher has a hard time when asked how they are the only "exclusive" person seeing the entire elephant while everyone else is blind. The question puts the Philosopher in the position of having all the answers for religion yet they scolded a religion for having all the answers. By turning the Philosopher's question back on them, their idea crumbles.

The Lust of the Eyes comes in many forms. Seeking an easy way to get through life without commitment or completely denying God can become an idol. Idols can be science or philosophy instead of God. The reason for choosing these idols usually boils down to two things. First they are avoiding accountability to God. Some people want to live their life their way and not have "rules" to follow to keep them from worldly pleasures. The second thing is a severe hatred of God, even when they do not believe in God. I've found it very ironic how much someone can hate something that does not exist in their mind. They blame God for all the problems in their life and seek other idols to bury their pain.

Sadly chasing idols never leads to satisfaction. Idols require more and more stimulation from sin to feel pleasure. With an atheist there is no moral limit to sinning so it takes more and more drugs, alcohol, pornography, sexual encounters, power, and greed until their life spirals out of control. Those who hate God rarely keep it to themselves. Eventually they speak out against God but that's not enough. They attack God in the schools, government, and even churches to satisfy their hatred for Him. They are miserable and want everyone to be miserable with them. It's a challenge to find how these people actually build others up for the betterment of mankind. They are so negative and usually seek those of like mind to be around so they can all dig a deeper pit of a hopeless future without a loving God.

LUNCH WITH COLLEGE STUDENTS

My friend and I asked to join a table of two university students at a local restaurant. This is where our accountability group lunch had been meeting every Wednesday for over ten years. Unfortunately the workers there frequently forgot to put out a reserved sign on our table in a private room and two students had sat at our regular table. The two students were drinking water and using Wi-Fi so they said we could join them.

My friend asked one of the students what God meant to him now that he was in college. The student proudly boasted of his atheism. I asked if he was an evolutionist and he agreed and went on to say it was proven like gravity was proven.

I let my friend love on him for a moment and then I asked this question, "If you farted in this room would the gas come together, form a turd, and drop out on the table?" He looked at me like I was crazy. I told him this is what his textbook tells him about evolution. He argued his books didn't say that but I explained how the big bang was considered one gas that exploded, I call it the cosmic fart. It formed all the elements of the universe, that's called alchemy. I let him have the alchemy miracle and asked him how did the gas condense and form the sun, the solar system and us the turds? I explained gasses will not condense without an external pressure. They expand so everyone can enjoy the smell. His answer was, "The laws of physics must have been different then." I told him it must be convenient to change the laws of the universe for his beliefs to be true.

I began questioning him about all sorts of amino acid experiments and other creation verses evolution topics and he could not answer one question. I knew he wouldn't be able to answer tough science questions because he was an English-Philosophy major. I asked him about a previous statement he had made about being an evolutionist. I told him he couldn't call himself an evolutionist because he didn't know the first thing about the science of the theory of evolution. I explained that I could call myself a Chiropractor because I went to school, passed boards, and practiced chiropractic. I shared with him I was not mad at him I was mad at Satan for squashing his spiritual gifts.

Then I asked him the tougher question, 'Why are you so mad at God?" He quickly puffed up and stated he was not mad at God because there is no God. I pressed him more and asked, "What happened to you to make you hate God?" He tried to side step the question but I finally found out his Dad died when he was 16 years old. Still clinging to his disbelief, I asked him if he had ever given his heart to Jesus. His face paled as he admitted being heavily involved in Campus Crusades before his Dad died. He was a believer at one time but he explained how he began to believe the professors and took the path of atheism. I told him he was trying to save people's brains when he was supposed to be saving people's hearts. I told him he was 18 inches off target for what he was created to do.

"For the time will come when people will not put up with sound doctrine. Instead, to suit their own desires, they will gather around them a great number of teachers to say what their itching ears want to hear. They will turn their ears away from the truth and turn aside to myths."
2 Timothy 4:3-4

I wish I could tell you he kneeled down and repented of his disbelief but it did not happen then and there. He was a very large person that towered over me but he was a big ole teddy bear. I saw him on a few occasions and he would always give me a big hug. I would hug back and always say a prayer for him. I hope I mended some of the holes in his Armor that the teachers put there in a vulnerable time of his life.

Are you one of those teachers that prey on vulnerable students? Do you teach freedom with Christ or bondage to the world? Do your teachings help students find their true path they were created to follow? Do your teachings Help students find the love of Jesus? Are you mending the holes made by others?

"Your word is a lamp for my feet, a light on my path."
Psalm 119:105

Have you shut off the lamp for your feet? Are you staggering down a dark path with no direction? What right do you have to snuff out the light of others and mess up their life? You have the right to choose to wander in the dark for the rest of your life but you were not created to be in the dark. Fan the small ember of Faith inside of you and ignite the flame of God to light your path. He is reaching out to you with the plans for your life. He has been patiently waiting on you to take His hand!

"The eye is the lamp of the body. If your eyes are healthy, your whole body will be full of light. But if your eyes are unhealthy, your whole body will be full of darkness. If then the light within you is darkness, how great is that darkness!"
Matthew 6:22-23

STOP dragging people into your pity party world to worship your idols.
LOOK at the never-ending cycle of depression and despair you have created for your life and others around you.
LISTEN to God's truth and crawl out of your pit of despair with the help of Jesus and other people of Faith.
BE WHAT GOD CREATED YOU TO BE; an example of truth for all those around you to see.

"The devil knows if he can capture your thought life he has won a mighty victory over you."[70]   -Smith Wigglesworth

PRIDE of LIFE:
Gift-Killers from Selfish Ambition

"You, then, why do you judge your brother or sister? Or why do you treat them with contempt? For we will all stand before God's judgment seat."   Romans 14:10

The spiritual gifts represented by the Belt of Truth can become arrogant as they fall deeper and deeper into the sin of pride. Picture the person as a know-it-all with a lot of head knowledge and no grace or forgiveness for other's mistakes. They look down on others that do not live up to the perfect standards of the Old Testament laws and feel like they are God's police, jury and judge of all things wrong.

Their obsessive compulsiveness demands perfection from others and they become rigid with "their" values and leave no margin of error. They control others by saying they are God's voice and everyone should listen to them and obey them. They can have fits of rage and anger if people do not follow them.

> *"Now this was the sin of your sister Sodom: She and her daughters were arrogant, overfed and unconcerned; they did not help the poor and needy."* Ezekiel 16:49

Eventually judgement becomes more about their own views and less about God's Word and everything revolves around them. They only look after their own desires and give up helping others. Preachers can say, "If you just do things the right way, God will bless your bank account." They ask people to send them money in order for God to bless them. They lean more on their own words and less of God's Words as they become crooks to take money from the gullible.

They think they are full of the truth and they claim to be the voice of God and they can never be wrong. They become the wolf in sheep's clothing and target the spiritually weak as easy prey. They love honors, titles, connections and great offices for personal recognition. They lie to get personal gain by twisting God's Word. This is literally using God's name in vain. If they had true Faith they would pray for God's provision.

> *"Do not add to what I command you and do not subtract from it, but keep the commands of the Lord your God that I give you."* Deuteronomy 4:2

If you see a person adding or subtracting from the Word of God, run away! They will lead others down some very bad paths and even to death. Jim Jones led almost a thousand people to be murdered with poisoned Flavor-Aid in Jonestown, Guyana. David Koresh led many to follow him and they willingly allowed his sexual perversions with under aged girls in Waco, Texas. His cultish actions led to a 2 hour firefight which left him and 79 others dead.

Fortunately these extremes are rare but this shows how far the sin of pride can take a person. Many of these people could have been saved from such horrible deaths if they had relied on God's truth rather than false Prophets and Teachers given over to depraved minds. God is not going to call a person to give their underage daughter over to a man for sex. These types of people manipulate God's Word for their own selfish gain. Remember if someone is delivering a message of God they should be pointing people back to God's Word and not making up new commandments.

FAKING IT

"Whatever happens, conduct yourselves in a manner worthy of the gospel of Christ. Then, whether I come and see you or only hear about you in my absence, I will know that you stand firm in the one Spirit, striving together as one for the faith of the gospel."   Philippians 1:27

Sadly many in church may appear to *"conduct"* themselves as good church members but they are completely lost behind their smiling churchy mask. The people in this group of gifts can appear to have it all together in their lives but they are very good at hiding the deep wounds inside of themselves. Hiding the wounds slowly destroy them as they fester like an unattended infection.

When Christians fake their life at church it can create dangerous spiritual situations. It can keep the unsaved from being saved as they think they are too dirty for God. It can make others feel they could never fit in with those perfect church people because of their own problems. Being fake keeps young Christians from their full freedom in Christ. They think they need to show how they have it all together and show no weakness. Casting Crown's song, Stained Glass Masquerade, speaks of how Christians hide their pain behind their smiles in church even though their hearts are broken. Maybe, one day we can be real with each other and help each other heal through Christ's genuine love.

Unfortunately showing weakness at church can be dangerous because Christians tend to shoot their own wounded. No wonder people feel like they need to put up a front and act like they have no problems. This group of gifts hides a lot of their pain behind their mask of comedy, their knowledge or by overworking. They are masters at deflecting the conversation away from what is really eating away at their insides. Ironically they usually know their faults but may feel unable or unwilling to make steps to improve them. Usually because they think everyone else has it all together and they are avoiding being shot.

Unfortunately Pastors can be greatly affected when they show weakness to their church. It can end in humiliation and their termination. It is difficult for a Pastor to confide in others about their weaknesses in fear of being exposed. Many have been burned trying to be accountable as they found their secrets betrayed to the church.

> *"Being a pastor is like death by a thousand paper cuts... You're scrutinized and criticized from top to bottom, stem to stern. You work for an invisible, perfect Boss, and you're supposed to lead a ragtag gaggle of volunteers towards God's coming future. It's like herding cats, but harder."*[71]
> -Forbes Magazine – Ranking the 9 Toughest Leadership Roles

I know many Pastors who struggle with their ministries. Having to deal with the everyday corporate running of the church brings them down and keeps them from using their true spiritual gifts. They think heavily about leaving the ministry because of the constant struggle of day-to-day problems. Because they avoid accountability they will keep showing no weakness until it's too late. They fall so hard and so deep it seems there is no one to help them out of the pit they are in.

I had a friend who could never engage in a deep conversation. He was like talking to a squirrel trying to cross the road with cars coming both ways. We had many things in common but I had to give up on the relationship due to the difficulty of just carrying on a conversation with him. Later on he came to me seeking spiritual advice and finally allowed me a small glimpse of what was really inside of him.

I think he was so scared of opening up his soul he missed out on all God was offering for him and his wife. Unfortunately, because of his verbal diarrhea, things did not work out and he and his family did some major damage to their close friends. He really needed those close friends so he could be accountable with them and stay close to God on life's journey. Instead he pushed away the ones that could help him. I still have hope he is continuing to mature in Christ and will eventually restore the friendships he lost.

STOP speaking your own gospel for your own gain.
LOOK to God and repent of your pride before you destroy yourself and others.
LISTEN to God's Word not your own words.
BE WHAT GOD CREATED YOU TO BE; a child of God who humbly leads people back to God's Word with gentleness and respect.

"Pride must die in you, or nothing of heaven can live in you."[73]
-Andrew Murray

PROTECTING YOURSELF FROM THE GIFT-KILLERS OF THE BELT OF TRUTH

LIVING IN GRACE

"Live in harmony with one another. Do not be proud, but be willing to associate with people of low position. Do not be conceited." Romans 12:16

The two most powerful abilities of this group of gifts is hearing from God and pointing others back to His Word. Their most important tool is their mouth. Statistics vary widely about how many words we speak on a day to day basis but it ranges from 2-7 million words a year! What percentage of those words is used to build up other people? What percentage is used to tear down other people? What percentage speaks of Jesus?

> *"Or take ships as an example. Although they are so large and are driven by strong winds, they are steered by a very small rudder wherever the pilot wants to go. Likewise, the tongue is a small part of the body, but it makes great boasts. Consider what a great forest is set on fire by a small spark."*
> James 3:4-5

Words can steer people in good or bad directions. What direction are your words steering people? Words can spark a huge fire. Are your words sparking controversy and division among the Body of Christ or do they unify the church? How judgmental are your words? Are they full of grace and forgiveness or condemnation? Do you arrogantly say "God told me to tell you" or "Thus sayeth the Lord?" You can gently say God put you on my heart or God gave me a message from His Word for you. But wait for them to ask you for help.

> *"I have come into the world as a light, so that no one who believes in me should stay in darkness. 'If anyone hears my words but does not keep them, I do not judge that person. For I did not come to judge the world, but to save the world."*
> John 12:46-47

If we are to become as much like Christ as possible while we are here on Earth, it appears we should not judge others. Jesus came here to save the world and that should be our goal as well. Grace was freely given to us and we should extend that same grace to others. This is the same grace that frees people from addiction and the bondage of a multitude of sins. It allows people to take a totally different direction for their lives so they can serve Christ and help others. The purpose of this group of gifts is to help others find the right direction for their lives. If they feel as if they are being judged they will most likely not listen and run in the opposite direction. Do not judge the world; concentrate on saving it!

> *"There is a judge for the one who rejects me and does not accept my words; the very words I have spoken will condemn them at the last day."*   John 12:48

There will be an eventual judgment for those that reject Jesus but that is not for us to decide. Our job is to keep as many as possible from entering into that judgement. We need to love people to Christ. It can be done in a variety of ways like being patient with others as they grow in Christ. Showing small random acts of kindness like opening doors, smiling, hugging, sending encouraging texts, donating used goods, saying hello, please and thank you. We are supposed to be known by our love so show Christ's love to others.

Love is really nothing unless an action shows the love. Are you showing love through your spiritual gifts to others? Do your actions draw people close or push them away? Do you show the joy you have as a saved Christian on their way to heaven for an eternity? Are you known by your love?

> *"Rejoice always, pray continually, give thanks in all circumstances; for this is God's will for you in Christ Jesus."*
> 1 Thessalonians 5:16-18

Be grateful for what you have and stay clear of jealousy of other people's things. Being thankful helps build up others and shows your appreciation for them being in your life. When you are with others, stay away from bragging about your stuff and your accomplishments. Focus on the other person, keep eye contact and honor them by asking questions about their lives and engage in real conversations.

Learn the names of people's children and ask how they're doing. Be there for your friends and celebrate their happiest moments and weep with them in their times of sorrow. Pray for people every chance you get. Say you are sorry when you make a mistake. Forgive when others are wrong, especially if they ask. Take apologies and move on to a better future. Do your best not to keep a tab of all the wrongs done to you and all the wrongs you have done to yourself.

Making a lasting impression on people through your words and actions can change people's lives. I once met Gene Stallings in an airport in Dallas Texas and he made a lasting first impression that I still use to this day. Being the head coach of Alabama and winning a National Championship gives him quite the reputation with Alabama fans. Meeting him was a huge honor. Teresa was so start-struck with him she said to him, "We were in L.A. yesterday and we never saw a star and here we are sitting with you." Gene answered her back in the most humble Texan accent, "Honey, you still haven't met a star." By this time people were gathering around him to ask questions and get autographs.

There was a small boy about 8 years old in front of the crowd trying to get a question in but the adults were talking over the boy. Gene knelt down to the boy and looked him in the eye and completely focused on him and asked if he had anything to say. It was a wonderful moment I will never forget. As Gene spoke with the boy I decided to make his action a priority in my life. If a child is being good and looks like they need to say something I will focus on the child and give them my attention. I'm sure that boy remembers speaking with Gene Stallings at the airport and how important he made him feel as he autographed his hat and patted him on the head thanking him for being a fan. We are all called to build up others and help them feel the love of Christ.

"Love does not delight in evil but rejoices with the truth. It always protects, always trusts, always hopes, always perseveres. Love never fails..."   1 Corinthians 13:6-8

You are a truth-bearer for Christ and you should always rejoice with the truth and get excited for the power it has to change lives. When you give a message to others through your mouth, your writings or your actions, remember the great responsibility for the message in other's lives. You are speaking the greatest power on earth through God's Word and the same mouth should be clean and free from foul language and divisive words? Is your mouth helping people protect themselves from Satan's attacks by providing them with the Words of God to keep their Sword of the Spirit sharp? Are you helping others increase the size of their Shield of Faith to stop Satan's fiery arrows? Are you giving the hopeless a hope for their future so they can get up off the ground and fight the good fight?

The Words you share show God's love for us and His *"love never fails."* Are you showing His love when you speak the Word of God? Are you allowing God's love to flow through you or are you clogged up and spiritually constipated with a lack of grace for others? Everyone in the Bible was a sinner, except Jesus, and if God could use them to accomplish His Will; He can surely use you and me, no matter where we are in life. When He does use you, give Him all the credit and all the glory!

> *"Grace and peace be yours in abundance through the knowledge of God and of Jesus our Lord."*
> 2 Peter 1:2

STOP thinking you have the right to judge others.
LOOK to God's Word for loving and grace-filled ways to give corrective messages to others. Remember you may have to eat your words someday so I hope they were well seasoned!
LISTEN to the voice of God; it's what you do best.
BE WHAT GOD CREATED YOU TO BE; a forgiven and willing vessel that allows the Word of God to flow through you to others.

Amazing Grace, How sweet the sound
That saved a wretch like me
I once was lost, but now am found
T'was blind but now I see
-John Newton

GROWTH IN CHRIST
The Spiritual Gifts Related to
The Belt of Truth

UNDERSTAND "WHOSE" YOU ARE

"Though the mountains be shaken and the hills be removed, yet my unfailing love for you will not be shaken nor my covenant of peace be removed," says the Lord, who has compassion on you."   Isaiah 54:10

This group of gifts has the knowledge of whose they are but sometimes they lack the emotions and experiences of God. You may know whose you are but do you actually feel whose you are? God has an *"unfailing love for you"* and has *"compassion on you."* He wants you to feel His love, compassion and peace in your life. Many miss this mark by 18 inches, the distance between the mind and the heart. Those 18 inches may be keeping you from experiencing miracles, healing and amazing experiences from God. Open your heart and receive all God has to offer you. Get out of your own head and let God fill your heart and direct your mind. Make sure you love yourself the way Christ loves you so you can love others in the same way.

CONFESS AND PROGRESS

"Repent, then, and turn to God, so that your sins may be wiped out, that times of refreshing may come from the Lord..."   Acts 3:19

Do you regularly beat yourself up over the stupid things you've done? Do you file those actions away into "things I will never do again" but soon fall right back into that same sin again? You can't escape everything that keeps you in bondage by yourself. Bring the "stupid things" into light with others you trust. By being accountable to them it will help you break free from the things that bind you. God will help you so *"your sins may be wiped out!"*

COMMUNICATE WITH GOD

"The Lord is righteous in all his ways and faithful in all he does. The Lord is near to all who call on him, to all who call on him in truth. He fulfills the desires of those who fear him; he hears their cry and saves them."
Psalm 145:17-19

This group of gifts is really good at communicating with God through His Word and His truth. But sometimes they miss the experiences of life found between the lines. Cry out to Him and desire the experiences of God. Do not be like the Pharisees who thought they had all the knowledge of God and missed the experience of Jesus while He was standing in front of them!

"May the God of hope fill you with all joy and peace as you trust in him, so that you may overflow with hope by the power of the Holy Spirit."   Romans 15:13

Seek to become more like Christ and be filled with His Word and His Hope. Do not miss out on all God has planned for you. Do you enjoy God's Word? Does His Word bring life to you and those around you? If you are not sharing, you're despairing, so make the Word of God be an action in your life to build up God's people and God's Kingdom. There you will find joy!

USING THE SPIRITUAL GIFTS REPRESENTED BY THE BELT OF TRUTH WITH THE FRUITS OF THE SPIRIT

LOVE: Do you love people like Christ loved the church or do you carefully weigh their sins and shortcomings to give out your love based on your measurements? Remember Jesus showed you mercy and grace when you were still a sinner and gave you his full unconditional love. He met you where you were and lovingly built you up. Do your best to love people the way Christ loves you.

JOY: Joy comes from a mission well-done for Christ. Are you doing your mission well for Him? Do people become excited or cry when you deliver a message? Are people moved to make changes in their lives when they hear God cares about them? Stay in the Word and be available to deliver God's perfect message at the perfect time and experience the joy of being a good and faithful servant.

PEACE: Are you running around like a chicken with its head cut off trying to fix everything for God? Do you lack peace because of all the things needing your attention? Jesus said his burden is light. Are you trying to add more and more to your load? Make time for God. Slow down and drink some coffee or tea with Him during a quiet time with just you and Him. Allow Him to show you the things you need to be patiently working on and the ones you need to faithfully turn over to Him.

PATIENCE: Can you drive to the store without losing your patience? Do you call other drivers idiots while listening to Christian music in your car? Those drivers may be going through the hardest time of their lives and they may not be focused on their driving. You need to pray for them and their families because they may be having an incredible painful day and you may be the only one praying for them. Remember how patient God was with you.

KINDNESS: Are you kind to others or do you judge them constantly? Does your attitude draw people in or push them away? Be sure to be kind when correcting others. You may have to eat your own words one day and do the very thing you told them to do.

GOODNESS: Are you doing good works for others so they build a relationship with you and trust you? Doing good things helps make the messages more receivable to others. By serving someone's needs, they are much more willing to hear what you have to say. Continue doing good things for others and show the integrity of Christ so they will follow God's Word.

FAITHFULNESS: Are you working everything out under your own power? Are you allowing God to work in your life and show He is God? Do you allow Him in every little detail of your life? He cares deeply about not only the big things but the little things so stop working frantically and give it all over to God. Trust Him with your life!

GENTLENESS: Do you want God to humble you more in order for you to be gentler? Go back to 1 Peter 3:15 and ask yourself if you are delivering God's messages with gentleness and respect for those who ask. When you point your finger at someone who is not ready to hear from God they will only look at the three fingers pointing back at you? Be gentle to others so your message is well-received.

SELF-CONTROL: Is your belt too tight? Are you a strict religious nut for Jesus? The Pharisees had all the head knowledge about the Savior and completely missed Jesus. Are you so caught up in religion you're missing the relationship with God? Sometimes we get wound up so tight and become so obsessive compulsive that we expect everyone, including ourselves, to follow the rules to the letter. Self-control could mean loosening your belt and allowing yourself to enjoy the experience of Jesus.

TAKE THE MIRROR TEST

When you look in the mirror do you see a person people love to dump their problems on, even if you do not know them? Do you ask why they come to you for answers to their problems? Do you look in the mirror and see the beacon of light God created in you so others find refuge to safely receive His Word? Do you see a person working diligently to complete tasks that seem to get harder and harder to fix? Have you ever wondered why projects in your life are hard to finish?

God sees you as a "completionist" and trusts you with the hard things because He knows you will finish the job. It's a bit frustrating to know you were created for such things but there has to be people who will push to finish the job because Satan never gives up. You are designed to push against Satan and his forces to take the ground he has stolen. Work diligently on maturing your spiritual gift to gain ground for Christ and bring joy to yourself and others for finishing a job well done.

> *"If God were not my friend, Satan would not be so much my enemy."*[73]   -Thomas Brooks

> **"Dear children, let us not love with words or speech but with actions and in truth."**   1 John 3:18

STOP being overwhelmed by the brokenness in the world and yourself.
LOOK for the broken people needing to hear God's Word.
LISTEN to God because it's your number one gift, second only to showing others a message through God's Word.
BE WHAT GOD CREATED YOU TO BE; a holy ear tuned into God's voice willing to spread His message through a holy mouth.

PONDERING POINTS

What are the gifts related to the Belt of Truth?

How is the Belt an important piece of Armor physically?

How is the Belt an important piece of Armor spiritually?

What does the Belt need to be attached too?

What is the goal of the gifts of the Belt of Truth?

What is the purpose of the gifts of the Belt of Truth?

What is the strength of the gifts of the Belt of Truth?

What is the main weakness of the gifts of the Belt of Truth?

Are you so busy in life you don't have time for God?

Have you ever thought someone was unworthy of God's grace?

What are the dangers of judging other people?

How can you increase your grace and compassion for others?

What happens when you share God's truth with others?

Have you ever spoken a word from God that changed a person?

Have you ever disobeyed God by not giving a message?

How can the gifts in the Belt & Breastplate work together?

Is more important to know God or to experience God?

What do you do when others will not listen to God's Word?

What fears can stop these gifts?

CHAPTER ELEVEN
THE SANDALS OF READINESS

"Stand firm then, with the belt of truth buckled around your waist, with the breastplate of righteousness in place, and with your feet fitted with the readiness that comes from the gospel of peace. In addition to all this, take up the shield of faith, with which you can extinguish all the flaming arrows of the evil one. Take the helmet of salvation and the sword of the Spirit, which is the word of God."

Ephesians 6:14-17

If you've ever been to Disney World you know the importance of good shoes when walking 10 miles a day and standing in lines for half the day. This principal of good shoes works the same for Armies. Shoes are of upmost importance for moving an Army quickly and efficiently to battle. The Roman sandals used in battle were built for speed over rough terrain. They were cleated with nails or spikes for traction to hold them in position and help keep them from slipping and falling down in battle. They were literally made to *"stand firm"* in battle. Good foot wear is a must for any army to be effective on the battlefield.

"Readiness" implies a preparation beforehand like building a good foundation to make a structure stronger. A strong soldier needs to have a similar solid foundation through training, preparation and experience. This education will prepare them for battle and being ready for battle is a top priority for winning them.

"And how can anyone preach unless they are sent? As it is written: 'How beautiful are the feet of those who bring good news!'"

Romans 10:15

The spiritual gifts represented by the Sandals of Readiness are the perfect example of preparing a foundation for others to spread the Gospel of Peace and the good news of Jesus Christ. They carefully get ready all the things needed to allow God's Word to be preached throughout the world. The Sandals are literally the foundation of the Body of Christ as they go about their purpose of building up the Kingdom.

SPIRITUAL GIFTS REPRESENTED BY THE SANDALS OF READINESS

Giving
Helps
Ministry

This group of gifts works very well as a team to build up the Kingdom of God. The perfect example is when a church decides to build another church in a third world country. The project details are worked out by leadership and the gifts of Giving step up to fund the project. The gifts of Helps hit the road to build the new church. Then the gifts of Ministry prepare the way to spread the Good News of Christ in the new church. They set up classes for children and adults, lead worship and help people feel warm and welcome. This group of gifts works well together to build the foundation for spreading the Gospel.

Without this group of gifts it would be almost impossible to get the message of what Jesus did for us to the masses. They're responsible for making it possible to train up disciples in large and small groups. Their diligent work behind the scenes allows worship, preaching and ministry to flow effortlessly to those who need it. If we did not have this group of gifts where would we meet and who would make sure we have heat, a/c and plumbing? Who would care for the children, plan events and make things possible through their giving? They are disciples making disciples.

WE ALL HAVE SPIRITUAL GIFTS PLURAL

This group of spiritual gifts builds up the Body of Christ from the Cradle to the Grave. They are involved with Children, Youth and Adult Ministries with Discipleship and Mentoring. The provide Worship and Hospitality to help people feel welcome at church. They also use Outreach, Counseling, Prayer and Benevolence to help people in need.

There are so many areas of service and obvious ways for anyone to help. What excuse is there for a Christian to not be a part of the Body of Christ and serve others? Some may be able to swing a hammer or paint while others care for children. Someone has to make lemonade and sandwiches for the helpers while others could pray! We all have spiritual gifts, Plural!

Some may feel like they don't have much money give but Jesus recognized the Widow giving what she could. Your service may not seem like much but God uses what you give Him to multiply His Kingdom. He sure did a lot with a little fish and bread. He will use your service and your giving.

THE GOAL OF
THE SANDALS OF READINESS
"To Help Others Feel Warm and Welcome for a Purpose"

"And do not forget to do good and to share with others, for with such sacrifices God is pleased."
Hebrews 13:16

The people using these gifts are the ones remembering to *"do good"* which means "to make and do it well" which is exactly what they do to serve the Body of Christ. They prepare well thought out foundations to build up the church in all areas of Service. This group of gifts also knows how to *"share with others."* The Greek word for "share" is "Koinonia" which is a familiar Christian term meaning fellowship and community. It's like sharing Communion together. This group is well designed to provide opportunities for the community to get together and hear about Jesus Christ.

They help usher in the Holy Spirit through actions directed by God. Their actions soften the hearts of those needing to receive a message of Christ. It can be from hospitality that helps a person feel as if they are part of a family or hearing a well thought out set of worship songs that opens their hearts to God. They have a way of blessing others with the perfect thing at the perfect time through their service and actions. It may be helping build a home through Habitat for Humanity or simply giving someone the money to pay their power bill during a financially tough month. It can come from a simple act of kindness like a well-thought-out card or gift delivered at just the right time. They love to provide meaningful acts of kindness in Christ for others specific needs.

THE PURPOSE OF
THE SANDALS OF READINESS
"To Guide, Support and Relieve Others Though Action"

"...if it [the Spiritual Gift] is serving, then serve..."
Romans 12:7

These gifts are the ideal versions of a servant's heart. They are generally found volunteering behind the scenes doing large and small works for the church. They are not usually seeking the Spotlight and just want to serve like the Scripture states. They sacrifice great amounts of their talents, time and money to help others build up the Kingdom. They are very loyal and will carry out a task to completion and need very little direction from leaders to finish their mission. They take great joy in seeing their project become the welcoming and warming atmosphere it was created to be.

I had a family member in a tight financial spot and they were in need of an oven and clothes dryer. I was planning on purchasing both but I was getting some finances together and waiting for a sale on the appliances. I mentioned this to a patient and described the situation. I told him how I was worried about their young girls going to the laundry mat to wash clothes and I felt an urgency to get them the dryer. This man is a very nice man and I was not asking him for help but without me knowing, he gave my wife $400 toward the dryer! The family now has both appliances thanks to this man. This is an example of the Godly actions of the people with the spiritual gifts related to the Sandals of Readiness.

"We who are strong ought to bear with the failings of the weak and not to please ourselves. Each of us should please our neighbors for their good, to build them up."
Romans 15:1-2

Those with these gifts are people pleasers. They love to help people feel warm and welcome for a purpose and are created to *"please our neighbors for their good, to build them up."*

THE STRENGTH OF THE SANDALS OF READINESS
"Serving Others So Others Can Learn to Serve Others"

"...and if you spend yourselves in behalf of the hungry and satisfy the needs of the oppressed, then your light will rise in the darkness, and your night will become like the noonday."
Isaiah 58:10

The gifts related to the Sandals have a motto: "See a need fill the need!" They understand the needs of others and seek ways to provide for those needs. When they are tuned into God, He gives them the ability to provide amazing platforms for others to spread the Gospel of Christ. They truly allow God's light to shine in the darkness as they *"satisfy the needs of the oppressed."* Huge events like Promise Keepers and Billy Graham Crusades didn't just happen. There were many behind the scene workers planning the event and many more carrying out the physical duties of running the show.

Those with these gifts completely understand the need to serve others so others can be built up to serve others. They know lighting, sound, and seating along with good music helps others feel comfortable in church. Internationally they understand the importance of fresh water wells next to churches and schools to help spread the Gospel in a third world country. They carefully prepare a foundation no matter where they are to welcome people into the arms of Jesus.

> *"I have no greater joy than to hear that my children are walking in the truth."*   3 John 1:4

They also know that a children's musical or drama program can teach Bible stories and songs to build their Christian foundation. Many from this group of gifts serve in the children's ministries and build up our children with a solid foundation in Christ. Our children desperately need God's Word in their lives to prepare them for their life's journey. Thank you so much to all the men and women who serve our children. It may be a thankless job at times but you are preparing Godly foundations for the children to build on for a better life in Christ. It will be worth all the blood, sweat and tears! You will reap great rewards in heaven for your sacrifices here on earth!

> *"The only way you can serve God is by serving other people."[74]*
> -Rick Warren

THE GOOD OF
THE SANDALS OF READINESS
(Going Forward)
"Good People doing Good Works for Others"

> *"...being confident of this, that he who began a good work in you will carry it on to completion until the day of Christ Jesus."*   Philippians 1:6

Those using these gifts begin with good works and are efficient at completing the works they start. They are a steady work force for God that continually builds a foundation for others. They love helping people feel welcome in settings like Sunday school classes, church services and their own home.

While filling in one Sunday morning for a class, I decided to buy doughnuts to help keep the class awake during my talk. It was Valentine's Day and I remembered Krispy Kreme sold heart shaped doughnuts. I stopped and bought enough for the class of fifty only to realize, on the way back to church, I didn't even get napkins. Fortunately the church had plenty so I put the doughnuts on a table with some napkins and began to read over my notes for speaking. I noticed a lady member of the class come in and take notice of the doughnuts and leave. She came back in with small plates and forks in a cup and placed them on the table. She then opened each box to make it easy to access the doughnuts for the class.

Her actions gave me my opening lines for my lesson. I told the class I saw this lady help make everyone feel more welcome. I asked who in the class has this type of gift that helps people feel warm and welcome. Three people raised their hands out of the fifty. I told those three it means 94% of us do not do what you do! When those of you using these gifts are worried about the blue plates not matching the blue napkins, relax. The vast majority of us feel the effort you put into making us feel welcome and part of a family.

> *"For God has not given us a spirit of fear, but of power and of love and of a sound mind."*   2 Timothy 1:7

This is the life verse for this group of gifts. When the people using these gifts understand this verse and put it into action they are unstoppable. They allow their power to be multiplied by God to bless others through their actions of love. When they realize their fear is driven out by God's perfect love; they gain peace in their lives through self-discipline.

I've seen some amazing acts of service come from these people when they realize the power God gives them through His love to build the Kingdom.

THE BAD OF
THE SANDALS OF READINESS
(Going Backward)
"Seeking Recognition for Good Works"

The Bad actions of these spiritual gifts are not necessarily sin. They start to slip away from God due to stresses, overwork, and burnout. They can take on to many projects and spread themselves thin. This produces more and more stress, lack of sleep, and attitude changes. The "Bad" is like the check engine light on the dash of a car. It can be a warning of slipping into the "Ugly" sins of these gifts as they drift from God.

"WORKS" TRAPS:

> *"For it is by grace you have been saved, through faith— and this is not from yourselves, it is the gift of God— not by works, so that no one can boast. For we are God's handiwork, created in Christ Jesus to do good works, which God prepared in advance for us to do."*
> Ephesians 2:8-10

As these gifts begin to over-work and rely on themselves rather than God they fall into "Works" Traps. They may begin to seek love and praise from other people rather than God. They can begin to ignore what God wants done and do what they want to do in order to boast of their own accomplishments. They may even feel as if they are unforgivable and do works out of guilt or as a penalty for their sins. Here are the three "Works" Traps and one true *"Good Works."*

SALVATION WORKS

"I believe it's easy to serve God if we learn to hear from Him before we struggle to do things for Him that He never asked us to do."
-Joyce Meyer

Salvation Works are motivated by impressing God so He will forgive us. They cause people feel empty because human works are never enough for complete salvation. They become trapped in a never-ending cycle of not being good enough for God as they struggle with simply allowing God to forgive them. This endless cycle and the feelings of emptiness can lead to a "why bother" attitude and they stop serving others and become bitter. They may live out the rest of their life burdened by the pain of shame and regret by living in a prison of made from not living in forgiveness. You do not have to work off your salvation; Jesus already paid the price for you!

In him we have redemption through his blood, the forgiveness of sins, in accordance with the riches of God's grace [8] that he lavished on us..." Ephesians 1:7-8

GUILTY WORKS

"If you live for people's acceptance you will die from their rejection."[75]
-Lecrae

Guilty Works are motivated by others expectations, not God's expectations. They fall into a trap of never being able to say "no." This leads to "burn out" by taking on too many projects. It's hard to say "no" when trying to please all the people all the time. This can lead to anger and frustration which causes them to stop serving.

"...let us draw near to God with a sincere heart and with the full assurance that faith brings, having our hearts sprinkled to cleanse us from a guilty conscience and having our bodies washed with pure water."
Hebrews 10:22

You are of value to God; He sent His Son to die for you! He has prepared a place for you to live with Him forever. God, the judge of all creation, declared you "not guilty!"

SELFISH WORKS

"You can't let praise or criticism get to you. It's a weakness to get caught up in either one."[76]   -John Wooden

Selfish Works are motivated by the praise from others, not God's praise. This traps people with a constant need for a pat-on-the-back for a job well done. They feel unappreciated for their hard work if they do not receive praise from others and become angry then they quit serving.

"One person gives freely, yet gains even more; another withholds unduly, but comes to poverty."
                                                    Proverbs 11:24

Are you heading toward being the one who **"withholds unduly?"** Have you been working hard for God and no one recognizes all your good works? Does this make you angry and tempted to quit serving? Stop looking for worldly praise and please the one true God who created you for! **"Give freely"** so you gain more of what you really need in your life; love, joy and peace. Give out of the great love the Father has for you so your mind and heart can be free to learn more about Him. There you will find His promise and direction.

"Teach me, Lord, the way of your decrees, that I may follow it to the end. Give me understanding, so that I may keep your law and obey it with all my heart. Direct me in the path of your commands, for there I find delight. Turn my heart toward your statutes and not toward selfish gain. Turn my eyes away from worthless things; preserve my life according to your word. Fulfill your promise to your servant, so that you may be feared."   Psalm 119:33-38

Beg God to calm your mind so He can teach you His plan for your life so you can *"follow it to the end!"* Ask for your heart to be protected from selfishness so you can understand the path in front of you. Psalms is a book of songs and is the largest book in Scripture. The song writer is crying out for God to clearly help them learn to follow His laws and statutes and put them into action. They also cry out to turn their heart and eyes away from selfish gain and worthless things.

> *"Who is wise and understanding among you? Let them show it by their good life, by deeds done in the humility that comes from wisdom. But if you harbor bitter envy and selfish ambition in your hearts, do not boast about it or deny the truth. Such "wisdom" does not come down from heaven but is earthly, unspiritual, demonic. For where you have envy and selfish ambition, there you find disorder and every evil practice."* James 3:13-16

God calls people's *"selfish ambition"* *"earthly, unspiritual, demonic,"* and where you find *"disorder and every evil practice!"* To break "works traps" we must seek God's heavenly wisdom and submit to His call on our life even if we don't receive worldly praise. Our job is to reap a harvest of righteousness and not *"harbor bitter envy and selfish ambition."* Stay the course God planned for you since you were created, do greater things for Him and avoid falling into an *"evil practice."*

What if Noah listened to the mockery of the crowd when he was building the Ark for 120 years with no rain in those days? What if Joseph gave up on following God's morality because of being sold into slavery by his brothers? What if Ester selfishly thought about only her own life instead of doing what was right in God's eyes? What if Jesus only looked for praise from those in charge? Where would our future be? All of these obedient actions of others gave us a Savior and a hope for our future. Will your selfless actions bring a future of hope to others through your unselfish good works??

GOOD WORKS

"Unless God has raised you up for this very thing, you will be worn out by the opposition of men and devils. But if God be for you, who can be against you? Are all of them together stronger than God? O be not weary of well doing!"[77]   -John Wesley

Good Works are motivated by our love of God. Since He loves us we can love others and show the love of God to them. Freedom in good works produces amazing results when the Holy Spirit is allowed into the works to bless others. The power of the Good Works is magnified to be more than just a good deed. These works will speak the power of God through the hands willing to serve Him!

"Whoever sows to please their flesh, from the flesh will reap destruction; whoever sows to please the Spirit, from the Spirit will reap eternal life. Let us not become weary in doing good, for at the proper time we will reap a harvest if we do not give up. Therefore, as we have opportunity, let us do good to all people, especially to those who belong to the family of believers."   Galations 6:8-10

By staying faithful and not growing weary our Good Work's will reap a harvest of *"eternal life!"* That is Power!

"Good works is giving to the poor and the helpless, but divine works is showing them their worth to the One who matters."[78]
                    -Criss Jami

"And do not forget to do good and to share with others, for with such sacrifices God is pleased."
                    Hebrews 13:16

DISTRACTIONS

"Let the word of Christ dwell in you richly in all wisdom; teaching and admonishing one another in psalms and hymns and spiritual songs, singing with grace in your hearts to the Lord."   Colossians 3:16

This group of gifts can become distracted with perfectionism. I was speaking with a man about his Spiritual gift of Ministry with music. He was trying out for a stage position in his church and I could tell he was nervous about his own abilities and wanted to be perfect. I told him how important his gift was for opening the door to allow the Holy Spirit to fill the place.

Music and songs soften the hearts of people to receive God's Word. I told him how important it was for him to *"let the Word of Christ dwell"* in him. By staying in Scripture and listening to God for what songs need to be played he could help welcome in the Holy Spirit. Some people will listen to the song more than the sermon so the songs need to speak the truth of God.

Sometimes musicians get in a rut of playing what is popular to please the crowd thinking this is the perfect song choice. God may have a different song request that fits His message better and it may be out of the musician's comfort zone. The message for this man was to carefully listen for God's Will and play what He needs people to hear not what they want to hear. By allowing God to choose the music for him it could reduce his anxiety of picking the wrong songs and feel imperfect. By loving and trusting God with his music talents He could allow himself to teach others *"spiritual songs"* that will be sung with grace in their *"hearts to the Lord."*

"As Jesus and his disciples were on their way, he came to a village where a woman named Martha opened her home to him. She had a sister called Mary, who sat at the Lord's feet listening to what he said. But Martha was distracted by all the preparations that had to be made. She came to him and asked, 'Lord, don't you care that my sister has left me to do the work by myself? Tell her to help me!' 'Martha, Martha,' the Lord answered, 'you are worried and upset about many things, but few things are needed—or indeed only one. Mary has chosen what is better, and it will not be taken away from her.'"   Luke 10:38-42

Mary chose to be with Jesus and not miss the experience of listening to Him while sitting at His feet. Martha was *"distracted by all the preparations"* for the worldly needs but she was missing the most important thing, experiencing Jesus. Many in this group of gifts can miss worship, discipleship, and lose out on building relationships with others because they are distracted by preparations. Giving up precious time with Jesus can give a foothold for the enemy to sneak in and nudge us toward the "Ugly" sinful side of these gifts related to the Sandals.

STOP trying to please everyone else but God.
LOOK to God for a pat on the back and don't rely on others flattery.
LISTEN to God for what He wants you to be involved with. Avoid unnecessary distractions and don't give up important time with Him and miss out on experiencing Jesus.
BE WHAT GOD CREATED YOU TO BE; A forgiven child of the Most High who lovingly helps with the needs of others.

"So many times we say that we can't serve God because we aren't whatever is needed. We're not talented enough or smart enough or whatever. But if you are in covenant with Jesus Christ, He is responsible for covering your weaknesses, for being your strength. He will give you His abilities for your disabilities!"[79]

-Kay Arthur

THE MAIN GIFT-KILLING WEAKNESS OF
THE SANDALS OF READINESS
"Un-Forgiveness and Fear"

"Not that I have already obtained all this, or have already arrived at my goal, but I press on to take hold of that for which Christ Jesus took hold of me. Brothers and sisters, I do not consider myself yet to have taken hold of it. But one thing I do: Forgetting what is behind and straining toward what is ahead, I press on toward the goal to win the prize for which God has called me heavenward in Christ Jesus."
Philippians 3:12-14

Many with the spiritual gifts represented by the Sandals of Readiness have trouble *"forgetting what is behind"* and their goals become clouded by un-forgiveness. They cannot see what is ahead from being blinded by their past. They are hindered by the shame and regret of their past and stop *"straining toward what is ahead."* Their joy is stolen by Satan as they begin a journey into self-hatred and depression as their fears and anxiety grow larger and larger. Anger, rage and bitterness can then take over their hearts and their lives.

"Yes, let God be the Judge. Your job today is to be a witness."[80]
Warren Wiersbe

Because they hold back forgiveness, being judgmental gets a foothold in their mind and emotions. A strange turn of events happens as they judge the one who hurt them. They sit themselves on the Judgement Seat of Christ. When they take over God's job of judging, the one judging becomes judged. The Judgement Seat compares them to the perfection of Jesus and they quickly fall short.

They will never meet God's standards so their self-esteem collapses. They become so super sensitive to rejection they will avoid new social events in fears of how others will judge them. They fear criticism and become world class worriers. They fear looking foolish in front of others and become very hurt by the disapproval of other people. They become upset at their own inability to relate well with others due to their fears and anxieties. They then start tearing others down around them in order to build themselves up. They usually end up having less and less friends and family around them because of their bitterness.

These issues can be crippling in our social media society and so can the job of judging everyone including your own faults. Allow yourself to be set free so you can be a mighty witness to God's power. Forgiveness is the Gospel of Jesus Christ. His forgiveness not only set us free from the bondage of sin but it allows us to spend an eternity with Him in heaven. It's kind of a big deal! Imagine sin being the chains holding us in a prison while forgiveness is the key that unlocks the chains and sets us free. Forgiveness is mentioned several times in and around one of the most recognized Scriptures in the Bible; let us pray the Lord's Prayer.

"This, then, is how you should pray:
Our Father in heaven,
hallowed be your name,
your kingdom come,
your will be done,
on earth as it is in heaven.
Give us today our daily bread.
And forgive us our debts,
as we also have forgiven our debtors.
And lead us not into temptation,
but deliver us from the evil one.

For if you forgive other people when they sin against you, your heavenly Father will also forgive you. But if you do not forgive others their sins, your Father will not forgive your sins." Matthew 6:9-15

This can be a hard Scripture to swallow for this group of gifts. There are three times we are asked to forgive those who have hurt us in these Scriptures. Three times God states how important our forgiveness is toward others. It even says God will not forgive our sins if we do not forgive others! Un-forgiveness can become a hindrance to our prayers and reduce our conversations with God. This stifles our growth in our Faith and can reduce our mental, physical and spiritual health. Please, forgiveness is selfish and frees you from the bondage of being controlled by others. Forgive others, move forward and live in God's freedom!

Imagine being in an accident and someone hits your car. You find out they have no insurance and cannot pay for the damages. You get so mad you pull out a five gallon bucket of nails and pour them in front of their car to stop them from leaving without paying for your car. They simply back up their car and pull away to avoid the nails. You jump into your car and scream and holler at them but you are unable to move forward because of the nails on the road in front of your car. During the accident your car's rear end was pushed into a guard rail so you cannot go backward.

After sitting there all day you become tired and hungry. You even missed your child's birthday party. You pick up the cell phone and call God and say, "Hey God, I would like to forgive the person who hit my car. Can you help me move on with my life, I don't want to miss any more of it?" God sends out A.A.A. (Another Anxiety Averted) and they clear the nails in the road and the mess from the accident. This road service is so amazing they repair the damage to your car so you can get on with your life.

Un-forgiveness slows or stops our forward motion. Many times it can put us into reverse and lead us down the road of destruction. Notice how *"lead us not into temptation"* follows forgiveness. It's there for a purpose because holding in un-forgiveness weakens us spiritually. The next line clearly states the danger, *"but deliver us from the evil one."*

The Scriptures are in this order because un-forgiveness opens a door to allow Satan a foothold in our lives. On the other hand forgiveness allows God to send out the clean-up crews so we can get moving again. Forgiveness is selfish; it's more for us than the one who hurt us.

I've watched several people go down this road of un-forgiveness. It usually looks about the same every time. The person is diligently working for God and then someone hurts them. They wonder why God allowed it to happen because they were working so hard for Him. They begin to work harder to please God only to get more tired and more burned out. They never try to fix themselves because they think they aren't the one with the problem. They become so judgmental of the one who hurt them that their emotions become toxic and pour out on those around them. Those people leave and they end up alone with a festering wound. Eventually they blame God for all of their problems and they stop serving and drift into a life of sin.

> *"Therefore I remind you to stir up the gift of God which is in you through the laying on of my hands. For God has not given us a spirit of fear, but of power and of love and of a sound mind.."*   2 Timothy 1:6-7 NKJV

This is the life verse for this group of gifts. When the people using these gifts understand this verse and put it into action they are unstoppable. Their power can be multiplied by God to bless others through their actions of love. When they realize their fear, the same word for timid, is driven out by God's perfect love they gain peace in their lives through self-discipline.

This word for *"fear"* is only used once in Scripture. This word is "reticence" meaning a silence in speech due to a fear coming from cowardice or doubt. It is used to describe someone who lost their moral gumption and falls short of following Jesus. This is the opposite for the other words used for fear which can mean a reverent or respectful Fear of God because of their awe for Him.

Are you living in so much fear you are scared to speak out for our Lord and doubt the abilities He gave you? Do you want *"Power"* from God to conquer your fears? The word for that power is "dynameos" and is where we get the word dynamite? Dynamite comes in small packages and has tremendous power. No matter how small you feel you still have the use of God's power to complete the mission He gave you.

Being full of fear which stops you from speaking about your life with others can be a result of feeling unloved and unworthy to be a spokesperson for God? Being able to receive the unconditional love of God can drive out those fears and allow your life's story to bless others going through the same trials. Do you crave a well-balanced direction from God that gives a sound mind that regulates your outward behavior with self-control rather than being controlled by doubt, cowardice and fear? God is offering this through His amazing love!

Fear and un-forgiveness may be a great power couple for destruction but you were given the *"Power"* of God to combat a defeated enemy! Satan will try to put the fear of not being good enough to receive and live in God's forgiveness in your head. You have the *"Power"* to guard your *"Sound Mind"* with the *"Love"* of God and block Satan's attacks. I've seen some amazing acts of service come from people when they realize the power God gives them through His love to build the Kingdom. God's perfect love gives you the ability to set yourself free from the prison of your own making.

"The voice of sin is loud, but the voice of forgiveness is louder."[81]
-Dwight L. Moody

THE UGLY OF
THE SANDALS OF READINESS
(Going Sin-Ward)
"Worrying What the World Thinks"

The Ugly use of the Spiritual gifts is when a believer chooses to disobey God and use their God-given talent for evil. God gives us the choice to follow Him or not. He also gives us the choice to use our talents for good or bad and when they are used to sin they become Anti-Gifts. Here is the ugly side of wrongly used talents represented by the Sandals of Readiness. They have been broken down into the three areas of sin discussed in chapter 6:

LUST of the FLESH:
Gift-Killers from Sins of the Body
"Seeking Approval from People Rather than God"

"Flee from sexual immorality. All other sins a person commits are outside the body, but whoever sins sexually, sins against their own body. Do you not know that your bodies are temples of the Holy Spirit, who is in you, whom you have received from God? You are not your own; you were bought at a price. Therefore honor God with your bodies."

1 Corinthians 6:18-20

Warning: The temple is now within our body so be careful what you bring into the Temple of God. A negative self-esteem in the people using these gifts can fall victim to flattery and praise. I know someone who received compliments at their work place that made them feel pretty. This led to an emotional attachment which led to an affair. Their poor self-image was like a hungry fish going after the bait of flattery and compliments and eventually it was a hook in their mouth with Satan at the other end of the rod.

I've seen people, whose spouse committed adultery, deny forgiveness and become bitter and enraged. They were so toxic to be around they lost many of their friends. I'm not saying everyone has to stay with someone who has committed adultery. This is a very difficult road to travel. I will say that having the support of Godly people around you will be an important part of the recovery process if you decide to forgive and stay together. The most important thing is to forgive those who've hurt you to avoid becoming bitter and toxic.

"Christian morality prefers remorse to precede lust, and then lust not to follow."[82]   -Karl Kraus

STOP looking for attention from the wrong people.
LOOK closely at the edge of the cliff you are about to fall off of.
LISTEN to God for how beautiful and important you are to Him.
BE WHAT GOD CREATED YOU TO BE, a builder of Godly foundations to build the Kingdom of God upon.

LUST of the EYES:
Gift-Killers from Idol Worship or Coveting

"Then he said to them, 'Watch out! Be on your guard against all kinds of greed; life does not consist in an abundance of possessions.'"   Luke 12:15

The gifts related to the Sandals can be fixated on the beauty of people and things but desiring something more than Jesus is an idol. Do you fish and hunt more than you spend time with God? Do you spend more time looking in the mirror each week than you spend at church? Do you spend more time in your yard trying to impress neighbors rather than talking about Christ with others? Does your time with TV, movies and music far outweigh your quiet time with God? Do you spend more on collectables than your donations to the church and the needy? Do you spend more time going to ball games than serving others and attending church?

BOYCOTTS

"Verily, we know not what an evil it is to indulge ourselves, and to make an idol of our will."[83]   -Samuel Rutherford

Lust of the eyes can be very deceiving and it tries to justify the idol and keep it alive in your life. I saw some people act very strange when the Southern Baptists decided to boycott Disney many years ago. They boycotted because of Disney's decision to give gay couples the same employee benefit rights as married couples. They also sited Gay Day at Disney as an issue which was not an officially sanctioned Disney event. I listened to a couple defend the Baptist position and say they were not going to buy any Disney merchandise nor take their family to Disney World. Ironically they had very little money and these things were not in their budget so it was no real boycott for them.

The problem with the boycott was Disney owned ABC and ESPN. Southern Baptists love their sports and were watching their team idols on the stations religiously. I asked the husband of this couple about the situation since he was a huge sports fan. He thought it was fine to watch the games since he was not giving them any money. I explained they get more money from the commercials by the amount of people who watch the games.

I'm not supporting Disney's decisions nor condemning the Southern Baptists. They both have the right to their opinions. I attend a Southern Baptist church that I love. I want to show how Idols can make us compromise our choices. Ironically Disney did something similar by announcing their boycott of the film industry in Georgia. Disney made the decision because of the state's new stricter abortion law. Yet Disney continues to film in other countries like China where they kill gay people and give no rights to women. The double-minded hypocrisy is what drives me crazy.

When the Baptist Boycott began I had a completely different view of what to do. If the homosexual community can rally together for a Gay Day then the Christian community could rally together for a Christian Month. Christians could take the month of July and plan a vacation to Disney and show the love of Christ to hundreds of thousands of people from all over the world. It's a huge mission field. They could wear their Jesus T-shirts, hats, backpacks and toe rings then go out and do random acts of kindness for the tourists. They could pray openly, pay for meals, pick up things people drop, speak kindly and do what Jesus would expect them to do, show His love.

Some people boycott Target for some of their political views but both Walmart and Target sell a majority of items from China. China has horrible work conditions for their employees and they imprison and kill Christians simply for their belief. Which store is better if they both sell the same or similar products? I don't see Christians standing up for the boycott of items from China because it would be too inconvenient for their lifestyle.

I never saw where Jesus boycotted a Bacon Express or shun a prostitute. He kept the Jewish laws but he showed an immense love for others and met them where they were in their lives. The ones He had the most problem with were stiff-necked Pharisees who thought they were better than everyone else.

Is it more important to show love rather than hate? We now live in a culture of hate and cancel culture. Where did they learn this behavior, was it boycotts? What is the difference between cancel culture and boycotts other than it is just an increase in hatred. Both seek to kill and destroy what they hate and it sounds a lot like what Satan would do. If there is something for us to hate it should be the lack of love.

WHICH MASTER DO YOU LOVE?

"No one can serve two masters. Either you will hate the one and love the other, or you will be devoted to the one and despise the other. You cannot serve both God and money."
Matthew 6:24

Insert any of these words for the word *"money"* in this Scripture: Cars, Trucks, Motorcycles, 4 x 4's, Name Brands, Clothes, Sports, Famous People, Actors, Singers, Collectables, Possessions, Entertainment, Food, or your own Appearance. If you are not sure you are dealing with an Idol just check where you spend your time and money and it will become clear. You cannot *"serve two masters"* in your life. Christ must be the priority in your life in order to have people, places and things not become a form of idol worship in your life.

"If anyone has material possessions and sees a brother or sister in need but has no pity on them, how can the love of God be in that person?"   1 John 3:17

Having nice things is not a sin but how they are obtained and how they are used can be the sin. When you receive a raise do you use more of your income to help others in need or do you simply adjust your lifestyle upward when you are blessed with more income? Most of us have had a helping hand from someone at a low time in our lives. Are you a helping hand for others or do you get in more debt due to the upward lifestyle change and continue being a slave to *"money?"* Even in debt you could still use your possessions to cook someone a meal that lost a loved one or take someone to a doctor's appointment. There is always a way to give back to God.

"You don't have to go to heathen lands today to find false gods. America is full of them. Whatever you love more than God is your idol."[84]
-Dwight L. Moody

While serving on Tres Dias I began writing many skits for the Men's weekends. I have accumulated hundreds of props and costumes over the years. I have spent thousands of dollars on them and try to keep them in good shape in order to use them over again. Occasionally people ask to borrow some costumes and I cringe. I have had so many bad experiences with loaning them out and getting them back either damaged or with missing pieces.

The worst experiences seem to come from a really nice set of Disciple outfits that were made by a very generous patient. I bought the material and cut out the patterns and she sewed them for me. I loaned the outfits to a group and told them not to loan them to anyone else and they did. They got mixed up with another set of outfits and pieces were lost. Another time a friend borrowed them and left them in the trunk of his car for months. He was a chain smoker and I had to wash and iron all of them a week before using them in my own skit.

> *"Good will come to those who are generous and lend freely,*
> *who conduct their affairs with justice.*
>
> Psalms 112:5

I wrestle with being stingy with the outfits and using them only for my skits. When I die, I don't want to hold up the outfits to Jesus and say, "Look, I kept these in mint condition" and Jesus would say, "Why weren't they used until they were rags in order to share the Gospel and tell the world about Me." I do not want the costumes to become idols. I want them used to spread the good news of Christ. So please, when you borrow things bring them back quickly and in better shape than you received them so Satan cannot get a foothold through your negligence.

> *"Do to others as you would have them do to you."*
>
> Luke 6:31

STOP allowing your eyes to rule your mind and body.

LOOK for what God wants in everyone's heart, His love!

LISTEN to Godly messages and moral entertainment. Be careful when choosing worldly versions of entertainment that can corrupt your mind and body.

BE WHAT GOD CREATED YOU TO BE; a forgiven preparer for the Gospel of our Lord Jesus Christ.

> *"...we are quick to rationalize our entertainment and priorities yet are slow to commit to serving God."*[85] -Francis Chan

PRIDE of LIFE:
Gift-Killers from Selfish Ambition

> *"Search me, God, and know my heart; test me and know my anxious thoughts. See if there is any offensive way in me, and lead me in the way everlasting."*
>
> Psalm 139:23-24

This Scripture probably gives anxiety to those with the gifts related to the Sandals. They seem to have *"anxious thoughts"* a lot of the time. They can worry about everything even their own forgiveness from God. Their low self-esteem is a target for *"any offensive way"* because they can see themselves as flawed and unusable for the Kingdom. Feeling unworthy of God's love makes them a prime target of Satan's lies about God's forgiveness.

THE PRIDE OF UN-FORGIVENESS

When God revealed un-forgiveness to me as being the main Gift-Killer of the spiritual gifts related to the Sandals of Righteousness, I did not accept it. I tried looking in every other direction but it kept on proving itself correct as I spoke with people with these gifts. It is so sad to see a person when they are asked about un-forgiveness. They drop their eyes and then their head in embarrassment as they own up to not doing what God has asked them to do. It is strange how this un-forgiveness can lead to a problem with pride.

The pride which comes from un-forgiveness leads to becoming judgmental of others. It was mentioned earlier about how they will sit themselves in the judgment seat of Christ and their butt doesn't fit in the seat! They quickly realize they cannot measure up to the seat as it judges them. Pride comes in as they make themselves feel better by judging others more harshly. To compensate for their own short comings they tear others down to build themselves up. They will compare everything from weight, appearance and possessions, to spouses, occupations and clothing. They are scared to look inward so they keep their eyes focused on the outward appearance of others.

Pride can kill all love except the love of self. This self-love is never satisfied and it always craves attention and needs to be constantly fed. It makes someone feel more important than other people and causes them to overestimate their self. They become insensitive to other's needs and discount their value. They become blinded to their own faults and only see the faults in others. They become the know-it-all and drive others away only to be left in isolation and loneliness. Many burn out and stop serving in their retirement years when this should be the time they have more time to spread God's love.

If you find yourself heading in this direction accept God's forgiveness and run back to Him, it's never too late! Get your butt out of the judgement seat and live the life God has planned for you.

> *"It's Satan's delight to tell me that once he's got me, he will keep me. But at that moment I can go back to God. And I know that if I confess my sins, God is faithful and just to forgive me."*[86]
> -Alan Redpath

PRIDE IN OUR ABIBLITIES

Pride is very dangerous to our physical bodies. I've heard about many people who were injured during church projects. Sadly a local person was trying to cut a tree limb at church while standing in the bucket of a backhoe and he slipped and the chainsaw killed him. Remember Satan wants to kill, steal and destroy! Just because you are doing a church project does not give you immunity from accidents. You cannot cut corners on safety just because you're doing something for God. If it says, "Do not stand on or above this step" then don't! If you need help, ask others and don't let your pride get you hurt or killed.

I've watched people who were good at the gift of Helps become unable to do the physical jobs they did in the past because their body was failing them. I've talked with several people in my office who were down on themselves for not being able to do the projects for the church any more. They would often help with things like Carpenters for Christ projects but found themselves unable to swing a hammer because of their physical condition. I'd ask them, "Can you make a sandwich?" They always answered yes. I'd ask, "Can you make and pour lemonade? Yes again. I'd ask, "Did they ever serve you sandwiches and lemonade on those projects?" Their eyes began to brighten as I say, "Why aren't you there serving sandwiches and lemonade?"

It's like a light bulb comes on in their head as they begin to see a purpose for their life again. I went a little further and told them that a problem could come up that they may know how to fix and their experience could come in handy to tell how to fix it. I told them the most important thing is they may get the chance to talk about Jesus to others while they are there.

Pride can come in many forms and thinking you are useless because you can no longer do grand things is actually a source of pride. By placing a higher value on certain abilities you can devalue others. If you find yourself no longer able to do what you thought of as the important abilities for the church, they still need sandwiches, lemonade and someone to talk about Jesus! Suck-it-up-buttercup and learn that every part of the body of Christ is important. Get back in the game and share a sandwich and share Jesus. Then pour lemonade and pour out His love on others.

> *"Faithful servants never retire. You can retire from your career, but you will never retire from serving God."*[87]
>
> -Rick Warren

"Whoever can be trusted with very little can also be trusted with much, and whoever is dishonest with very little will also be dishonest with much." Luke 16:10

Jesus was speaking directly about the love of money in this verse but it can be applied to any idol we desire over God. We can have pride in our own abilities even if our abilities are not as good as we think they are and they become an idol. Sadly some people may have a dream to sing solos in front of the church but their voice is not as good as several singers already doing the job. I've watched people think they're an awesome singer and try out for solos, but they only get a spot on Wednesday night and not Sunday mornings. Their love of self eventually devastates them and they quit because they think they are too good for Wednesday nights and deserve the spotlight on Sundays.

Maybe God is training you, but you need to be **"trusted with very little"** at first. Maybe singing with the children or at Elder Care homes is more important than the big spotlight. Let God use you where He knows you will have the most impact and growth so later you will **"be trusted with much."**

"Some people have a warped idea of living the Christian life. Seeing talented, successful Christians, they attempt to imitate them. For them, the grass on the other side of the fence is always greener. But when they discover that their own gifts are different or their contributions are more modest (or even invisible), they collapse in discouragement and overlook genuine opportunities that are open to them. They have forgotten that they are here to serve Christ, not themselves."[88]
                                                              -Billy Graham

STOP feeling useless for God because your body is broken or you're not as good as others in the spot lights.

LOOK for little things that need to be done to bless others. Remember dynamite comes in small packages but has great power.

LISTEN for opportunities to be a witness and share Jesus with others as you serve in the big and small things.

BE WHAT GOD CREATED YOU TO BE, even if it's a sandwich-making-Jesus-lover if necessary!

PROTECTING YOURSELF FROM THE GIFT-KILLERS OF THE SANDALS OF READINESS

LIVING IN FORGIVENESS

"If we confess our sins, he is faithful and just and will forgive us our sins and purify us from all unrighteousness."
1 John 1:9

The group of spiritual gifts related to the Sandals of Readiness has a tough time with this Scripture because many of them do not feel forgiven. God states very clearly He will ***"purify us from all unrighteousness"*** because of His Son's sacrifice for us. Still many people have a tough time "forgiving themselves" which is not a Biblical statement.

We cannot forgive ourselves of our sins, only God can forgive us of our sins. It's really about feeling unworthy to live in the freedom of forgiveness! When someone believes the lies from Satan they will live in his condemnation and become trapped in the bondage of their past. Satan convinces them they are too dirty to be forgiven. They need to resist the devil and allow themselves to live in God's forgiveness with a life full of joy in His freedom.

> *"...let us draw near to God with a sincere heart and with the full assurance that faith brings, having our hearts sprinkled to cleanse us from a guilty conscience and having our bodies washed with pure water."*   Hebrews 10:22

God gives us an unimaginable freedom from the shame and guilt of our past through His grace and forgiveness. God wants to *"cleanse us from a guilty conscience"* and free us from the bondage of our sins forever. When we *"draw near to God"* we can experience the love of our heavenly Father which drives out fear. His perfect love drives out the fear of not measuring up. It drives out the fear of what others think. It drives out the fear of feeling useless. It also drives out the fears from our past and gives us hope for our future with Him.

> *"The Lord is compassionate and gracious, slow to anger, abounding in love. He will not always accuse, nor will he harbor his anger forever; he does not treat us as our sins deserve or repay us according to our iniquities. For as high as the heavens are above the earth, so great is his love for those who fear him; as far as the east is from the west, so far has he removed our transgressions from us."*
> Psalm 103:8-12

Do you know how far the *"east is from the west?"* You can travel north and eventually begin to travel south yet when you travel east you will never travel west! God is *"abounding in love"* for you and wants you to live in the freedom of forgiveness so you can find joy in building His kingdom. He is for the broken hearted and He wants you to live guilt-free and have peace in this life. He does not want you to worry; He has your life in His hands.

> *"Who of you by worrying can add a single hour to your life?*
> *Since you cannot do this very little thing, why do you worry*
> *about the rest?"*   Luke 12:25-26

When my wife worries, I ask her how many times the imaginary catastrophic event has ever happened? She constantly worries about what others think about her. Her "on time" is 15 minutes early so she doesn't disappoint anyone by being late. She worries about what to wear to church and what to bring to potluck dinners. When choosing an outfit she asks me what I think and I tell her, then she usually chooses another one. I'm beginning to think I am her anti-advice counselor for choosing clothing. She worries about the day-to-day troubles in our lives and has a difficult time allowing God to work His peace in her.

> *"I have told you these things, so that in me you may have*
> *peace. In this world you will have trouble. But take heart! I*
> *have overcome the world."*   John 16:33

"In this world you will have trouble" but God says *"I have overcome the world!"* What is your attitude during troubling times? Do you know and understand that all things work for the pattern of good for those who love Him? Do you have peace in all circumstances? Do you really know whose you are and do you know how much He loves you? Remember His perfect love drives out fear!

> *"... in all these things we are more than conquerors through*
> *him who loved us. For I am convinced that neither death*
> *nor life, neither angels nor demons, neither the present nor*
> *the future, nor any powers, neither height nor depth, nor*
> *anything else in all creation, will be able to separate us*
> *from the love of God that is in Christ Jesus our Lord."*
>   Romans 8:37-39

With that much love from our Father in heaven do you live daily in an attitude of gratitude? Forgiveness creates a path to gratitude and gratitude creates a path to joy in your life. Do you see the peaceful joy filled plans He has for you?

BEING A CHILD OF DIVORCE

"So do not fear, for I am with you; do not be dismayed, for I am your God. I will strengthen you and help you; I will uphold you with my righteous right hand."
Isaiah 41:10

When I was a child and my Mom and Dad were going through a divorce I didn't see God's plans for my life. I was full of fear and only saw the heartache and pain in my life. Everything was turned upside down. I was crying and giving my Mom fits and asking her to take my Dad back every day. I was 9 years old I did not understand everything going on around me.

One day, early in the divorce, I received some fund raising pamphlets for magazine subscriptions from my elementary school. I begged Mom to take me to my Dad to ask if he wanted any of these subscriptions to help my school. Keep in mind he was living in a motel at the time.

My Mom took me to his motel. His car was out front and we knocked on the door but he did not answer. Mom and I walked around the back of the Motel and a woman was getting dressed as she was leaving out the back door of Dad's room. I looked up at my Mom's face and even though she was a beautiful petite redhead her face looked like Maude from the old TV show. Maude always looked so angry and mad to me; now my Mom looked like her.

We went in Dad's room and I started to show him the magazines available and I saw some toys for a child younger than me. I asked, "Are those toys for me?" Dad answered, "No, those belong to the lady's son that just left." After I left I never gave Mom any more trouble. I saw clearly what was happening; Dad did not want me anymore. This was the moment that shaped my life for decades to come and I lost my childhood that day.

Fast forward 45 years and in an interesting turn of events I received a letter while the writing about forgiveness in this chapter. The letter was from the "woman at the back door." She was asking me for forgiveness. I had forgiven her and my Dad many years before this but the letter brought so much to my attention about forgiveness.

The vast majority of bad things that happened to me as a child were a result of her and my Dad's choices. I felt so alone because Dad was not paying his child support and my Mom had worked many hours to keep us fed and in our home so I did not see much of her. I was bullied at school and I was bullied by a neighbor's son when I got off the bus. It was a miserable life but I buried my pain. My Mom would let my Dad see me on occasion but he was involved with other more important things so I was not a priority in his life. It was also very awkward being at Dad's home with his new wife; the "woman at the back door."

My Dad and I had no real relationship and I rarely saw him for many years. In my senior year of High School my Dad must have begun to experience guilt about what he had done to me through his life choices. He offered to "buy me back" and showed his "love" through financial means. He was doing pretty well financially and my Mom and I were struggling. Mom had moved us to Davenport Iowa for her to attend Chiropractic College in the middle of my junior year of High School.

It was a miserable time in my life. My girlfriend broke up with me due to the long distance relationship. I found myself drinking heavily at keg parties to cope with the break-up and leaving my friends in Alabama. My Dad was doing very well financially and offered to pay for an apartment near my old High School to let me finish my senior year with my friends. He offered me his 1979 Trans Am in 1980 to drive along with a Shell credit card. I guess he was feeling pretty guilty for his past behaviors. It was dreams come true for a teenager, what kid wouldn't jump at that offer so I jumped.

I was so glad to be happy again. I didn't even throw a party at my apartment until my last day there for fear of losing it. I was actually a pretty good kid compared to the path I was on in Iowa. Unfortunately the emotional baggage from my past warped my heart and I left a string of empty relationships in Alabama.

After High School, I moved back in with Dad and the "woman at the back door" in Louisiana. He offered to pay for my college and put me in a dorm. I worked for my Dad remodeling homes with a group of friends and my girlfriend. We fixed them up and Dad rented them. I learned quite a lot of remodeling skills that have served me for a lifetime. Life was pretty good for an older teenager.

> *"See to it that no one takes you captive through hollow and deceptive philosophy, which depends on human tradition and the elemental spiritual forces of this world rather than on Christ."* Colossians 2:8

Unfortunately church was never a priority when I was young and I definitely was not seeking a closer relationship with Christ. I don't even remember praying one time through my tough times in Iowa. I had no discipleship or positive male role models in my life to help give me good guidance. I was trapped by the world.

I had no real relationship with God but I loved science. I began to believe all the professors with all the letters after their names and they became my role models. I was held *"captive through hollow and deceptive philosophy"* which I chose to believe. I wrongly believed God did not care personally about me or anyone else on the planet. I thought God wound up the universe and stepped back to watch. I became a theistic evolutionist, believing God used evolution to create the universe. This caused me to drift even further from Him and do bad things accordingly. But God was still working in my life even as I was drifting from Him. He never let go of me!

Around this time in my life the "woman at the back door" was trying to become a better person. She was trying to clean up her life by attending church and she tried to play match maker for me with a girl from her church. Florine and I did not hit it off as a couple but I brought my friend Dewayne over to the house and she was there for a shower. It was love at first sight for Dewayne and he said he was going to marry her one day. I thought he was crazy!

He arranged a first date with Florine to go canoeing in the bayou at our college. She was too young to drive and her best friend, who lived next door, brought her in a Subaru Brat to the parking lot behind our dorm next to the bayou. The elevator was not working in our 11 story dorm and I happened to be coming down the stairs and met the driver. It was Teresa, who is now my wife of over 40 years and the Mother of my over 29 year old son. Florine and Dewayne married and have two girls who have given them several grandchildren. We all continue to be best friends to this day. There is so much more to this story and it took decades for me to see how God was working in my life.

My Dad and I drifted apart for several reasons and I had not seen him in 20 years. I was contacted by his fourth wife, Mary Jo, a few years ago telling me my Dad had dementia. I feared they wanted me to care for him and I could not take on that burden. I was caring for my Mom with Alzheimer's and I had cared for other family members in the past. I really did not want to add caring for my Dad to the list.

My son decided, on his own, to contact Mary Jo and see what she wanted. He found out my Dad wanted to apologize to me and ask for forgiveness and it had nothing to do with caring for him. I called my Dad and had a few conversations with him and he seemed genuinely sorry and very humble. It felt like I was giving a dying man his last wish.

Some time passed and Mary Jo had to put my Dad in a home. At that time I received a letter from the "woman at the back door" asking for forgiveness for what she had done. Do you think God has some amazing timing? This was during the time I was writing on forgiveness! God touched my heart and prompted me to drive to Louisiana to see my Dad for the first time in 20 years on November 2, 2019.

Dad was sitting in his rocking chair. He looked older and a bit more humped over because of his osteoporosis. He still had his old habits from clearing his throat to his childlike grin. We talked and he asked me who I was and I told him I was his son, Michael. He processed for a moment and asked who my mother was and I told him Brenda. I could tell the memories were not all there. As we talked I realized God had erased all the bad memories in his life. He seemed at peace!

We talked for a couple of hours. We laughed and cut up a bit. He was in a good mood except he was sad about being in the home and having to do what he was told to do. He just wanted to be at his home. I reassured him it was for his safety. Having been through this with my Mom, I explained that when we have trouble with our brain we could have a lapse of judgment. In that moment we could leave our home and get lost and even die of exposure or starvation in the woods. He nodded but was still unhappy about not being home. I told him I needed to leave and we stood up and hugged. I could not help but say to him, "I love you." It felt right and I had a Dad for that moment in time. God gave me a Dad who was free from all the bad things in the past as a gift for my obedience of seeing him.

As we were walking out Mary Jo entered the building and my Dad lit up like a Christmas tree. He gave her a sweet compliment and got a hug. She was carrying a box of Ginger Snap cookies and told me how he had gotten down to 105 pounds. She was doing everything she could to help him put on some weight. I caught up with her about her two children and more about my Dad's condition. We all hugged and I went on my way.

While driving home I began processing all the emotions, actions and information of the day. I thought it was funny how Mary Jo gave Ginger

Snaps to my Dad. My son was just telling me about how he was going to be giving out Ginger Snaps during the Christmas parties at Disney World in front of the Jungle Cruise where he works. It reminded me of when I told my Son I would never want to go back and change anything in my life because I could never duplicate the ability to have him as my Son.

While Teresa was driving home from Louisiana, I wrote a Facebook post about my time with Dad and received many encouraging comments and reactions. The first comment was from Florine. Instantly I had an amazing message from God. He revealed to me that if it were not for the "woman at the back door" I would have never been introduced to Florine. She would have never met Dewayne, gotten married and had their children and grandchildren and I would have never met Florine's best friend Teresa. I would have never married her and had my son, Brody. What does Romans 8:28 say…

> *"And we know that in all things God works for the good of those who love him, who have been called according to his purpose. For those God foreknew he also predestined to be conformed to the image of his Son, that he might be the firstborn among many brothers and sisters. And those he predestined, he also called; those he called, he also justified; those he justified, he also glorified."*
>
> Romans 8:28-30

God is working in thousands of places in your life you cannot see! I had never really put it all together to see how God worked a horrible time in my life for good. But when God says He *"works for the good of those who love him,"* I get it now! The "woman at the back door," a terrible childhood, being bullied and living selfishly has all eventually worked *"for the good"* in my life to be called to serve God. He showed up and showed me how all those imperfections can work to become perfections from Him! I was extremely fortunate to see it happen while I was still alive.

You may be blessed to see it during your lifetime or you may need to wait for heaven to have God's goodness revealed from past hurts but His Word is truth! Will you allow Him to work during those dark times in your life? Will you stay close to Him through thick and thin? Will you allow God to help you *"conform to the image of His son?"*

> *"Therefore we do not lose heart. Though outwardly we are wasting away, yet inwardly we are being renewed day by day. For our light and momentary troubles are achieving for us an eternal glory that far outweighs them all. So we fix our eyes not on what is seen, but on what is unseen, since what is seen is temporary, but what is unseen is eternal."*
>
> 2 Corinthians 4:16-18

You received Grace, so give Grace to others. Grace got you saved, so you are forgiven; act like it and live in that freedom! Grace takes us from worthless to worthy and from orphans to belonging to a family! The *"momentary troubles"* we go through are a drop in the ocean compared to the *"eternal glory"* we will receive. Fix your eyes on the eternal and *"do not lose heart!"* Allow yourself to be *"renewed day by day"* so you *"do not lose heart."*

HOW TO FORGIVE OTHERS

Since you've been forgiven show forgiveness to others. This is a problem area for this group of gifts in the Sandals. To let someone off the hook and let go of the hurt feels like we are saying it was ok for them to have hurt us. Satan wants us to hold on to the hurt because he knows the more hurts we hold, the less effective we are for God and His Kingdom. What Satan tells us goes against everything Jesus said about forgiveness.

Imagine if I was hiking with a friend and I put a few rocks in their backpack every time we took a break. Eventually they would slow down more and more until they were unable to carry the pack. This is what un-forgiveness does to a Christian as they load hurt after hurt into their backpack and try to keep moving. How much weight of your un-forgiveness can you carry and for how long?

Forgiveness may be difficult but it's necessary to mature in Christ and build up the Body of Christ. As you go through the process of forgiving others, think about the grace and forgiveness God has given you for your past. Think about the eternal plans He has for you. Here are some helpful steps toward forgiving others:

1) Say, "I Forgive Them."

> *"Bear with each other and forgive one another if any of you has a grievance against someone. Forgive as the Lord forgave you."*   Colossians 3:13

This is out of your obedience to God. Think of the grace God shows you every day of your life to begin this process. The first step of forgiveness may be the hardest but just do it! If you have to say it through gritted teeth, do it! Just say you forgive them. It may take years to get to the next step but it's possible, so don't give up.

2) Say, "I Forgive Them." Then Pray for Them.

> *"Do not judge, and you will not be judged. Do not condemn, and you will not be condemned. Forgive, and you will be forgiven."*   Luke 6:37

This is out of your love for God. Think about the forgiveness you received from God as you pray for those who have hurt you. Think about the times when you needed prayer to get out the mess you were in. It can be a quick, "God bless them" or something more specific but start praying for them. Your forgiveness and prayer may open some doors in heaven to help change the person for the better. At this point you have most likely begun healing from the hurts you received. Now it is time for you to help others going through similar hurts. Share with them how forgiveness has helped heal your heart.

3) Say, "I Forgive Them." Then Pray For Them and Rejoice When Something Good Happens to Them.

> *"But to you who are listening I say: love your enemies, do good to those who hate you, bless those who curse you, pray for those who ill-treat you."*   Luke 6:27-29

This is out of God's love for us. Remember you do not deserve anything but death but Jesus forgave you and is giving you a free home in heaven for eternity. Think eternal because the short time you're here will be nothing compared to an eternity in heaven. Forgive and be set free. Stop worrying about the "why" of life and focus on "how" you can live for Christ. There you will find peace.

> *"We win by tenderness. We conquer by forgiveness."*[89]
> -Frederick W. Robertson

> *"Be kind and compassionate to one another, forgiving each other, just as in Christ God forgave you."*
> Ephesians 4:32

CONQUERING YOUR FEARS:

> *"God is love. Whoever lives in love lives in God, and God in them. This is how love is made complete among us so that we will have confidence on the day of judgment: In this world we are like Jesus. There is no fear in love. But perfect love drives out fear, because fear has to do with punishment. The one who fears is not made perfect in love."*
> 1 John 4:16-18

Faith knows God, trusts God and loves God. God already loves you more than you could ever imagine so rejoice, be grateful and feel loved by Him. His *"perfect love"* casts out fear! Being fearful punishes yourself and keeps you from reaching your full potential in Christ. Be the *"whoever lives in love lives in God"* and have Him do amazing things through you. Open your heart to God and tell Satan "Not Today" when he tries to cast fear in your life! Replace his attacks with Scriptures about how much God loves you and remember His *"perfect love drives out fear."*

> *"I sought the Lord, and he answered me; he delivered me from all my fears. Those who look to him are radiant; their faces are never covered with shame."*
> Psalm 34:4-5

Living in un-forgiveness leads to some serious issues as anger, hate and rage take over your life. It starts with worrying over stupid minor mistakes, missed opportunities, what others think about you and replaying bad life events over and over in your head. This spirals into regret, depression, shame and self-hatred as fear takes over your life.

Fear left unchecked can lead to an Avoidant Personality Disorder. People become over sensitive to rejection and criticism from their feelings of inadequacies and insignificance. They begin to avoid activities with personal contact, especially those where they have to meeting new people. This leads to becoming socially inhibited to the point of isolating themselves from others. This disorder feeds on itself as their fear of disapproval and embarrassment causes more social distancing. Avoiding strangers causes less interaction with others which causes more isolation which causes more anxiety about rejection and ridicule. This vicious cycle steals the life of a person buried under a mountain of fear.

> *"Worry does not empty tomorrow of its sorrows; it empties today of its strength."*[90]
> -Corrie Ten Boom

You need to remember God is with you every step of the way. You are not alone; your Creator cares about you and your anxieties. He wants you to overcome your fears and be all that He created you to be. There are several things you can do to help calm your fears:

KNOW WHO'S IN CONTROL

"When I said, 'My foot is slipping,' your unfailing love, Lord, supported me. When anxiety was great within me, your consolation brought me joy." Psalm 94:18-19

Being fearful is equal to being out of control. God is always in control of every circumstance; allow Him to be in control of your circumstances. You have an eternal security with God: what is this day compared to an eternity with Him? Allow God to support you during times of great anxiety. Let His Word and His perfectly timed hugs bring you joy!

REALIZE EXPERIENCING FEARS IS NORMAL

"Even though I walk through the darkest valley, I will fear no evil, for you are with me; your rod and your staff, they comfort me." Psalm 23:4

There would not be the topic of "Do not fear" written at least 365 times in Scripture if it were not a common problem with people. Fear can protect you in situations but it can cripple you in others. Much of conquering fear is controlling it to work for you. Most fears are learned and can be unlearned. You have 3 choices; one is to solve the problem that is making you anxious. Another way is to control your level of anxiety to manageable levels through self-control. The last choice is to live in fear and allow Satan to gain a foothold in your life and reduce your ability to serve God.

IDENTIFY YOUR FEARS

"So do not be afraid of them, for there is nothing concealed that will not be disclosed, or hidden that will not be made known. What I tell you in the dark, speak in the daylight; what is whispered in your ear, proclaim from the roofs. Do not be afraid of those who kill the body but cannot kill the soul." Matthew 10:26-28

There are fears of open spaces, confined spaces, animals, insects, snakes, storms, needles, flying, etc. You should have more of a fear of hell than the fears in your life. Are you able to help save someone from Hell if you are controlled by your own fears and cannot push past those fears? Is it worth bringing someone to Christ and keeping them out of Hell by pushing past your fears?

Learn the difference between a good fear that protects you and the fears that cripples you. Study your fear and learn the actual statistics of falling off a building by accident or getting bit by a bat. Identify triggers like caffeine, alcohol, smoking, not eating and stressful situations. Eliminate or avoid them if at all possible. Continue to think eternal when fear creeps in on you.

VISUALIZE OVERCOMING YOUR FEARS

"The Lord is my light and my salvation - whom shall I fear? The Lord is the stronghold of my life - of whom shall I be afraid? When the wicked advance against me to devour me, it is my enemies and my foes who will stumble and fall." Psalm 27:1-2

Look at yourself as God sees you. You are an overcomer and He sees your value. See yourself through God's eyes as His loved child positively completing the task that brings you so much fear. Imagine your *"foes who will stumble and fall"* Imagine being a *"well done good and faithful servant of God"* who has the power of God behind you!

TACKLE YOUR FEARS AS QUICKLY AS POSSIBLE

"Do not be afraid of them; the Lord your God himself will fight for you." Deuteronomy 3:22

Delay gives strength to fear, so avoid talking yourself into putting off the problem or completely talking yourself out of tackling your fears. Most of the time, the delaying of something fearful becomes worse than the actual fear. Delay also allows more problems to tag on to the one you are dealing with. Do your best to focus on one issue at a time and tackle it quickly. Practice and prepare then take the fear head on all-the-while giving it all you got. Do what you fear to do and watch your confidence grow.

GET OUT OF YOUR COMFORT ZONE

"Have I not commanded you? Be strong and courageous. Do not be afraid; do not be discouraged, for the Lord your God will be with you wherever you go." Joshua 1:9

Seek God's Will for your life no matter where He takes you and *"do not be afraid."* The world seeks comfort; God seeks the results outside your comfort zones. Don't settle for being average for Christ. If it's Biblical and He's calling you to do it then get off your rump and do it because *"God will be with you wherever you go!"*

"But he said to me, 'My grace is sufficient for you, for my power is made perfect in weakness.' Therefore I will boast all the more gladly about my weaknesses, so that Christ's power may rest on me." 2 Corinthians 12:9

You must trust God in your weakness to see His perfection take place on Earth. Gather the courage you need to take the first steps of His Will for your life and be amazed at the wonders He will do through you and your gifts.

RENEW YOUR MIND

"The mind governed by the flesh is death, but the mind governed by the Spirit is life and peace."

Romans 8:6

Fill your mind with the good things of the Holy Spirit. Listen to Christian music, read God's Word, talk to God and do not give up meeting with other Christians. By doing these things you will easily recognize what is from God and what is of Satan. Idle minds give Satan a place to plant his lies. Stop giving him the fertilizer to grow bad thoughts into bad actions. Let God continually help you through every hour of every day of your life by keeping your mind on Him.

KNOW THE BASICS TO FIGHT FEAR

"The Lord himself goes before you and will be with you; he will never leave you nor forsake you. Do not be afraid; do not be discouraged." Deuteronomy 31:8

Get plenty of good sleep, eat healthy, exercise and avoid unnecessary stimulants, drugs, smoking and alcohol. Give yourself rewards and develop good friendships. Use friendships to carefully share your life with and build each other up in Christ. Speak life into each other with kind texts and sharing uplifting memes and videos. Little acts of encouragement can go a long way in helping with stress filled times. But be sure to speak life into yourself. When you find yourself in a tough situation think about what you would say to a friend going through the same thing.

You either have to fight your battle or run from it and Elijah ran from Jezebel when he was afraid of being killed by her. God helped Elijah and had him rest, sent angels to feed him and then asked him to get some exercise through walking. God tried to get him out of his "fight or flight" mechanism from stress and get him into the "rest and digest" mechanism so his body and mind could rest and repair. It is very important to physically take care of what God gave you when you start tackling your fears

BE THANKFUL

"Let the peace of Christ rule in your hearts, since as members of one body you were called to peace. And be thankful."
Colossians 3:15

Practice an attitude of gratitude and thank the Lord for all He has done for you. Thank Him for His priceless eternal blessing of heaven. Be thankful for having access to God's Word so you can learn more about Him and grow your trust in Him for your life's purpose. Thank God for the spiritual gifts He freely gave to you to make you special. Be thankful you can use those gifts to show Christ to others and lead them to heaven with you.

"Gratitude produces deep, abiding joy because we know that God is working in us, even through difficulties."[91]
-Charles Stanley

GROWTH IN CHRIST
The Spiritual Gifts Related to
The Sandals of Readiness

UNDERSTAND "WHOSE" YOU ARE

"Your eyes saw my unformed body; all the days ordained for me were written in your book before one of them came to be. How precious to me are your thoughts, God! How vast is the sum of them! Were I to count them, they would outnumber the grains of sand - when I awake, I am still with you."

Psalm 139:16-18

You are not just a slave to accomplish God's "to do" list! He knew you before you were born and you are a loved child of God. He sees you as perfect because of Jesus' sacrifice and gives you a home in heaven. Does God have a purpose for you? Yes He does. Does He have some things He wants you to do? Yes He does, but His "to do" list not only helps others it also helps bring you joy and purpose!

CONFESS AND PROGRESS

"But thanks be to God! He gives us the victory through our Lord Jesus Christ."   1 Corinthians 15:57

Worry, anxiety and fear can result in stopping the use of your spiritual gifts. You were given the spirit of power, love and a sound mind by God! If He is for you who can be against you? He gave you *"victory through our Lord Jesus Christ!"* Confess your shortcomings to God and allow Him to work through your weaknesses. This will only magnify how much He loves you. Allow His perfect love to drive out every last ounce of fear left in you. Move forward one step at a time working side by side with God to accomplish an awesome life through the building up of His Kingdom. Then watch as you are amazed beyond your wildest imagination!

COMMUNICATE WITH GOD

"I have told you this so that my joy may be in you and that your joy may be complete."   John 15:11

How do you know what to give to a person at just the right time? How do you know their needs at that very moment? God tells you these things so you can bless others and *"your joy may be complete."* There are needs all around us 24/7 but you know the ones that make big differences in people's lives by communicating with God. Let Him show you the "who" and "how" to help and be obedient to your calling. Listen carefully and make sure you are not just saying "yes" to please others or gain popularity. Use God to confirm your activities to help you be free from burnout and fatigue. Be sure not to serve out of guilt; serve out of His love for you so His *"joy may be in you."*

USING THE SPIRITUAL GIFTS REPRESENTED BY THE SANDALS OF READINESS WITH THE FRUITS OF THE SPIRIT

LOVE: Do you love praise from people or from God? Are you serving out of an appreciation of the love of God or from trying to make up to Him for your life's mistakes? Let His love flow through you freely without hang up's from your past hurts or shame.

JOY: Do you still receive joy for a job well done for Christ? When you finish a project, Is there a moment when you sit back and relax into His presence? God took a break on the seventh day to admire His work. He wants you to receive a joyful moment for your well done works. Lay back into the arms of Jesus and receive that joyful moment, get rested and then say, "Here I am send me!"

PEACE: Does worry and un-forgiveness destroy your peace? Take time to dwell on God's Words for the peace He desires for your life. Feed your servant's heart with God's love to drive out anxiety and fear. Pray and read, but most of all get your hugs from Jesus.

PATIENCE: Do you get frustrated when you seem to be the only one doing anything for God? Do you take away tasks from others to get them done faster and better? Your impatience runs others off because they feel they can't do anything right for you. Stop running workers off and build them up so they can develop the skills needed to finish the task. Show them their potential and train them up in a loving way so you can build up an army to help create even bigger projects!

KINDNESS: Do you have time to do special things with your family? Are you too busy to spend time with those you love? Is what you're doing worth sacrificing your family? A "burned-out schedule" leaves little room for kindness.

GOODNESS: Are you cheerful with others and take time to ask how their life is doing? Are you so busy that you rush through any meaningful conversations to work on the projects? If someone asks how are you doing do you only speak of yourself and never ask how they were doing? It's not all about you, slow down and build Godly relationships with others.

FAITHFULNESS: Do you ever completely allow God to handle even one of your projects or problems? Having Faith is trusting God in all circumstances. Let's face it, you have trouble letting anyone including God handle your projects or your problems. When you get tired of doing everything by yourself He will be patiently waiting to help you. He knows what is best for you. Have Faith in God's Faithfulness, not your own Faith.

GENTLENESS: Are you short with waiters and cashiers? Are the kids with you when you aren't acting exactly gentle? You may brush it off as having a bad day or a stressful work problem but what about the other person. What if they just lost a spouse or they were wondering how they are going to pay bills this month. Your gentleness may be the only face of Jesus they ever see and it may change their lives. Your actions influence others, especially those closest to you.

SELF-CONTROL: Do your fears and worries run out of control when you think of the worst possible outcome? The ever increasing fear of failure will keep you from reaching your full potential and stop the use of your gifts. Ask yourself if these "worst possible outcomes" ever come true. Imagine yourself doing your best in the upcoming project and imagine Jesus cheering you on to do your best.

TAKE THE MIRROR TEST

"I no longer call you servants, because a servant does not know his master's business. Instead, I have called you friends, for everything that I learned from my Father I have made known to you." John 15:15

What was that blur in the mirror? Wait, please stop and be still for a moment. Yes you look great today, stop primping and worrying about what you are going to wear to church today! Please listen! Stop worrying so much about your outward appearance and whether or not it lives up to what others think about you. Look in the mirror and see what the Creator of the universe sees in you. You are a wonderfully-crafted child of the Most High! He sees you as a friend with whom He has shared some of His most innermost thoughts! You have so much potential that you have buried beneath the worries, riches and pleasures of the world. Let God help you dig yourself out of the self-made grave of fear. God has plans for you that will blow your mind and take you further than you could have ever imagined.

STOP burying yourself under your fears.
LOOK at the ways God continually loves on you.
LISTEN to His promises of perfect love and let it drive out the fears in your life.

BE WHAT GOD CREATED YOU TO BE; a fearless child of God helping prepare a way to build up the Body of Christ.

> *"Fear is a self-imposed prison that will keep you from becoming what God intends for you to be. You must move against it with the weapons of faith and love."*[92]   -Rick Warren

> **"I know what it is to be in need, and I know what it is to have plenty. I have learned the secret of being content in any and every situation, whether well fed or hungry, whether living in plenty or in want. I can do all this through him who gives me strength."**   Philippians 4:12-13

PONDERING POINTS

What are the gifts related to the Sandals of Readiness?

How are the Sandals an important piece of Armor physically?

How are the Sandals an important piece of Armor spiritually?

What is the goal of the gifts of the Sandals?

What is the purpose of the gifts of the Sandals?

What is the strength of the gifts of the Sandals?

What is the main weakness of the gifts in the Sandals?

Are your works based on Salvation, Guilt or Selfishness?

Are you trying to work off your sins through good works?

Are you forced into works from not being able to say, "No?"

Do you look for a pat-on-the-back for your good works?

What makes good works good?

Do you have un-forgiveness toward others in your life?

Do you allow yourself to be forgiven?

Do you live in God's forgiveness?

Do you judge others?

Do you leave time to train others so they can be used of God?

Do you justify any worldly idols in your life?

Do you have fears in your life?

Have you conquered the fears in your life?

What drives out fear?

What are you grateful for in your life?

What fears can stop these gifts?

"When we stray from His presence, He longs for you to come back. He weeps that you are missing out on His love, protection and provision. He throws His arms open, runs toward you, gathers you up, and welcomes you home."[93]   -Charles Stanley

CHAPTER TWELVE
THE SHIELD OF FAITH

"In addition to all this, take up the shield of faith, with which you can extinguish all the flaming arrows of the evil one."
Ephesians 6:16

Faith is represented by a door sized shield capable of protecting the entire soldier from attack. It was well-built with wood and metal and was designed to stop arrows and javelins. On the front of the shield was cloth or leather that could be soaked with water to help *"extinguish all the flaming arrows"* shot at them from the enemy. The shields could be lined up side by side to form a wall and block the enemy's attacks.

Another highly effective defense was for soldiers to hold up their shields and work together to form a rectangle of shields around the outside of the formation. This allowed them to be protected from any direction. The soldiers in the middle would hold their shields overhead forming the Testudo Formation to form a tortoise-like shell of protection. If anyone moved out of place, whether they were moving too slow or too fast, it would create a weak spot for attacks. This maneuver took great obedience and unity within the group of soldiers.

It states, *"...take up the shield of faith"* indicating an action is required by the user of the shield. *"Take up"* literally means to aggressively receive what is available. The soldier is given a shield to use by the army they are serving just as God gave Christians the Shield of Faith. Just as we are too eagerly desire spiritual gifts, we are to actively take the Faith God is offering for our protection.

The shield is held in place with the less dominate hand while the dominate hand holds the Sword of the Spirit. What are you doing with your hands? Does one hand hold your shield in place and the other hold the sword? Is there anything more important to hold in your hands when the enemy attacks?

For Christians, the Shield of Faith is important in Spiritual Warfare. Notice the one who is shooting the flaming arrows in the Scripture is called *"the evil one."* When flaming arrows are coming from the sky in battle they are very distracting. It is hard to put out fires and fight an enemy at the same time. Satan loves to distract us with these flaming arrows to take our focus and direction off the main battle. Fortunately the shield helps extinguish the flames of the arrows but it takes unity in the Body of Christ to cover each other's back in battle.

> *"I appeal to you, brothers and sisters, in the name of our Lord Jesus Christ, that all of you agree with one another in what you say and that there be no divisions among you, but that you be perfectly united in mind and thought."*
> 1 Corinthians 1:10

Being alone in your Christian walk is full of dangerous roads where Satan is waiting to destroy you. It's best to have others covering your back and head with their shield as you hold yours in place to protect both them and yourself. *"Don't give up meeting together"* and remember "iron sharpens iron." We not only need to build each other up but we need to protect each other from Satan's attacks. We are more powerful against Satan when we are *"united in mind and thought"* than we are divided over minor issues.

> *"Be on your guard; stand firm in the faith; be courageous; be strong."* 1 Corinthians 16:13

You always need to *"be on your guard"* and *"stand firm in the faith"* against Satan's tactics to kill, steal and destroy. The Shield is designed to protect the entire Christian Soldier while wearing the Armor of God and the bigger the shield the better. Do you want an itty bitty shield or a big door sized shield when going up against Satan's fiery arrows in your life? What is the state of your Faith? Is your shield large or small? Your shield's size is dependent on your trust in God. Who you trust more, yourself or God?

"For we live by faith, not by sight." 2 Corinthians 5:7

With flaming arrows flying toward you it's hard to take a look at what is going on in front of the shield for fear of being hit in the head with an arrow. We need to trust in our commander in chief for instructions. As we stand firm behind the shield we need to wait until we are commanded to move.

We need to stand next to our brothers and sisters in Christ and keep the defensive blockade of shields tight so no arrows go through the front line. We must have confidence, trust and assurance in our Creator that He will give us the proper command to move at the proper time. By ignoring orders and moving out of line too quickly or to slowly, we will create a weak link in the line of shields. Proper shielding from the enemy requires unity in the Faith!

I am a fan of some sci-fi but I like it to be morally decent and believable. This tremendously limits the amount of sci-fi I enjoy. With that said, I have a strange vision of the Shield of Faith. I see the Shield being like an invisible force field. When a laser is fired at us while standing behind an invisible force field we shouldn't flinch. We should feel protected because we know the shield will stop the laser. If we *"live by Faith"* and *"not by sight,"* can we get to the point in our own lives to trust the Shield of Faith so we don't flinch when Satan shoots his flaming arrows in our direction?

"It's a weak faith that only serves God in times of blessing. The book of Job teaches us that true faith, genuine faith, great faith is revealed only when we serve and trust God in the hard times, the times of suffering, loss, and opposition. That's the kind of faith that makes the world sit up and take notice."[94]

-Ray Stedman

SPIRITUAL GIFT REPRESENTED BY THE SHELD OF FAITH

Faith

When you are around people overflowing with the spiritual gift of Faith they seem to have a comfort bubble around them. It's like a warm blanket and a hug from Jesus. A person overflowing with Faith understands God's Grace and is usually a very humble servant of God. They are completely dependent upon Him and they trust Him to guide their lives. They are filled with peace and tranquility and give hope to those without hope. They seem to always have extra portions of Faith to pass around to those needing it the most.

Here is the Scriptural definition of Faith from three different Bible translations:

> *"Now faith is confidence in what we hope for and assurance about what we do not see. This is what the ancients were commended for."*   Hebrews 11:1 NIV

> *"Now faith is the substance of things hoped for, the evidence of things not seen. For by it the elders obtained a good report."*   Hebrews 11:1 KJV

"Now faith is the assurance (title deed, confirmation) of things hoped for (divinely guaranteed), and the evidence of things not seen [the conviction of their reality—faith comprehends as fact what cannot be experienced by the physical senses]. For by this [kind of] faith the men of old gained [divine] approval."

Hebrews 11:1-2 AMP Amplified Bible

The Amplified Bible version for this Scripture really defines Faith. It reads like a legal contract with God giving us a *"title deed"* for our home in heaven! I love the expressions *"confirmation"* and *"divinely guaranteed"* being used to describe our future home with God. The Men and Women of Scripture who were given *"[divine] approval"* for their Faith never fully received their promises from God on this Earth. Moses never saw the Promised Land, Abraham never saw a nation of people from his son, and all of them never saw their Messiah, Jesus Christ, until they reached heaven.

"These all died in faith, not having received the promises, but having seen them afar off, and were persuaded of them, and embraced them, and confessed that they were strangers and pilgrims on the earth."   Hebrews 11:13 KJV

They all had moments of Faith which helped prepare for the arrival of Jesus; some were even in the bloodline of Jesus. It is amazing what can be accomplished through acts of Faith no matter how large or how small! You never know what the smallest acts of Faith done in the name of the Lord can accomplish in the future.

"Be faithful in small things because it is in them that your strength lies."[95]   -Mother Teresa

"In the same way, faith by itself, if it is not accompanied by action, is dead."   James 2:17

James states *"faith by itself"* is not what we should be striving for in our relationship with God. It is the beginning of our relationship but Jesus told us even the Demons believed in Jesus. True Christian Faith should be a complete belief and trust in God. But it is more of a verb than a noun. To grow in Faith one's Faith needs to be *"accompanied by action"* and the action should complete a purpose. Think of it like a carpenter building a house. His action is to complete the house so someone can live in the house. The action of your Faith is becoming what God created you to be in order to accomplish your purpose. In everything we do, no matter how large or how small, we should know our purpose is sharing the Faithfulness of God with others.

"God has written us a book, and now we have the opportunity to respond with our words and actions."[96] -Jared Brock

THE TRI-UNITY OF FAITH ALIGNS WITH THE HOLY TRINITY

Faith is more than a spiritual gift or a piece of the Armor of God; it is also a Fruit of the Spirit. Faith is similar to the Trinity of God because it is also one thing with three parts. The Father, Son and Holy Spirit combine into the one true God. As humans we have a mind, a body and a spirit yet we are one. The Tri-unity of Faith is a spiritual gift, a Shield and a Fruit yet it is one thing when the object of Faith is directed toward God.

"The Lord is my rock, my fortress and my deliverer; my God is my rock, in whom I take refuge, my shield and the horn of my salvation. He is my stronghold, my refuge and my savior—from violent people you save me."
2 Samuel 22:2-3

The Shield of Faith represents Father God's protection and His promise of an eternity with Him no matter what happens here on Earth. Father God is described by being our rock, fortress, deliverer, refuge, shield, and our stronghold. He has a safe place for us in heaven that Jesus is preparing for us.

> *"But the fruit of the Spirit is love, joy, peace, forbearance, kindness, goodness, faithfulness, gentleness and self-control. Against such things there is no law. Those who belong to Christ Jesus have crucified the flesh with its passions and desires. Since we live by the Spirit, let us keep in step with the Spirit."* Galatians 5:22-25

The Fruit of the Spirit, Faithfulness, is represented by Jesus who showed all of the qualities of the Fruit of the Spirit especially love. Christians are supposed to copy these attributes and use them in their daily walk just as Jesus did when He walked the Earth. Jesus showed us the greatest Faith as He followed the Father's instructions without hesitation, even to His death!

> *"There are different kinds of gifts, but the same Spirit distributes them."* 1 Corinthians 12:4

The spiritual gift of Faith is represented by the Holy Spirit and He distributes all of the Spiritual Gifts. The spiritual gifts are designed to build up the church and the Holy Spirit helps teach us how to carry out God's Will and purpose here on Earth. The Holy Spirit is our Teacher, Advocate, Comforter, Helper, Reminder, and He convicts us of sin, testifies of Christ and helps us pray. He is also a source of wisdom, Revelation and helps us not to sin. These actions represent the majority of the Spiritual gifts purpose.

> *"The God who has claimed us for himself if Father, Son and Holy Spirit; not just Father, not just Son, not just Spirit. God is God FOR US – Father. God is God WITH US – Son. God is God IN US – Spirit"*[97] Darrell W. Johnson

FAITH IS A DIRECTIONAL FORCE

Faith is a direction, a group of Vector Forces! Hang on, I know this is higher math but let me explain. A vector is simply a line from point A to point B with a direction. The length of the line is the magnitude of the vector. The longer the vector is the greater the magnitude. So think of your life following Christ as a Vector. You started at point A, your Salvation, and the length of your Vector is how much you have become like Christ.

Now think about having 3 Vectors of Faith you are trying to keep pointed at Jesus to become more like Him. When we as Christians align the three parts of Faith and focus them with our trust in God, we can move mountains. Jesus said we can do greater things than what He did while He was on earth. When Peter kept his focus on Jesus, at least he got out of the boat and walked on water. But when Peter took his focus off Jesus and looked at the storm he sank and Jesus said to Peter, 'You of little Faith, why did you doubt?" Peter changed the direction of one of his Vectors of his Faith and moved it toward the storm. This weakened his Faith.

The application of the Tri-unity of Faith is more about what you as a Christian are doing with each part of your Faith. Are you living out the Fruit of the Spirit and becoming more like Jesus? Are you 110% assured of the promises of Father God and believe with all of your heart you are going to spend an eternity with Him? Are you allowing the Holy Spirit to guide you when you use your spiritual gifts so God's Will is accomplished through your actions? When you align these areas of your Faith you will experience the presence and power of God! But the reality is how much are you willing to live like Christ, Trust your Father God and Serve the Holy Spirit?

> *"Trust in the Lord with all your heart and lean not on your own understanding; in all your ways submit to him, and he will make your paths straight."* Proverbs 3:5-6

When you submit *"all your ways"* (plural) to Him; *"He will make your paths (plural) straight."* As Christians we obviously trust Jesus to be our Lord and Savior and we believe He is the Son of God but do we truly put our Faith and trust in Him. But how much Faith do we put in Him? Whose *"understanding"* do we lean on? Is our Faith directed inward toward ourselves or outward to what others think or do we have an upward Faith that will *"submit to Him"* and allow Him to make our *"paths straight?"* If He knows the best paths for our life then how much more should we trust Him?

"It is one thing to believe in God; it is quite another to believe God."[98]   -R.C. Sproul

WE ALL HAVE SPIRITUAL GIFTS PLURAL

We all have the spiritual gift of Faith? Faith is what led us to our salvation. Faith is the foundation of Christianity and that foundation should be firmly established in our lives. Faith believes in something unseen but our Faith should be seen by others around us; including our family, neighbors, and co-workers. Even though there are people with great Faith, we are all called to show our Faith no matter how much Faith we have.

THE GOAL OF
THE SHIELD OF FAITH
"To Overflow Faith to Others"

"For by the grace given me I say to every one of you: Do not think of yourself more highly than you ought, but rather think of yourself with sober judgment, in accordance with the faith God has distributed to each of you."
Romans 12:3

"Distributed to each of you" means using a measuring device for something dry or liquid. It's like a ruler or a cup. This means each of us

was *"distributed"* the same measure of Faith when we believed Jesus is the Son of God. What makes the amount of Faith in each person different is how you grow the seed of Faith inside of you.

Knowing we all have the spiritual gift of Faith makes us responsible to humbly put the gift into action and spread the Faith of God. We are responsible to Love God, Love Others and tell them about Him! Anyone who says they do not have a spiritual gift needs to know we all have a measure of Faith as a spiritual gift from God.

> *"...for everyone born of God overcomes the world. This is the victory that has overcome the world, even our faith. Who is it that overcomes the world? Only the one who believes that Jesus is the Son of God."*   1 John 5:4-5

Being *"born of God"* there are three primary ways to function in Faith and the first way is to love God with everything we have. If we love Him we trust Him for the next steps in our lives. Second is putting His love into action by loving others as we love ourselves and the third is telling people about our own Faith in Jesus. With these three actions we overcome the world!

Many Christians would love to have more Faith but struggle with how to grow their Faith. This is a touchy subject since it can lead to the "Name It, Claim It and Frame It" style of religion. Some people feel if they prayed with enough Faith then God will give them a new pink Cadillac. They think they could be healed if they only had more Faith or the people around them had more Faith.

True Faith's ultimate goal is to spread Faith. True Faith trusts God in all circumstances. True Faith looks for ways to carry out God's will for their life. It's not looking at the problems of life and expecting God to repair it the way we think it needs to be repaired. True Faith is looking to the Creator of the Universe for His guidance no matter the circumstance and obeying His Will. True Faith is not trying to force God to do what we want done for us.

If you love God and believe He has your best interests in mind for your life then submit to Him and allow His Will to be worked out in your life. God may allow you to have a pink Cadillac but are you are taking meals to the needy and take people to church with it? He doesn't care about the Cadillac because it will all be rust eventually. God cares about people and the relationship He has with them.

> *"For it is by grace you have been saved, through faith-and this is not from yourselves, it is the gift of God-not by works, so that no one can boast."* Ephesians 2:8-9

God, the object of our Faith, tells us not to boast about ourselves and our works because we are supposed to know where grace, mercy, and forgiveness come from. We know we are to love God, love our neighbors, and tell them about our Faith. Telling others is as easy as sharing your Faith with the people around you and telling them how Jesus changed your life. These people could be your family, friends, co-workers or church members.

Maybe you are called to go half-way around the world to share your Faith with perfect strangers and find amazing joy in telling others about your heavenly Father. Maybe you need to tell someone sitting next to you on a bus or plane about a God who loves them very much. A random act of kindness coupled with your testimony goes even further when expressing your Faith.

> *"Consequently, faith comes from hearing the message, and the message is heard through the word about Christ."* Romans 10:17

Many people are wasting away because they have never heard the message of the saving grace of Jesus Christ. This verse states *"faith comes from hearing the message"* but how will they hear if no one is speaking to them? Are you speaking to others about how Jesus saved you? Are you staying in God's Word so you can deliver the right messages at the right time to the right person? Are you staying in God's Word to strengthen and grow your Faith? Do you have the Faith to deal with the troubles in your own life by trusting God with those troubles?

> *"Do you not know that your bodies are temples of the Holy Spirit, who is in you, whom you have received from God?"*
> 1 Corinthians 6:19

If God is omni-everything and infinite in power and you have a mustard seed size of Him inside of you then how much of Him do you have? You have the infinite God living inside of you, so what are you afraid of? Do you think you do not have enough Faith to carry out the plans God's has for you? Even the Disciples had similar doubts about their Faith but look at what they accomplished.

> *"The apostles said to the Lord, 'Increase our faith!'"*
> Luke 17:5

Jesus answered their question by saying they could do miraculous things with the Faith of a mustard seed. Do you know what a single mustard seed can do? It can make another mustard plant and that plant can make more seeds and those seeds can make more plants which make more seeds… Get the picture? You have an infinite source of power within you from only one tiny seed and you only need to believe! All Christians have a portion of Faith and are responsible to share their Faith and help others trust God. In order to share your Faith you need to grow the seed inside of you and let your Faith grow into a complete trust in Him. Let your trust grow into action and tell others about Jesus.

> *"Direct my footsteps according to your word; let no sin rule over me."*   Psalm 119:133

Are you allowing God to *"Direct my footsteps?"* Are you sinning less and repenting when you do sin? Do you trust God with all of your heart for those footsteps in your life? Are you speaking about the greatness of Christ and how he loved you even as a sinner?" Are you growing your Faith and allowing it to overflow to others?

"Whoever believes in me, as Scripture has said, rivers of living water will flow from within them."
John 7:38

"God is the only source of hope that'll never disappoint. When we place our faith in him, he provides joy, peace, and hope that overflows."[99]
-Rick Warren

THE PURPOSE OF
THE SHIELD OF FAITH
"Giving People Hope for a Future with God"

"May the God of hope fill you with all joy and peace as you trust in him, so that you may overflow with hope by the power of the Holy Spirit." Romans 15:13

When missionaries travel to unreached parts of the world they are told to look for "people of peace." These people seem to already know the peace and love of God. They are generally ready to accept Christ and become willing to help spread the Gospel in their area of the world. They understand God wants to bring joy and peace to themselves and to others around them. They seem to already have known God cares for them and wants a future with them. It is as if they were patiently waiting for Him to show up in their lives.

"We wait in hope for the Lord; he is our help and our shield. In him our hearts rejoice, for we trust in his holy name. May your unfailing love be with us, Lord, even as we put our hope in you." Psalm 33:20-22

The people operating with the spiritual gift of Faith trust God to help give hope for the future. They are the beacons of the message, *"Everything is going to work out for the pattern of good for those who love God"* as they point people to the promises of God. Their trust and hope in the Lord spills over to others as they share their Shield of Faith and show His unfailing love.

> *"Every word of God is flawless; he is a shield to those who take refuge in him."*   Proverbs 30:5

Faith's trust and hope comes from knowing the Word of God and experiencing God. As we read of His promises and experience them, we have a hope in our future with Him. Every Christian has the gift of Faith yet it looks different with each person. We are all supposed to share the Faith we have been given and when we share our Faith we offer others a place to *"take refuge in Him."* Can you imagine passing out shields on a battlefield to soldiers where the sky is filled with flaming arrows. Passing out Faith is even greater!

> *"Trusting God does not mean believing he will do what you want, but rather believing he will do everything he knows is good."*[100]   -Ken Sande

THE STRENGTH OF THE SHIELD OF FAITH
"Trusting God Completely"

> *"But blessed is the one who trusts in the Lord, whose confidence is in him. They will be like a tree planted by the water that sends out its roots by the stream. It does not fear when heat comes; its leaves are always green. It has no worries in a year of drought and never fails to bear fruit."*
> Jeremiah 17:7-8

Those blessed with an abundance of Faith let it overflow to the people around them. When those using the spiritual gift of Faith stay close to God they are a never-ending spring of joy and hope for others. Even during tough times in their lives, Faith *"never fails to bear fruit"* because of their deep roots in Christ.

By trusting in God they can always draw from His everlasting living water and show love and compassion to others even in the droughts of their own lives. The spiritual gift of Faith bears fruit when they help others trust God in all circumstances.

> *"You will keep in perfect peace those whose minds are steadfast, because they trust in you."*
> Isaiah 26:3

"Steadfast" means "to lean" or "rest." You can rest your mind by trusting in God and enjoy the *"perfect peace"* of His Will. Whatever happens in your life it is for the pattern of good for those who love Him. Knowing you have an eternity with Him makes the problems of this world seem very small. The message of this Scripture is what people are desperately seeking today, peace! People today are running around doing so much busy work they willfully forget to live for a purpose other than their own self-centeredness. This is a lonely dead end road. They need peace in their lives and you are the one to tell them the message of Christ that delivers peace! Your trust in Him will help others trust His Will for their life.

> *"But I trust in you, Lord; I say, 'You are my God.' My times are in your hands..."*   Psalm 31:14-15

> *"I have complete confidence that God is able to take care of any situation and provide an answer to any question or problem - He has all the resources of the universe to draw upon in helping each one of us through any type of crisis if we will trust Him."*[101]
> Charles Stanley

THE GOOD OF
THE SHIELD OF FAITH
(Going Forward)
"Sharing the Promises of God"

"I will say of the Lord, 'He is my refuge and my fortress, my God, in whom I trust.' Surely he will save you from the fowler's snare and from the deadly pestilence. He will cover you with his feathers, and under his wings you will find refuge; his faithfulness will be your shield and rampart. You will not fear the terror of night, nor the arrow that flies by day..."   Psalm 91:2-5

The good of the Shield of Faith is having a simple trust in God's promises and sharing them with others. Our trust in Him frees us from the *"fear"* and *"terror"* of this world. No matter what happens we have a place in heaven. The good of Faith is having confidence and assurance even if we never see it all work out in this lifetime. The worst-case scenario is being in heaven with God for an eternity!

"The future is as bright as the promises of God."[102]
-William Carey

THE BAD OF
THE SHIELD OF FAITH
(Going Backward)
"Losing Faith"

The Bad actions of these spiritual gifts are not necessarily sin. They start to slip away from God due to stresses, overwork, and burnout. They can take on to many projects and spread themselves thin. This produces more and more stress, lack of sleep, and attitude changes. The "Bad" is like the check engine light on the dash of a car. It can be a warning of slipping into the "Ugly" sins of these gifts as they drift from God.

"'Lord, if it's you,' Peter replied, 'tell me to come to you on the water.' 'Come,' he said. Then Peter got down out of the boat, walked on the water and came toward Jesus. But when he saw the wind, he was afraid and, beginning to sink, cried out, 'Lord, save me!' Immediately Jesus reached out his hand and caught him. 'You of little faith,' he said, 'why did you doubt?'" Matthew 14:28-31

Give Peter a little credit for a few things in this verse. Peter first tested the spirit by asking if it was the Lord to see if he was actually seeing Jesus and not something else.

"...do not believe every spirit, but test the spirits to see whether they are from God..." 1 John 4:1

Jesus said, *"Come"* and then Peter was obedient to the call and he got out of the boat while the others stayed in the boat. Then Peter *"walked on the water"* because of his obedience to Jesus' call.

"...observe what the Lord your God requires: Walk in obedience to him..." 1 Kings 2:3

Peter did great at first. Are you the Lord; check! Obey His command; check! Walk with Jesus, even on the water; check! At this point, I'm sure the other disciples in the boat thought of him as an over achieving Teacher's pet but they were probably more concerned the boat was going to sink. I heard this old saying while on rough seas during a scuba diving trip, "If you are having trouble on the water look at the Captain. If he's not nervous then stay calm and ride out the storm." Keep in mind this must have been a pretty bad storm if a bunch of fishermen were afraid of sinking!

Even in a raging storm Peter got out of the boat, but he took his eyes off Jesus. Peter needed to keep his Faith focused and directed on Jesus but he failed! He changed the direction of his Faith and focused on the winds and the storm. This allowed Satan to shoot a flaming arrow of fear directly at him and he sank like the rock he would become. Jesus asked, *"You [Peter] of little faith, why did you doubt?"*

"Doubt" means to waver or hesitate between two positions. When we waver or hesitate in our direction of Faith it opens an opportunity to be hit by a flaming arrow shot at us by Satan. The arrow gets past our shield as we move it back and forth trying to make a decision. These arrows come in all sorts of shapes and sizes like doubt, fear, shame, regret, blame, anger, greed, and jealousy. They are all dangerous.

If we were traveling in a boat of Faith these arrows could put small holes in our boat that would cause leaks. We may be able to bail water and keep our boat afloat but one of the most dangerous situations on a boat is a fire. While you are concerned about bailing out the water coming into the boat there is fire spreading from the flaming arrows on the other side of the boat. Eventually the end results will be disastrous.

Faith is deeply rooted in believing in a good and hopeful future but life is full of trials and tribulations that poke holes in our boat. Faith, our trust in God, is what gets us through those trials of life and helps us patch the holes. It may feel like we are in a burning building trying to climb down a dark stairway. We can only feel one step at a time but knowing there is an exit at the bottom of the stairs keeps us moving. Faith provides the hope to move us forward despite the destruction left behind us. It provides a purpose and a direction to follow.

> *"But the Lord is faithful, and he will strengthen you and protect you from the evil one."*   2 Thessalonians 3:3

Without Faith it is impossible to do life. You sit in a chair because you have Faith the chair will hold you up. We get in planes, buses and automobiles having Faith they will get you to your next destination. Without Faith how can you move from moment to moment in life? When bad things happen to you it may get worse before it gets better.

Faith reminds you about surviving tough times before. It reminds you of hope!

A focused Faith in God reassures you that in the toughest of times *"He will strengthen you"* and be there with you through it all. God is also faithful to *"protect you from the evil one"* and give you a home in heaven forever. You can be reassured that all of your pain was for a reason to help grow your character and grow your Faith.

> *"Not only so, but we also glory in our sufferings, because we know that suffering produces perseverance; perseverance, character; and character, hope. And hope does not put us to shame, because God's love has been poured out into our hearts through the Holy Spirit, who has been given to us."*
> Romans 5:3-5

Sometimes the holes in our boat from our sufferings seem like too much for our Faith and we don't repair the holes. Eventually we have so many un-repaired holes we cannot bail out the water fast enough and we sink. Many times we are trying to do things under our own power and we miss out on God's direction from the fear of the water flooding into the boat.

If we focus on Him, He would tell us to repair the largest hole first and then bail some water. Patiently sitting in a little water to repair the large hole first is much better than sinking with too much water later. Our trust in Him develops our character and gives us more hope for our lives. Through the trials we see how much God loves us and our Faith grows as we trust Him more and more.

Faith has direction. To keep from sinking you need to keep your Faith focused in only one direction, Jesus Christ! Do you have a Focused Faith looking in the proper direction? Are you quick to change your direction when the water rises? Are you willing to sit in a little water and let God direct the repairs of your boat?

"Consider it pure joy, my brothers and sisters, whenever you face trials of many kinds, because you know that the testing of your faith produces perseverance. Let perseverance finish its work so that you may be mature and complete, not lacking anything." James 1:2-4

"The danger of loss of faith in God is not that one will believe in nothing, but rather that one will believe in anything."[103]

-Gilbert K. Chesterton

THE MAIN GIFT-KILLING WEAKNESS OF THE SHIELD OF FAITH
"The Misdirection of One's Faith"

"Some trust in chariots and some in horses, but we trust in the name of the Lord our God" Psalm 20:7

Faith is a direction and it can be changed. Having Faith in *"chariots and horses"* is an example of directing Faith in government and its army for protection but our ultimate Faith should be in the *"Lord our God."* We need to be careful where we direct our Faith because people with authority over us can manipulate and control us and lead us away from God. Professors, teachers, politicians and bosses can slowly erode away at the morality of God through their teachings, demands and laws. Some may threaten your college grade or your job income if you don't do things their way even if it goes against your morals as a Christian.

Do you trust a just God or an ever-changing government? Do you trust an all knowing God or a professor who changes their books every few years? Do you trust a God who gave you rules to help or do you trust someone telling you to break the rules for their personal gain? Do you trust in a God of morality or a society saying to do whatever you want as long as it feels good? Do you trust a God who loves you or do you trust Satan who wants to kill you?

"I will conduct the affairs of my house with a blameless heart. I will not look with approval on anything that is vile. I hate what faithless people do; I will have no part in it. The perverse of heart shall be far from me; I will have nothing to do with what is evil." Psalm 101:2-4

"Faithless people" swerve and fall away from Faith and head toward *"vile"* worthless things. If we are not paying attention to the road in front of us we will eventually have to swerve to try and get back on the road. Many swerve and fall away into ditches, trees or even over a cliff. Keep your eyes on the road in front of you! Keep your eyes on Jesus and *"have nothing to do with what is evil."*

My son took a Dirty Jobs course in college for a social science elective. After the drop-add date the professor explained he would be going over strippers as a dirty job. He said he would be showing videos of naked strippers over the next two classes. He said if any student missed those classes he would fail them. By the way, this was not in the course description.

The world is full of people whose life's purpose seems to be "misery loves company." They love to drag people down to their level of immorality to make their selves look better. The videos were unnecessary because most people can imagine the poor choices involved in choosing a life as a stripper. My son kept his eyes down during the videos and completed the class.

I noticed parents asking about electives on a parent's page for the college and I told what happened in my son's class. A parent was very grateful for my post but another parent attacked her online. That parent argued for college students having the right to see these kinds of videos because they were old enough to see them. So sad, just because you are old enough to watch pornography or smoke or drink doesn't make it right!

There is a constant bombardment of evil Satan throws at us daily. Have the Faith to stand firm while wearing your Armor to withstand those attacks. Direct your Faith to God and never take your eyes off of Him throughout every circumstance of your life. Keep your Faith directed at God and Trust in Him!

FAITH IS:
Praying for a miracle from God and not knowing HOW
Trusting God and not knowing WHY
Waiting on God and not knowing WHEN
Following God and not knowing WHERE

THE UGLY OF
THE SHIELD OF FAITH
(Going Sin-Ward)
"Faith Directed at Darkness"

"This is the message we have heard from him and declare to you: God is light; in him there is no darkness at all. If we claim to have fellowship with him and yet walk in the darkness, we lie and do not live out the truth. But if we walk in the light, as he is in the light, we have fellowship with one another, and the blood of Jesus, his Son, purifies us from all sin."   1 John 1:5-7

Darth Vader made a choice to point the direction of his Faith toward the Dark Side but Luke Skywalker made the decision to keep his faith pointed in the right direction despite the intense trials and tribulations forced upon him. It is the same in Christianity; will you continue to keep your direction of Faith pointed at Jesus no matter what happens in your life? Or will you choose to *"walk in darkness?"*

The Ugly use of the spiritual gifts is when a believer chooses to disobey God and use their God-given talent for evil. God gives us the choice to follow Him or not. He also gives us the choice to use our talents for good or bad and when they are used to sin they become Anti-Gifts. Here is the ugly side of wrongly used talents represented by the Shield of Faith. They have been broken down into the three areas of sin discussed in chapter 6:

LUST of the FLESH:
Gift-Killers from Sins of the Body

"When tempted, no one should say, 'God is tempting me.' For God cannot be tempted by evil, nor does he tempt anyone; but each person is tempted when they are dragged away by their own evil desire and enticed. Then, after desire has conceived, it gives birth to sin; and sin, when it is full-grown, gives birth to death." James 1:13-15

A misguided or misdirected Faith puts more trust in anyone or anything more than Jesus Christ. Directing one's Faith toward a Cult Leader is an example of misguided trust. Many followers of these leaders are tempted into a life of peace and purpose. Unfortunately this bad choice of the direction of their Faith leads to financial ruin, brain washing and sexual immorality. Would you allow a Cult Leader to marry and have sex with your wife? What about your nine year old daughter? How does a person ever get to that point in their life and be *"dragged away by their own evil desire?"* Jesus would never ask you to give your daughter to a man for sexual sin.

This misdirection of Faith does not have to be as obvious as a cult leader. It can be a neighbor or someone at the office who seems to "have it all together" with their life. Slowly, but surely, your Faith drifts away from God and gives in to desire. *"Then, after desire has conceived, it gives birth to sin"* and it ends in an affair or a relationship that is unpleasing to God.

The most common outcome of these affairs is feelings of shame and regret. The most common outcome of these affairs is feelings of guilt, shame and regret. This makes it harder to look God in the eye and your direction of Faith is taken off course. Satan wins the battle and keeps you from accomplishing God's Will for your life. Keep your Faith directed on the light of Jesus and not the darkness of the world.

STOP blaming God for tempting you. You make the ultimate choices of where to direct your Faith. You know there will be consequences when you choose to direct your Faith on anything other than God.

LOOK at how your own *"evil desire"* enticed you to misdirect your Faith.

LISTEN to the warnings when dealing with the temptations trying to destroy your Faith.

BE WHAT GOD CREATED YOU TO BE; a Faith-filled child of God keeping their Faith directed at Him.

> *"Temptation usually comes through a door that has been deliberately left open."*   Anonymous

LUST of the EYES:
Gift-Killers from Idol Worship or Coveting

> *"We know that we are children of God, and that the whole world is under the control of the evil one. We know also that the Son of God has come and has given us understanding, so that we may know him who is true. And we are in him who is true by being in his Son Jesus Christ. He is the true God and eternal life. Dear children, keep yourselves from idols."*
> 1 John 5:19-21

As *"children of God"* we should know *"the whole world is under the control of the evil one."* We should also know Jesus is the one *"who is true."* We need to avoid directing our Faith at any form of idols which take us away from God's truth. We need to keep our Faith directed at Jesus at all times to avoid being deceived by false teachings and false idols. This deception can put us under the control of Satan.

FAITH IN IDOLS

A misdirected Faith can be a belief or trust in someone or something that eventually becomes an idol. An idol can even be a belief in false sayings like "good people go to heaven." Everyone has fallen short of being good enough for heaven and is in need of a Savior for their sins. Being good does not cover our sins; they can only be covered by Christ's sacrificial blood.

Believing "God helps those who help themselves" is another example of making an idol out of a saying. Most of those using this saying are selfish and are looking for ways to avoid helping others. This statement makes God sound like an Egyptian guard yelling at a fallen slave, "Get up now and work or you will never eat again!" Jesus is clearly for the beaten-down and He meets us where we are and helps us in our circumstances. His sacrifice for us does not say to get up and help yourself! His love asks what He may do for us.

False sayings can be found in songs, wall art, media, and books. They can misdirect our Faith. They can help us make excuses to not love and serve others in their time of need. We can be misled by the theology of man and not follow the Word of God. Many of us have spent our life believing and memorizing false sayings that are not scriptural. Make sure the "sayings" you are fond of line up with Scriptures so they don't deceive you and mess up your walk with God. You may find you will have to unlearn so much before you can learn the truth.

Faith can be misdirected towards a sports team and leave you depressed or mad after a loss. Faith could be a certain brand of vehicle that could let you down when it breaks down on the side of the road. Misdirected Faith could be placed in a computer brand that crashes and loses your saved work. Even a misdirected Faith in brands of clothing, shoes or food companies can be disappointing by finding out their worldly stand on political views. Faith can be misdirected at about anything or anyone but the only hope for your future is with Jesus Christ. Direct your Faith at the light of God and not the darkness of Satan.

"True faith is not a leap into the dark; it's a leap into the light."[104]   -Eric Metaxas

THE IDOL OF FAKE FAITH

"Thou shalt not take the name of the Lord thy God in vain…"   Exodus 20:7 KJV

Most of us learned the sin from this commandment was using God's name in vain by using the curse word "G..D…" Misusing God's name can look very different from using a curse word. ***"Vain"*** can mean emptiness, deception, worthlessness and lies. In reality using God's name in vain is using His name for personal gain. It is using a fake Faith to deceive others. Those doing this look to God as an idol to gain money, possessions, power or pleasure. They idolize the power in God's name but do not want the responsibility of a relationship with Him.

"Not everyone who says to me, 'Lord, Lord,' will enter the kingdom of heaven, but only the one who does the will of my Father who is in heaven."   Matthew 7:21

Imagine a man putting on fake smiles and doing everything "churchy" to look good to church people. Through his fake mask he sells insurance to members of the congregation. What if you are able to privately see what he does in his home? You might find him verbally or physically abusive to his wife and children. He may not be living a Godly life and he's using God's name for his own deceptive financial gain and God's name is empty to him other than what it can gain for him.

"You shall not misuse the name of the Lord your God, for the Lord will not hold anyone guiltless who misuses his name."   Exodus 20:7

Years ago a man came to my office and in a very animated way asked me if I was a Christian. He said he did not want anyone touching him who was not a Believer. I told him I was a Christian and adjusted him. He never paid for the adjustment. People seeking God could come away from such an experience and not want to be a part of Christians who steal from them.

He used God's name in vain and there are no telling how many people he has turned away from Jesus because of his actions. By the way, if you talk with a waitress about their problems and pray for them you better leave a big tip. Do not leave the table empty because it will empty their heart. Show the love of Christ through your actions and not just your words.

THE IDOL OF EDUCATION

"Woe to you, teachers of the law and Pharisees, you hypocrites! You are like whitewashed tombs, which look beautiful on the outside but on the inside are full of the bones of the dead and everything unclean. In the same way, on the outside you appear to people as righteous but on the inside you are full of hypocrisy and wickedness."

Matthew 23:27-28

Jesus gave an incredible description of those looking good on the outside but they were full of lies and evil on the inside. There are many like this on our college campuses today. They have the showy robes and multiple letters after their names but they have evil goals of destroying Christianity. I personally was a victim to this idol of knowledge for almost 20 years of my life. I believed their lies and drifted far from God. I made a lot of bad decisions along the way because of the weak relationship I had with God. Fortunately God is a God of Grace and He welcomed me home with open arms!

"I've graduated from three universities, and I can tell you that some of the dumbest people on earth are hiding out there."[105]

-John Hagee

About 20 years ago I had a woman come into my office who was overflowing with Faith. She was a joy and I looked forward to talking with her when she came in for adjustments. Unfortunately she came in about 5 years later and I asked her what happened? She was a ghost of her former self and had been drained of her Faith. She told me she had recently graduated as an older adult from a local university and had her Faith misdirected by the philosophy professors.

She had a bad back problem and had to come in several times over the next few months. I asked her if she was better off now with little Faith or was she better before when she had an abundance of Faith. I was so mad at the professors for stealing her wonderful gift of Faith and I was doing everything I could to repair the damage. I took the opportunity to speak truth into her life and patch the holes in her Armor made by the professors.

I saw her again about 10 years later and she was about half full of Faith. She was able to patch many of her holes and begin growing her Faith back. About 5 years after that visit, she came in overflowing with Faith. It was even greater than the first time I met her. She was full of life and thanked me for being one of three "angels" in her life that helped pull her out of the hole she was in following her graduation. It was good to see her Faith restored. She confessed she had reached a point of no longer believing in God in those darkest days. I detected a tone of regret as she said, "I wish my children could know what I know now." Her misdirected Faith during those dark days affected her children. Please send up prayers for her children, I know she would be forever grateful.

"Whoever is not with me is against me, and whoever does not gather with me scatters."   Matthew 12:30

If you think your Faith is just yours and yours alone, you are wrong. You will affect people all around you, especially your family. Do you help Jesus *"gather"* for the Kingdom or are you one who *"scatters?"* There is no gray zone here; you are either one or the other when it comes to the direction of your Faith. You are either for Jesus or against Jesus. A misdirection of Faith from philosophy professors can destroy you and your family. It took my patient almost 20 years to recover from the holes poked in her Armor. Some in her family still have holes needing repairs. Are you willing to let this happen to your family?

STOP misusing God's name in vain with lies for deception and personal gain.
LOOK inside yourself, are you full of everything unclean and have no room for God? Are you really better off without directing your Faith to God?
LISTEN to how you talk about and build up your idols; do you talk about Jesus in the same way?
BE WHAT GOD CREATED YOU TO BE; a gatherer directing their Faith toward Jesus!

> *"If you love anything better than God you are idolaters: if there is anything you would not give up for God it is your idol: if there is anything that you seek with greater fervor than you seek the glory of God, that is your idol, and conversion means a turning from every idol."*[106]   -Charles Spurgeon

PRIDE of LIFE:
Gift-Killers from Selfish Ambition

"And without faith it is impossible to please God, because anyone who comes to him must believe that he exists and that he rewards those who earnestly seek him."
Hebrews 11:6

When you direct your Faith toward anything other than trusting God you are saying His promises are not true. You are calling God a liar and this does not please Him. He loves you so much and only wants you to *"believe that He exists."* For those who *"earnestly seek Him"* He wants to give them a home in eternity with Him forever.

Without trusting God you turn to the only person you can trust, yourself. It is prideful when "Yourself" begins to make the decisions as to who or what you will have Faith in and who or what you will not. If you think God is a liar then your Faith doesn't stop it just changes directions. Directing Faith at yourself is pride and selfish ambition; you are making yourself to be like god!

> *"Blessed is the one who trusts in the Lord, who does not look to the proud, to those who turn aside to false gods."*
> Psalm 40:4

We all seem to be hard-wired for Faith in something whether it's in the one true God or little "g" gods. Our Faith can be in important people or even in ourselves. Faith will either be directed inward, outward or upward. Your Faith can be misdirected by needing oneness with the universe or rebelling against anything of God. It can even be directed at the destruction of Christianity. Misdirection of Faith has the ultimate goal to stop you from being a gatherer and make you one who scatters. This is the result of selfish ambition.

BLAMING GOD

> *"Those on the rocky ground are the ones who receive the word with joy when they hear it, but they have no root. They believe for a while, but in the time of testing they fall away."*
> Luke 8:13

Many people blame God for their problems and circumstances. They become prideful and act as if they deserve a better life than the one they have. Their dream life mostly wants more of the pleasures of the world and less of God. They look at the "rewards" of life as fame and fortune and not what is really best for them and their life. They eventually change their direction of Faith away from God and aim it at the world as *"they fall away"* during their *"time of testing."*

Sadly many Christians have made this destructive journey and now have no Faith in God. Many were by Christians in the church and sadly many from their own families. Many could not weather a storm in life because *"they have no root"* in God and they felt let down by Him. Now they're mad at God even though they may say He doesn't exist.

What can I say? If you made your opinion of God based on people and circumstances; then life can stink and people can too! Did God ever promise you an easy life in Scripture? No! Did He promise you that everybody you meet will treat you kindly and fairly? No! Did He say this world is perfect and righteous? No!

Did He promise health and wealth for you and your entire family for their entire life? No! Then why are you belly-aching about God not giving you special favor when people all over the world are suffering far worse things in their lives than you. Life is going to be hard but it's much better when you have Faith.

Make sure your roots are strong and deep enough by learning God's Word. You need those strong roots so you can draw water and nutrients from the rich soil. This way you can keep your wits about you in the storms of life.

EVOLVED FAITH

"For although they knew God, they neither glorified him as God nor gave thanks to him, but their thinking became futile and their foolish hearts were darkened. Although they claimed to be wise, they became fools and exchanged the glory of the immortal God for images made to look like a mortal human being and birds and animals and reptiles."
Romans 1:21-23

God knew man would turn to the things of this world to worship. He knew they would worship other humans, animals and things of the universe like the sun, planets and the stars. God gave a good description of the idol of evolution. He said they would exchange ***"The glory of the immortal God"*** for the worship of the image of ***"a mortal human being and birds and animals and reptiles."*** Evolution uses a row of animals leading to a mortal man for the image of their idol. They take their direction of Faith off God and focus it on the world and the universe as the creator of life.

Your Faith could become pointed at evolution. You may begin to trust people with an education and lots of letters after their name because you believe they have all the answers. You then believe the universe all started with cosmic flatulence and you ultimately have to believe in black holes because there is now one in your heart. That black hole is a God shaped hole that will never be satisfied by anything other than God.

I've watched myself and others go down this road of hurt, anger and bitterness. There is so little anyone could say to them when their ***"foolish hearts were darkened."*** This is a well-worn path and they don't realize what they are truly suffering from is ungratefulness. They can't appreciate what they have for focusing on what they've lost. They think God owed them something and He failed to deliver the life they think they deserved. They are so blinded by their misdirected Faith they do not even see themselves exchanging God for other idols in their life. God is not a liar, He is the truth!

THE VERY ANGRY EVOLUTIONIST

I debated, through email, with a very angry evolutionist more than 20 years ago. I was more interested in his list of "errors" in the Bible he posted rather than the creation verses evolution debate. I asked him if I came up with a reasonable explanation for the Biblical "errors" would he post my explanation next to the "errors?" He said he would and we began our debate.

His web page said the people who wrote the Bible had no idea what a bird was because it stated you could not eat a bird which walked on four legs. I explained to him that the Biblical word used for a bird was "fowl." In Hebrew it means a flying creature and gives no species of animal. As a biologist I quickly realized this was a bat. Bats walk on all four legs, 2 of them being their wings.

It was obvious why Leviticus told people not to eat bats because they're nasty animals and their caves are very dangerous for lung infections because of their feces. Ironically at that time Pterodactyl tracks were found and showed where they walked like bats. I told him these were also included in the "do not eat" section of Leviticus in the Bible. Sadly I gave good apologetic answers to his arguments for "errors" in Scripture but he would just cuss me and move on to the next "error" until he ran out. He never placed any of my arguments next to those on his website. By the way, COVID 19 is mostly from the bat genome. God knew bats were bad for us to mess with.

At the end of our debate I thanked him for proving the Bible to be 99.992% correct. I told him he had 11 pages of "errors" on his web site and my Bible had 1374 pages. I even graciously gave him his lengthy explanations and wide margins along with his last page only being a quarter of a page. I simply divided his 11 pages of "errors" by the 1374 pages of my Bible and calculated an error percentage of .0080% which showed the Bible was 99.992% accurate!

I pushed him on the accuracy of his information and asked him if he used the most up-to-date science books to prove his points about evolution and he said, "Yes." I asked if he used any 100 year old text books and he said, "No." Then I asked him what are people going say about his science in 100 years? No answer. Even if his errors were somehow correct I would still base my Faith on something thousands of years old that is 99.992% correct. Why would I put my Faith in ever-changing science books? It seems the only constant in science is change.

I did discover his father was a Nazarene preacher and he seemed to be in a state of rebellion against him. I did some recent research on him and found that he had written a book on the subject of creationism verses evolution. I read a few more arguments he had made many years ago and he continued with his angry cussing rants. His web page has been copied and is still viewable but no major changes have occurred in decades. I could not find out if he is still alive and sadly I do not think there was a conversion story.

I have seen people like this come to their senses decades later trying to sort out the mess of their own making. They realize the place they left had so much more life than the place they are now. The black hole in their heart was never filled as they went from one godless experience to another. If you are "mad at God" He is not surprised. He is big enough to take your anger towards Him. As mad as you are at Him, He is always waiting for you with open arms. Return to Him just like the story of the prodigal son returning to his Father.

> *"So he got up and went to his father. But while he was still a long way off, his father saw him and was filled with compassion for him; he ran to his son, threw his arms around him and kissed him."*
> Luke 15:20

STOP misdirecting your Faith because you didn't get everything you wanted in life.

LOOK at Scripture, there will be struggles we face while on Earth so be ready by being close to God.

LISTEN to God reassuring you He will be with you through all of those struggles.

BE WHAT GOD CREATED YOU TO BE; a guest invited to eternity's greatest feast!

"The difference between mercy and grace? Mercy gave the Prodigal Son a second chance. Grace gave him a feast." [107]

-Max Lucado

PROTECTING YOURSELF FROM THE GIFT-KILLERS OF THE SHIELD OF FAITH

KEEP YOUR FAITH FOCUSED ON JESUS

"...let us draw near to God with a sincere heart and with the full assurance that faith brings, having our hearts sprinkled to cleanse us from a guilty conscience and having our bodies washed with pure water. Let us hold unswervingly to the hope we profess, for he who promised is faithful."

Hebrews 10:22-23

The number one way of protecting yourself from the Gift-Killers of Faith is to *"draw near to God"* with a *"sincere heart"* and do it with the *"full assurance that Faith brings."* We are hardwired for Faith and it needs a direction and that direction is God.

Satan's forces will use interference to tempt you to change your direction of Faith to rely more on yourself and less on God. The world will cause a lot of static and distractions from the worries, riches and pleasures of the world. People will tickle your ears with what you want to hear but it will be filled with misdirection to take you down some ugly worthless paths. They will try to eat away at the truth in your *"sincere heart"* with lies that sound good and fill you with temptation that leads to guilt, shame, and regret.

> *"Every day I need to let God's Word interrupt me, rearrange me, and redirect me."*[108]   -Lysa TerKerurst

> **"And let us consider how we may spur one another on toward love and good deeds, not giving up meeting together, as some are in the habit of doing, but encouraging one another— and all the more as you see the Day approaching."**
> Hebrews 10:24

Keep your direction focused on the hope of our future with Christ *"as you see the Day approaching."* Gift-Killers will continually attack your relationship with God and the people you are trying to spur *"on toward love and good deeds."* Gift-Killers will do their best to destroy those relationships and change your direction of Faith. Keep encouraging others and never give up *"meeting together"* so you can renew your mind and grow your Faith and the Faith of others.

> **"Therefore I remind you to stir up the gift of God which is in you through the laying on of my hands. For God has not given us a spirit of fear, but of power and of love and of a sound mind."**   2 Timothy 1:6-7 NKJV

Keep fanning the ember of the spiritual gifts within you into a flame to overcome fear! Use His power and love to overcome Satan and his schemes against you. Seek His power and His love and a sound mind by being obedient to His Will for your entire life. When you're weak then lean on God's grace even more to carry you to victory.

"But he said to me, 'My grace is sufficient for you, for my power is made perfect in weakness.' Therefore I will boast all the more gladly about my weaknesses, so that Christ's power may rest on me. That is why, for Christ's sake, I delight in weaknesses, in insults, in hardships, in persecutions, in difficulties. For when I am weak, then I am strong."

2 Corinthians 12:9-10

Your Faith in God and His promises is not just a light for your path; it is the sole purpose for your existence. Knowing and trusting Him reveals your personal purpose by showing you what He created you to be. Your Faith in Him is what keeps you going when you run out of gas. When your tank is empty, His *"power is made perfect in weakness."* He exchanges your weakness for His strength. He replenishes the empty places in your heart and mind with the good and lovely things of God. As He works through your weakness your anxieties, shame and regret melt away as you stay focused on Him and His presence in your life.

Your problems will begin to look smaller in the grand scheme of things as He directs your next steps. Soon you find yourself on top of the mountain that was blocking your way and you will have conquered your giants. A focused Faith in God is the pathway to solving the problems of your life one step at a time. Trust Him today, tomorrow and every day after. Stop relying on your own strength, which is fleeting, so *"Christ's power may rest on"* you! Don't have Faith in your own Faith, have Faith in God's faithfulness!

"Imagine what God would trust you with tomorrow if you trusted Him more today..."[109]   -Simon Lawton

GROWTH IN CHRIST
The Spiritual Gifts Related to
The Shield of Faith

UNDERSTAND "WHOSE" YOU ARE

Those with the spiritual gift of Faith are good at knowing whose they are but there are levels to the trust they have in God to produce fruit in their lives. In Matthew 13 Jesus tells us how the seeds of the Gospel are planted and how they grow in people. Sadly the first group of seeds is thrown on the well-traveled road and the birds take the seed away and nothing grows. This represents Satan taking the seeds away and they never get planted and never grow. This is the unsaved. The three other seeds take root and grow in very different ways which represent the three types of Faith.

INWARD FAITH

"Some fell on rocky places, where it did not have much soil. It sprang up quickly, because the soil was shallow. But when the sun came up, the plants were scorched, and they withered because they had no root."   Matthew 13:5-6

The second group of seeds falls on rocky soil with little soil. Unfortunately the roots did not grow deep and strong. When the sun came out the plant withered because it could not draw water and nutrients from the lack of soil. Jesus explains:

"The seed falling on rocky ground refers to someone who hears the word and at once receives it with joy. But since they have no root, they last only a short time. When trouble or persecution comes because of the word, they quickly fall away."   Matthew 13:20-21

This group of seeds represents an "Inward" direction of Faith. They had no roots because their Faith was more about themselves. They were shallow in their relationship with God. When they encountered problems, even as a believer, they did not have deep enough roots to draw nutrients and moisture from the soil. They were not ready for the battle against Satan's schemes and *"they quickly fall away."*

"Fall away" is to sin, take offence, and cause to stumble. It can literally mean "to put a snare in the way to hinder the right conduct." It comes from the word meaning the trigger for a trap, does this sound familiar? Satan sees your shallow roots and brings on the heat. He sets the trap with bait designed for your weaknesses to stop your walk with God. Satan's interference will eventually take you so off course and you'll lose God's direction for your life. This will make you unable to build up His Kingdom and follow His Will. You are now in Satan's trap! Stay in the Word and grow your roots deep with God to avoid this trap! Do not put the direction of your Faith inward toward yourself.

OUTWARD FAITH

> *"Other seed fell among thorns, which grew up and choked the plants."* Matthew 13:7

The third group of seeds was planted among weeds and thorns which grew up around them and greatly reduced their harvest. The weeds steal the vital source of water and nutrients and grow over the crops blocking the sunlight and stunting their growth.

> *"The seed falling among the thorns refers to someone who hears the word, but the worries of this life and the deceitfulness of wealth choke the word, making it unfruitful."* Matthew 13:22

The weeds in this parable are described as the *"worries of this life and the deceitfulness of wealth"* which keep Christians from maturing. Luke 8 describes the plants being choked by the weeds of life's *"worries, riches and pleasures."* This seed represents an "Outward" direction of Faith which relies more on the world than God. They are constantly being drawn away from God by the world's cares, riches, temptations, pleasures and worries.

The weeds choke them till they are unfruitful and immature. They offer little in the way of expanding the Kingdom of God. The static of the world keeps them from fully hearing God speak to them and they willingly ignore His calling on their life. They can be more a culture of Christianity rather than a relationship! Unfortunately this represents a lot of Christians today. Their direction of Faith is pointed at the world and what it has to offer rather than God's and His truth.

UPWARD FAITH

"But the seed falling on good soil refers to someone who hears the word and understands it. This is the one who produces a crop, yielding a hundred, sixty or thirty times what was sown." Matthew 13:23

The fourth group of seeds landed on fertile soil with little to no weeds and developed a good root system. This is the ideal situation for a Christian to produce a harvest of up to a hundred fold. This is the "Upward" direction of Faith in God who provides the soil, sun and rain for the crops. Caring for a garden like this takes work to kill the weeds choking the crops. It also requires watering so the roots can grow deep but most of all it requires someone to pick the fruit of the crop to share with others.

Which type of soil is in your garden? Does your lack of good roots cause you to crumble under the trouble and pressures of the world? Are you growing up in the soil full of the weeds of worries, riches and pleasures of the world? Are they causing you to be choked and distracted from producing good fruit? Can you say you are planted in good soil with deep roots that allow you to produce a good harvest and more seeds? Maybe you represent the first seed that fell on the path and it was taken away by the birds and you never believed. If so I hope you come to a place in your life to ask Jesus into your heart and have the seed of the Gospel planted in good soil this time around.

USE YOUR SOIL TO GROW YOUR SEED OF FAITH

You should strive to be the seed planted on the rich fertile soil. Your Faith can grow from a tiny mustard seed and produce an amazing crop of new Christians that can produce even more Christians and so on and so on! The action of your love, trust and obedience helps you produce a hundredfold crop as God provides the good soil, sun and rain. Make sure you are properly tending to your garden by:

Removing Rocks:
These are the stumbling blocks of the world. Are you removing the idols blocking your relationship with God?

Fertilizing properly:
Are you doing the things that help Christian growth like church, Study, Sunday school, Serving? This is Hearing God's Word and following His Will.

Watering properly:
Are you confessing and progressing to your Lord and Savior every time you fall back into sin? Are you being accountable to others so you can sin-less??

Letting the "Son" Shine:
Are you keeping your shadow out of the way of the seed? Do you trust God with more and more in your life and get out of the way so God can work.

Plow the Soil:
Are you plowing the soil in those around you in order to plant the seed
of Faith in them? A broken soil is much more receptive to a seed. Are
you there when someone is broken and need you to share your Faith
with them?

Weeding:
Gift-Killers try to kill, steal and destroy your crop with the worries,
riches and pleasures of the world. Use the Word of God as weed killer
and miracle grow. Stay in the fight and finish the race God has set in
front of you so there can be a 100 fold harvest!

> *"I have fought the good fight, I have finished the race, I have
> kept the faith."*   2 Timothy 4:7

THE PURPOSE OF THIS BOOK

Early on I thought the purpose of my book was to get you to ask for
more Faith but it's actually asking you to grow the seed of Faith already
inside of you. It's already there and waiting on you to take the necessary
steps to give it the best soil, fertilizer, water and "Son-shine" to produce
amazing fruit! Get busy; it's not going to grow without your obedience.

> *"Let your life reflect the faith you have in God. Fear nothing and
> pray about everything. Be strong, trust God's word, and trust the
> process."[110]*   -Germany Kent

CONFESS AND PROGRESS

> *"Whoever conceals their sins does not prosper, but the one
> who confesses and renounces them finds mercy."*
>   Proverbs 28:13

Confess your worries and anxieties to Jesus so you can progress in His
mercy. Confess calling God a liar when you did not believe and trust

His promises. Get doubt and disbelief out of your home and fill it with the good things of Christ. Progress by tending the garden of your Faith so your crops can multiply.

COMMUNICATE WITH GOD

"I will give thanks to you, Lord, with all my heart; I will tell of all your wonderful deeds. I will be glad and rejoice in you; I will sing the praises of your name, O Most High."
Psalm 9:1-2

Thank God with all your heart for a planned future with Him. No matter what happens here on Earth, He is not surprised nor caught off guard by your circumstances. You are still a loved child of God and he will not love you any more or any less than the day you trusted Him to be your Lord and Savior. You are guaranteed a place prepared for you in heaven with Him for an eternity. Ask God to show you how to be His love in action for the ones needing to grow their Faith. Then go do some planting and watering and watch the fruit grow. God loves communicating with you but I bet He also loves when you tell others about His "wonderful deeds!"

USING SPIRITUAL GIFTS REPRESENTED BY THE SHIELD OF FAITH WITH THE FRUITS OF THE SPIRIT

LOVE: Do you love God with an unwavering Faith? Does the love from Him pour out of you to others? Do you still Love God when times are tough and Satan is interfering with your life?

JOY: Are you filled with joy when your Faith helps others love and trust God? Do you have joy and peace knowing life will ultimately all work out in the end? Are you thankful for the hard times in your life that grow your Faith? Do you find joy in the wonderful deeds God has done for you?

PEACE: Do you find peace and rest when you talk with God? Are you trying to do all of life under your own power or do you give your cares and worries to God? Do you find peace and self-control in God's love?

PATIENCE: Are you waiting on God's Word to move you or are you frantically searching for worldly answers to your problems? Are you bailing out your spiritual boat or are you repairing the holes?

KINDNESS: Does your life make people want what you have spiritually? Are you generous with your spiritual gift? Do your words show a confidence in Christ?

GOODNESS: Do you find people with holes in their spiritual boat and offer to help repair them? Do you allow time in your life to help others and share Christ with them?

FAITHFULNESS: Is your spiritual boat sinking or is it floating soundly? Can your spiritual boat take you to places to share the Gospel of Jesus Christ? Are you living your Faith daily?

GENTLENESS: Do you lovingly offer a helping hand for others to grow their Faith? Does your life pour out the truth, love and power of Christ to others? Are you wise as a wolf and gentle as a sheep when dealing with life's battles?

SELF-CONTROL: Are you able to slow down and fix the holes in your own spiritual boat? Are you able to avoid flinching when bad things happen and keep your Faith focused on Jesus?

TAKE THE MIRROR TEST

Do you see a loved child of God when you look in the mirror? Do you see where Jesus is hugging your DNA to help you to look like Him? Are there no worry lines on your face because you were able to cast your cares on Jesus? Can you see your confident unshakable trust in the Lord? Are your eyes open wide and shining brightly because of the future they see with God? Do you find yourself not needing to look at who you are as often because of whose you are?

STOP growing up in the weeds of worries, riches and pleasures of the world.
LOOK at God's Word and use it as Weed Killer and Miracle Grow.
LISTEN for those needing the seed of God planted in them.
BE WHAT GOD CREATED YOU TO BE; a Faith-filled child of God producing a hundredfold crop of more Faith-filled children of God.

"Faith doesn't always mean that God changes your situation. Sometimes it means He changes you."[111]

-Steven Furtick

PONDERING POINTS

What is the gift represented by the Shield of Faith? (Easy answer)
How is the Shield important to the other pieces of Armor?
What is the goal of the gift of the Shield?
What is the purpose of the gift of the Shield?
What is the strength of the gift of the Shield?
What is the main weakness of the gift of the Shield?
Where is your Faith directed in your life?
How long has your Faith been directed toward God?
Have you had your Faith challenged by an educated atheist?
Have you ever had weak moments in your Faith?
Do you use your Faith to help others trust God?
Do you have the spiritual gift of Faith?
What is an example of Rocky Soil and Inward Faith?
What is an example of Weed Infested and Outward Faith?
What is an example of Fertile Soil and Upward Faith?
Is there anything or anyone you trust more than God?
How much do you trust God with all areas of your life?
What fears can diminish your Faith?

"...The only thing that counts is faith expressing itself through love." Galatians 5:6

CHAPTER THIRTEEN
THE SWORD OF THE SPIRIT

"Finally, be strong in the Lord and in his mighty power. Put on the full armor of God, so that you can take your stand against the devil's schemes. For our struggle is not against flesh and blood, but against the rulers, against the authorities, against the powers of this dark world and against the spiritual forces of evil in the heavenly realms. Therefore put on the full armor of God, so that when the day of evil comes, you may be able to stand your ground, and after you have done everything, to stand."

Ephesians 6:10-13

A WEAPON OF MASS INSTRUCTION

There is an enemy literally hell-bent on destroying you and God is telling you how to *"stand your ground."* Satan will attack your weakest points with well-crafted *"schemes"* to kill, steal and destroy any joy you have from the Lord. Satan is trying to delay his future punishment by stopping you from expanding God's Kingdom with your God-given spiritual gifts. But God gave you the steps to freedom in this battle through His Armor and His Weapon, the Sword.

"Stand firm then, with the belt of truth buckled around your waist, with the breastplate of righteousness in place, and with your feet fitted with the readiness that comes from the gospel of peace. In addition to all this, take up the shield of faith, with which you can extinguish all the flaming arrows of the evil one. Take the helmet of salvation and the sword of the Spirit, which is the word of God."

Ephesians 6:14-17

Use each piece of Armor as it was intended and wield *"the sword of the Spirit, which is the "Word of God"* as your weapon against Satan. The Sword comes with a great power and with great power comes great responsibility. There is much for you to discover about the most powerful offensive weapon in the history of mankind! When "word" is used with "Spirit" it describes giving commands, promises, instructions, messages and doctrines from a living God. You may not realize it but you literally carry the power of life and death in your hand and speak His power with your mouth!

> *"The Spirit gives life; the flesh counts for nothing. The words I have spoken to you—they are full of the Spirit and life."* John 6:63

Do you speak and do more with the *"flesh"* which *"counts for nothing"* rather than Godly words and actions? Are your words and actions full of *"Spirit and life?"* Will any of your conversations or what you do for other people matter in 100 years? Are you self-centered or God-centered with your words and actions?

> *"Sing to the Lord, praise his name; proclaim his salvation day after day. Declare his glory among the nations, his marvelous deeds among all peoples."* Psalm 96:2-3

Do you *"sing to the Lord"* and *"praise his name?"* Are you sharing how God saved you with the lost? Will people be able to say they knew your Faith by your words and actions? Will your words help lead others to Christ?

> *"The tongue has the power of life and death, and those who love it will eat its fruit."* Proverbs 18:21

What fruit do you eat? Do your words reflect Scripture and build up the Body of Christ or do your words spew death and decay to those around you? Are your words the stale fruit cake no one wants at Christmas or do your words represent goodness, kindness and health for the Body of Christ?

"The words of the reckless pierce like swords, but the tongue of the wise brings healing."   Proverbs 12:18

How much healing will your words produce in others and yourself? Do people leave from your presence better than when they entered? Do your words build up people and give them hope? Do you wisely use your sword like a surgeon removing a cancer or do you flail your words around wounding others with quick jabs and cuts? Do you wound others to feel better about yourself and your knowledge? Do you speak to win the conversation or to win their soul? Do others want to be around you because your words are wise and bring healing?

"For the word of God is alive and active. Sharper than any double-edged sword, it penetrates even to dividing soul and spirit, joints and marrow; it judges the thoughts and attitudes of the heart. Nothing in all creation is hidden from God's sight. Everything is uncovered and laid bare before the eyes of him to whom we must give account."
          Hebrews 4:12-13

God's Word is *"alive!"* His Word is *"active!"* His Word declares promises to His children. His Word provides instructions for each step of your life and reveals the hidden evil set on destroying your life. God's Word gives you the commission to build His kingdom; are your words building His Kingdom? Do you gather or scatter, do you divide or unify?

"Do not merely listen to the word, and so deceive yourselves. Do what it says."   James 1:22

Thank you James for getting right to the point! Are you following in Christs footsteps? Are you even listening to His Words, much less obeying them? You've been given some amazing Armor along with an amazing Weapon of Mass Instruction! Please use the Sword. Learn how to care for and use the Sword. Tell others how Jesus came into your life when you were unworthy of forgiveness. Describe how He picked you up from the darkest valleys in your life and poured His mercy and grace into you. Describe to others the hope of a future you have with Him. A well placed word or action at just the right time can change the world.

> *"Don't fall into the trap of studying the Bible without doing what it says."[112]*   -Francis Chan

STOP thinking your words and actions do not matter to others.
LOOK for opportunities to share your Faith and put the Sword into action.
LISTEN to yourself; can you present the Gospel to others in an easy and understandable way?
BE WHAT GOD CREATED YOU TO BE; a Sword bearer in God's Army!

TRAIN WITH THE SWORD

Early sword training begins with wicker shields and wooden swords. The beginners shield and sword are heavier than the real ones in order to make the real ones feel lighter. This makes handling the real Shield and Sword easier as they advance in training. Sword training is similar to moving from Scriptural Milk to Scriptural Solid Food as Christians advance in their knowledge and Faith in God's Word. It's time for you to move from milk to meat!

MILK TO MEAT

"We have much to say about this, but it is hard to make it clear to you because you no longer try to understand. In fact, though by this time you ought to be teachers, you need someone to teach you the elementary truths of God's word all over again. You need milk, not solid food! Anyone who lives on milk, being still an infant, is not acquainted with the teaching about righteousness. But solid food is for the mature, who by constant use have trained themselves to distinguish good from evil." Hebrews 5:11-14

In the first chapter of Hebrews it speaks about the nature of Jesus and how He is the exact representation of God. It says He made the universe and sustains all things. It states He is above angels, purified our sins and sits at the right hand of God. Hebrews then warns us of unbelief and drifting away from the faith. It explains Jesus was fully God and fully human and was made lower than angels for a time to become a sacrifice to beat death and Satan. It reassures us of the promise made to Abraham to enter into God's rest still stands for those who are saved. It also states God's Word is alive and active and to hold firm to the Faith. This is a short list of the *"elementary truths"* being described in the early chapters of Hebrews needed to build a firm foundation of Faith in Christ.

There are many Christians still stuck on milk who *"no longer try to understand"* the *"elementary truths of God's Word"* or the *"teaching about righteousness."* They are choosing to be unable to *"distinguish good from evil."* They are basically lazy about going any further into God's Word and have purposely stopped seeking God's Will in their Christian walk. There is a time to build a foundation with Spiritual Milk but more importantly there comes a time to move on to Spiritual Meat. The move from Milk to Meat is a heart matter between you and God. It is time to take the next step to *"solid food"* in your Christian life!

Coaches love to remind their players to learn the basics in order to play the game properly and see the big picture. They tell the players to focus on their part and do it well and if everyone does their best, the team will do well. The basics are like the Spiritual Milk of the foundation of Christianity. The job of playing the game is like the Meat of Christianity. Eventually the Christian has to take the basics they have learned and get in the game.

Do you know the basics of Christianity? Remember the question, "How do you eat an elephant… one bite at a time!" Training with the Sword and learning how to use it is a process that takes time and effort. Be willing to put in the time to build a foundation of truth for your spiritual growth and maturity. By working through the elementary teachings and moving on to the maturity of solid food, Christians become able to teach and mentor others to grow in their Faith. In other words when you learn more then be sure to share your knowledge with others!

"Preach the Gospel at all times. When necessary, use words."[113]
-St. Francis of Assisi

Your foundation is made up of knowing the nature of Jesus and why He came to Earth. It should be an unshakable foundation in which to build your life upon. If you do not have enough of God's Word in you to tell **"good from evil"** you can be taken advantage of very easily. You can be misdirected by false teachings and fall prey to cults and false teachers because of your lack of knowledge of God's Word. Evil can tickle your ear and promise you the world but eventually you will find yourself trapped in Satan's snare.

"…my people are destroyed from lack of knowledge."
Hosea 4:6

Always continue training with the Sword God has given you; read your Bible and grow in your knowledge and Faith in Him. Graduate from Milk to Meat and become the best swordsman possible. Be sure to use it with love, forgiveness and grace to expand the Kingdom? Learn how Jesus wielded the Sword?

"We need to encourage new believers to feed on God's Word—it is nourishment for the soul."[114]   -Billy Graham

STOP making excuses for not laying down a good foundation of God's Word.

LOOK to the Sword as the source of knowledge to build your life's foundation upon.

LISTEN closely to God in order to be able to distinguish good from evil.

BE WHAT GOD CREATED YOU TO BE; a Well-Trained Sword Bearer in God's Army!

ALWAYS KEEP YOUR SWORD READY

"I went to Jerusalem, and after staying there three days I set out during the night with a few others. I had not told anyone what my God had put in my heart to do for Jerusalem."
Nehemiah 2:11-12

In the first chapters of Nehemiah, he was given a mission from God to rebuild Jerusalem. He fasted and prayed for his ancestors, family and for his own sins against God to be forgiven. He realized he had not kept God's Word and he turned to God's promise to restore Jerusalem to the Jewish people. He asked for God's strength and favor to carry out the promise. He went to Jerusalem and inspected the walls and gates and found them to be destroyed. Nehemiah had put his Sword, God's Word, down for a time. Fortunately he realized what happens when you drift away from God's Word and he began to seek God's Will again.

"From that day on, half of my men did the work, while the other half were equipped with spears, shields, bows and armor. The officers posted themselves behind all the people of Judah who were building the wall. Those who carried materials did their work with one hand and held a weapon in the other, and each of the builders wore his sword at his side as he worked."   Nehemiah 4:16-18

Nehemiah ordered his workers to use one hand to build the temple and the other hand to hold a sword to fight off potential attacks. Nehemiah was working to rebuild Jerusalem and its wall for defense but more importantly his goal was to rebuild the Temple. The Temple was where God dwelled for the Jews. These Words not only tell the story of the physical Temple being rebuilt but they tell how Christians can rebuild themselves today.

"Don't you know that you yourselves are God's temple and that God's Spirit dwells in your midst? If anyone destroys God's temple, God will destroy that person; for God's temple is sacred, and you together are that temple."   1 Corinthians 3:16-17

Since the destruction of the Temple, Christians have become the temple where God's Spirit dwells. Most Christians start with a pretty messed up Temple. They are laid waste to shame, guilt, sorrow and pain that has destroyed their walls of defense and allowed Satan to easily walk in and steal anything he sees of value.

Christians need to rebuild their defenses and protect their Temple from Satan's attacks. Nehemiah gives a picture of how that looks in everyday life. Christians should rebuild with one hand and hold God's Word in the other. Surround yourself with other well-armored and well-armed Christians with common goals who have your back. Pray, fast and seek God's Word and follow good leadership. Put God's Word into practice and be a doer of His Word.

> *"Therefore everyone who hears these words of mine and puts them into practice is like a wise man who built his house on the rock. The rain came down, the streams rose, and the winds blew and beat against that house; yet it did not fall, because it had its foundation on the rock."*
>
> Matthew 7:24-25

Before coming to Christ a person is like a house without a good foundation where the storms of life can easily destroy it. Christians need to fill themselves with God's Word to lay a new foundation so their home can withstand the storms and attacks from the enemy. Being a Christian requires standing up to an enemy with a temple built upon a firm foundation; *"the Rock!"*

DEMOLISHING SATAN

Christians are called to fight the enemy while fully suited in their Armor and holding the Sword in their hand. As a Christian you are up against a father of lies who wishes to kill, steal and destroy anything of God within you. There are no terms of peace or truce nor cease fire. If you give in to Satan he will get a foothold and never stop attacking. Keep your Armor on every day, use your spiritual gifts and take up the Sword to continue growing and maturing in the Lord! The Sword is what brought eternal life to you and those you love so use its power to build God's Kingdom. Never surrender, never retreat and never allow Satan to get in your head. Resist the Devil and he will flee! Replace evil thoughts with God's promises.

> *"For though we live in the world, we do not wage war as the world does. The weapons we fight with are not the weapons of the world. On the contrary, they have divine power to demolish strongholds. We demolish arguments and every pretension that sets itself up against the knowledge of God, and we take captive every thought to make it obedient to Christ."*
>
> 2 Corinthians 10:3-5

Studying God's Word allows His truth to *"demolish strongholds."* These strongholds can become prisons of your own making when you seek what you think is a "safe place" to escape reality. This is where we go when we are experiencing fear, shame and regret. These places we feel safe could be drugs, alcohol, sex, excessive shopping, over eating, etc. Satan would love to find you in these places and pound you with his thoughts. Don't let Satan tempt you by asking, "Did God really say…" If you know God's Word you will be able to distinguish between good and evil and not become an easy target for Satan and his attacks.

Studying God's Word allows His truth to *"demolish arguments."* Arguments are carefully crafted thoughts to reach a personal opinion. In other words it is what someone thinks about a subject based on their life and their knowledge. Unfortunately without proper knowledge of God's Word a person can fall victim to another person's poor opinion and poor interpretation of God's Word.

You are called to test these arguments by going back to His Word and seeing if they match up with the other person's opinion. Satan is a master at twisting Scripture. He gives a great deal of truth mixed with a little lie to slowly take you off course and change your direction. Always remember that rat poison is 99% good food and 1% poison!

Studying God's Word allows His truth to demolish *"every pretension."* Pretensions are things that are lifted high and exalted. This is anything placed above God in people's lives. It could be sports, cars, sex, food, shopping, self, drugs, alcohol, your own children, etc. It's any idol which creates a barrier that keeps you from fully reaching God. If we are to *"take captive every thought to make it obedient to Christ"* we need to know the Lord so well we never accept a counterfeit god. If something in your life is more important than God it is an idol.

It states we should demolish *"every pretension"* because God is a jealous God and there should be nothing in between you and Him. Make the one true God of the universe your one and only source of worship! Be ready with an answer to those strongholds, arguments and pretensions by staying in the Word of God. Doing so will give you *"divine power"* to take down the prison walls and find freedom. It will also keep you from becoming trapped by Satan and the false teachings of others. You have a mind; use it to make good choices. You have a heart; fill it with God's Word and be freed from the bondage of sin and Satan's lies.

CHRIST'S TEMPTATION AND GOD'S WORD

In the fourth chapter of Mark, Jesus was tempted during His 40 day fast in the wilderness. Satan tried to deceive Jesus by saying, *"If you are the Son of God, tell these stones to become bread."* Jesus came back with the Word and said, *"Man shall not live on bread alone, but on every word that comes from the mouth of God."* Satan took Jesus to the highest point of the Temple and told Him to throw Himself down.

He began to twist Scripture a second time and said because it is written, *"He will command his angels concerning you, and they will lift you up in their hands, so that you will not strike your foot against a stone."* Jesus replied, *"It is also written: 'Do not put the Lord your God to the test.'"* A third time Satan tempted Jesus by showing Him the kingdoms of the world and offered to give them all to Him. He only needed to bow down and worship him. Jesus said, *"Away from me, Satan! For it is written: 'Worship the Lord your God, and serve him only.'"* Then the real life application of the Scripture follows, *"then the devil left him."*

Eve failed all three of these same tests in the garden while she was speaking to Satan. Satan twisted God's Word about eating from the Tree of Life and Eve fell for the deception. She believed Satan's words over God's Word. The rest is our history.

> *"When the woman saw that the fruit of the tree was good for food and pleasing to the eye, and also desirable for gaining wisdom, she took some and ate it. She also gave some to her husband, who was with her, and he ate it."*
>
> Genesis 3:6

Eve saw the fruit as *"good for food"* just like Jesus would have been tempted to turn the stone into bread during His 40 day fast. But He used God's Word to shut down Satan. This is the temptation of the lust of the flesh.

Eve saw the fruit as *"pleasing to the eye"* just like Jesus would have been tempted with being given all of the nations and their treasures from all over the world. But He used God's Word to shut down Satan. This is the temptation of the lust of the eyes.

Eve loved the idea of *"gaining wisdom"* and becoming like God. Jesus would have been tempted by the pride of having angels catch Him in front of crowd to show His power. But He used God's Word to shut down Satan. This is the temptation of the pride of life.

But Jesus used God's Word to shut down Satan at every temptation. These three temptations should ring a bell. They are described in every piece of Armor's weaknesses and destroy spiritual gifts and people's lives. These are the three main attacks Satan has been using to kill, steal and destroy mankind for thousands of years.

> *"Do not love the world or anything in the world. If anyone loves the world, love for the Father is not in them. For everything in the world—the lust of the flesh, the lust of the eyes, and the pride of life—comes not from the Father but from the world. The world and its desires pass away, but whoever does the will of God lives forever."*
> 1 John 2:15-17

Jesus, in a weakened state from His 40 day fast, knew the Word of God. He used it to defend Himself against Satan's slick moves and defeated him. He used God's Word to defeat the temptations of *"lust of the flesh, lust of the eyes and pride of life."* Are you learning God's Word? Do you desire the power in the Word of God to defeat Satan? Do you want to be a *"whoever does the will of God?"*

"Imagine if we started raising generations of children who stood uncompromisingly on the Word of God, knew how to defend the Christian faith, could answer the skeptical questions of this age, and had a fervor to share the gospel from the authority of God's Word with whomever they met! This could change the world."[115]

-Ken Ham

STOP leaving the Sword on your nightstand or book shelf gathering dust.

LOOK into His Word daily and always keep it at your side.

LISTEN for the Good News God has for you today in His Word.

BE WHAT GOD CREATED YOU TO BE; a well-trained, ready at any moment, Sword Bearer in God's Army.

KEEP THE SWORD SHARP

Sadly, many Christians keep their dull rusty sword put up in a drawer, a closet, a shelf or out on a table gathering dust. They became a Christian, purchased a Bible and now have their free ticket to heaven so they play at worship. They become Easter Lilies and Christmas Poinsettias by attending church a couple days a year. There is so much more to the life of a Christian. God is patiently waiting to give you the extraordinary plans for your life! Dust off your Sword and live!

I learned a valuable lesson as an elementary school child during tomahawk throwing competition in elementary school. I was tied for first place and they arranged a tie breaker for the two of us. A string was tied around a large upright log and first to break the string wins. I won the toss to go first and threw my tomahawk. I sunk the tomahawk at least an inch deep on the middle of the string but the string held in the log. This was about exciting as a tomahawk completion could get!

There was only one thought in my mind as I walked up to the log to pull out my tomahawk and see if it had cut the string. I had neglected to sharpen my tomahawk before the competition. I reached for the handle and pulled down while pushing inward toward the string trying to "cut" it as I pulled the tomahawk from the log. The string popped right back out and was not cut! My opponent threw his tomahawk and cut the string. I came in second all because I had not sharpened my blade.

> *"So you also must be ready, because the Son of Man will come at an hour when you do not expect him."*
> Matthew 24:44

In my head I reasoned there was no need to sharpen my edge because the competition points were about placement of the tomahawk and not their cutting abilities. I felt confident in my capabilities to place the tomahawk in the correct position so I got lazy about the care of my weapon. When it came down to needing a sharp edge to win, I failed due to laziness and pride. God wants us to be ready every hour of every day of our lives and always keep the Sword sharp.

HOW TO SHARPEN THE SWORD

Sharpening a sword requires time, patience and cautious attention. It is not recommended to use power tools to speed up the process because the sword could overheat and it could warp the blade. Power tools can also remove too much of the sword too quickly making it weak and unbalanced. Removing too much of the edge can also cause it to chip or break easily.

Avoid any distractions while sharpening a sword. They may cause you to lose focus and damage the sword or cause injury to yourself. A slow and steady technique works best. Learning the proper techniques is best done by watching others familiar with the process. Jumping in with no training can cause severe damage to the sword or yourself. The focus should be on the entire sword as it is sharpened.

The first step of sharpening a sword begins with a thorough cleaning. The second step uses a file that creates a rough edge. Keeping the filing of the edge balanced is very important to keep the strength of the sword. It is necessary to count the strokes of the file on each side to keep it balanced. Patience is important so do not test the sharpness at this point; the blade needs more work.

The third step is a refining process to sharpen the roughness of the sword and allow the edge to reveal itself. This requires oil as a lubricant to keep the friction down when the sword is moved against the whetstone. There is a clear direction to the movement as edge is revealed along the entire length of the sword. A good light source is needed to constantly check the fine details along with testing the sharpness of the edge.

Finally the fourth step blends the edge with the entirety of the sword with a fine sanding. This is very dangerous as distractions could result in very deep cuts so keeping focused during this step is very important. Finally remove the residue and the sword is now sharp and ready to use.

The process of sharpening a sword is like the process of growing and maturing as a Christian. It starts with a thorough cleaning by God through His forgiveness, grace and mercy. The new Christian picks up the Sword and begins their journey to become more like Christ. The file begins to take off what kept the edge from being sharp. The process removes the habits that have kept the Sword from being sharp and the edge begins to forms its shape. At this point the Christian is not sharp and they are still on Spiritual Milk. They need to be patient and balanced as they learn the truths of God and build on their foundation with the Word of God.

The process of sharpening your Spiritual Sword needs to be slow and steady to avoid burn-out which can weaken you and those around you. The refining process can be dangerous if focus is lost. Looking to the world for answers can leave you injured and bleeding. Keep your focus directed at God to avoid unnecessary injury.

As the edge is revealed, use your Faith like the oil in an engine is used to reduce friction. There will be hard times which will create friction in life. Use the oil to let the friction sharpen you but not break you. Inspect the edge frequently with a good light source is like making sure your Bible studies are on point. Don't allow darkness to cause you to miss areas needing sharpening in your life. Learn to distinguish between good and evil!

Share your weaknesses with others you trust and exchange ideas about how God's Word can help. Allow God to reveal the sharpened edge of the entire Sword so you show balance and maturity. Finally, keep focused with the vast amount of knowledge you have gathered and don't allow the distraction of pride to cut you and others. Use your knowledge to provide wisdom to others so they can sharpen their Sword.

The next steps of using your Sword are like the instructions on a bottle of shampoo; wash, rinse, then repeat. With the Sword, the instructions are sharpen, use, then repeat. Always keeping the Sword sharp!

> *"If you have a Bible that's falling apart, you'll have a life that's not."* [116]   -Adrian Rogers

STOP sitting on the sideline with your free ticket to heaven, get in the game!

LOOK at the condition of the Sword God gave you. Is it dull, rusted and unused?

LISTEN to how God wants you to use the Sword and keep it sharp, available and ready at all times.

BE WHAT GOD CREATED YOU TO BE; a well-trained, ready at any moment sharp Sword bearer in God's Army.

HOW TO STUDY THE BIBLE AND
SHARPEN YOUR SWORD:
TIME

Try to read the God's Word every day or at least 4 times a week outside of church. Choosing the same time each day can help keep you regular with your study. Be consistent even if it's only a 5 minute Devotional.

> *"Be still, and know that I am God…"*
> Psalm 46:10

I grew up very hyperactive and for me to *"be still"* was nearly impossible. I could focus but I always needed something to do. It took me decades to come to realize I needed to stop and spend time with God. I look back and wish I could have learned that lesson early in my life. It doesn't have to be hours of study, it can just be a short Devotion or prayer and a Christian song or two. The main thing is to just do it. Learn to *"be still"* so you can know God better and trust Him with your life.

HAVE A QUIET PLACE

Have a quiet study place free from distractions. It should be a peaceful place that feels good to you. It also should be comfortable in case you need to spend more time with God.

> *"But when you pray, go into your room, close the door and pray to your Father, who is unseen. Then your Father, who sees what is done in secret, will reward you."*
> Matthew 6:6

Personally, I'm not much into staying in a closet to pray but I love to pray as I go about my day and I loved the movie *War Room*. In the movie Christians took their closet space and turned it into a command center of prayer. I do have dry erase boards on my walls in my closet and garage where I write my long term prayer requests to God. They help remind me to pray every day as I pass them.

It took me years to discover my "place" to meet God. I began my first studies like drinking from a firehose then I would spend time in a desert not drinking from God's Word. I would study in spurts and dive deep into Scripture only to stop for days or weeks and dry up spiritually. It took years but I found my best study time was sitting in my truck at the park or behind my clinic. I was free from distractions other than feeding squirrels and birds. God and I have a peaceful place where I pray, listen to Christian music, study His Word and jot down ideas for Christian skits and writing. I found my quiet place to get to know my God, trust my God and it has helped me become what He created me to be.

You can speak to God anytime and anywhere but having a regular place of peace to meet with God is important. Ask God to give you a special place where you and He can have unique moments of communication free from distractions. And when you find it, enjoy being in God's presence and thank Him for allowing you to speak with Him directly.

STUDY HELPS

Choose an easy to read and understand Bible like the NIV, ESV, or NASB. If you are a King James fan the New King James is easier to read. Feel free to highlight, circle, underline and write in your personal Bible. This will help you remember your conversations with God. Purchasing a Study Bible of these versions can be helpful but use several sources of commentary for a better understanding. Make sure you test the Spirit of the commentary you read, it should line up with God's Word.

Have a plan such as beginning with the Gospels or studying Bible topics. But remember distance is not as important as depth; dwell on one passage if needed. It's ok to just read and not study; let God show you what He wants you to learn. Daily Devotionals can help you study regularly when time is short.

If you are a verbal learner, listening to God's Word and others speaking online about Scripture can be helpful. Study groups are good ways to grow in Scriptural knowledge and share your life with others. It's also a good place to hear how God helped others in their lives. Consider a Journal of your studies and prayer times to see how God is working in your life. Don't worry if you learn differently from others. God will meet you where you are and build you up from there.

> *"All Scripture is God-breathed and is useful for teaching, rebuking, correcting and training in righteousness, so that the servant of God may be thoroughly equipped for every good work."* 2 Timothy 3:16-17

I started with an easy-to-read Bible but I wanted to be able to go deep into the Word when needed. I chose a NIV, Greek-Hebrew Study Bible decades ago. It's easy to read and I can look up words to learn more about their meaning. I also read different commentaries to learn what others think about certain Scriptures and Biblical topics.

I enjoy Christian books, music, Sunday school, church specialty classes, and listening to the preacher in church, online or on TV. The point is to find whatever helps you to learn more about God's Word and how to use it.

The internet has a vat amount of knowledge but be careful and test the information against God's Word. Remember, anyone can make a post or website. Just because it is on the internet or is someone's commentary does not make it the truth. I use topic searches along with different Bible translations and the Greek/Hebrew translations on line to speed up my searches. It's ok if this doesn't fit your style of study. If you want to listen to pod casts, that's fine. If you prefer a book in your hand, that's fine too. Just get into God's Word and let it fill your heart so you can become the best possible version of yourself and fight Satan along your way!

PRAYER

Communication with God is of upmost importance. If you want to know Him better then pray for wisdom and understanding of His Word. If you want to know God's Will for your life then pray He gives you the correct information to study and the right people to be around. If you are confused, pray to unlearn the wrong information stuck in your head in order to learn the truth. Pray to test the truth from others commentaries and opinions and learn to distinguish good from evil. Then choose good!

Most of all use prayer to ask God for the next steps in your life. Let Him put His knowledge into action through you to build the kingdom of God. Let Him mature you by teaching you how to turn knowledge into wisdom and grow your Faith. Pray for God's direction in your life to be shown to you through your study and pray even more to be more like Jesus.

> *"And pray in the Spirit on all occasions with all kinds of prayers and requests. With this in mind, be alert and always keep on praying for all the Lord's people."*
> Ephesians 6:18

Prayer helps you know and trust God. Part of your spiritual growth is learning how to tell good from evil. The more you pray and the more you study God's Word the more likely you will be able to recognize good from evil. The more you choose good the more God's steps and plans for your life becomes clearer. The more you follow God's plans for your life the more like Christ you will become.

RENEW YOUR MIND

Keep God's Word at your side and have it ready at all times. A way to personalize God's Word is to put your name in Scripture as you read. An example is, "For God so loved (Mike) He gave..." Use God's Word to renew the thoughts in your head and allow God to correct those thoughts and free you through His Word. You can also renew your mind with Christian music, books, blogs and Faith-based films. Try your best to keep your Faith directed at Jesus. Remember everything of God points to Jesus your Savior.

> *"You were taught, with regard to your former way of life, to put off your old self, which is being corrupted by its deceitful desires; to be made new in the attitude of your minds; and to put on the new self, created to be like God in true righteousness and holiness.*   Ephesians 4:22-24

The world will pull you away from God with the static it creates to keep you from hearing God's radio channel. It will distract you and do it's best to take up all your time with the things of the flesh that counts for nothing. I was distracted for decades before I realized the path I was being led down. I learned I needed a constant flow of God in my life to make any positive changes. I needed God to desperately renew my mind and transform my life.

I love to listen to Christian music and let it feed my soul in happy and sad times. The artist's words can speak truth to me when I do not feel like reading or studying. I enjoy Faith-based films with heartwarming stories that are good for the whole family and tell the world about Jesus. Do your best to *"put on the new self"* for your life and the lives around you.

START

Sometimes starting is the hardest part of a job. I do not like the prep work needed to begin painting a room. I do not enjoy getting all the tools together to work on a project but something cannot be finished if it's never started. There are lots of excuses for not starting but none outweigh the importance of spending time with God. Get out of the rut Satan has you in and dive into a relationship with God!

"Praise be to the God and Father of our Lord Jesus Christ, the Father of compassion and the God of all comfort, who comforts us in all our troubles, so that we can comfort those in any trouble with the comfort we ourselves receive from God."
2 Corinthians 1:3-4

People will ask me what is God's Will for their life and I will simply say, "If you have been through a trial and were comforted by God then help others get through the same trial. It's Biblical!" Go out and help others and you will begin to discover God's plan for your life. Most Christians will tell you they found God's Will and their purpose while helping others!

TELL OTHERS ABOUT GOD

"Preach the word; be prepared in season and out of season; correct, rebuke and encourage—with great patience and careful instruction. For the time will come when people will not put up with sound doctrine. Instead, to suit their own desires, they will gather around them a great number of teachers to say what their itching ears want to hear. They will turn their ears away from the truth and turn aside to myths. But you, keep your head in all situations, endure hardship, do the work of an evangelist, discharge all the duties of your ministry."   2 Timothy 4:2-5

We are all called to love God, love others and tell them about Jesus. Every Christian is called to use some level of the spiritual gift of Evangelism to *"preach the word."* This doesn't mean you have to be a polished and professional Evangelist but you do need to be *"prepared in season and out of season"* to carefully *"correct, rebuke, and encourage"* others. Gaining God's knowledge is fine for you but what about others trying to grow and mature in Christ with God's truth. Put your knowledge into action and help others learn more about God.

The best way to learn truth is to teach truth. Every Christian is called to use some level of the spiritual gift of Teaching to give *"sound doctrine"* with *"careful instruction"* to others. This may be your children, friends, family or co-workers. It could be teaching in a church classroom, a school or a stadium full of people. Your Faith pleases God! Don't be embarrassed by your level of teaching God's Truth; it's more embarrassing, as a Christian, if you're not teaching others about Christ.

In football there are many levels of players like Tiny-mite, Mitey-mite, Jr. Pee Wee, Pee Wee, Jr. Varsity, Varsity, College and Pro. It's similar with Christians and spiritual gifts. You may not be a Pro at Evangelism or Teaching but you may be at the Pee Wee level. You may not play at a domed stadium in front of tens of thousands of fans but you may have fun in a flag football game with friends in the backyard. In other words use what you have, wherever you are in the best way you can to please God and expand His Kingdom.

> *"We must be ready to allow ourselves to be interrupted by God."*[117]   -Dietrich Bonhoeffer

There must be a good reason that the Bible is the best-selling book of all time. Even though the exact number of Bibles printed is impossible to count, the Guinness Book of World Records estimated over 5 billion copies had been sold and distributed. The Bible out-sells every book every year with as many as 100 million copies sold or given away each year. Maybe you need to start reading your Bible and see what all the fuss is about!

> *"Put your nose into the Bible every day. It is your spiritual food. And then share it. Make a vow not to be a lukewarm Christian."*[118]
>   -Kirk Cameron

BIBLE STUDY STATISTICS:

I understand many people do not enjoy studying statistics but they are very important. Think of statistics as checking the Body's temperature to know if there is an infection needing care. There are several research groups who have been following Christian activities and behaviors for decades. Barna, Lifeway, Pew Research and the Center for Bible Engagement are a few of these research groups. They watch Christian trends in order to point out the needs of the church and give us warnings; but is anyone listening and acting on those warnings?

Generally speaking, being a practicing Christian who attends church regularly, shares their Faith and reads their Bible often tends to avoid many problems. They are more likely to avoid gambling, pornography, drunkenness and sex outside of marriage. They have longer marriages and are more generous and loving towards other people. These are great statistics and can really sell the idea of being a Christian.

Unfortunately most research is tracking a general downward spiral in Christian growth and maturity. I believe they would all say the world is in a desperate need of a revival. Some people would rather have a root canal than study research but you do not want to perish from the lack of knowledge. Christian research is of extreme importance and it's screaming for us to wake up and see the effects Satan and the world is having on Christianity.

There are very positive effects on Christians who read their Bible regularly but there has been a downward trend in Bible reading overall as time has passed. The general research goes on to show a rapid fall in those who identify as Christian in America over the decades. It is time to sound the alarm and take action to stop the bleeding.

"At that time many will turn away from the faith and will betray and hate each other, and many false prophets will appear and deceive many people. Because of the increase of wickedness, the love of most will grow cold, but the one who stands firm to the end will be saved. And this gospel of the kingdom will be preached in the whole world as a testimony to all nations, and then the end will come."

Matthew 24:10-14

Scripture describes some of the things that will happen in the end times. It clearly states the *"many will turn away from the faith"* but take heart in the fact *"the one who stands firm to the end will be saved!"* We all need to be doing everything possible to build up God's Kingdom and stand firm against Satan. If it says many will fall from the Faith, we need to share our Faith even more. If it says there will be many deceived by false prophets, then we need to keep our Sword sharp so we can distinguish between good and evil and show them the truth. If people's love is growing cold then we need to spread the love of Christ through our actions. Keep using your spiritual gifts to spread His Good News and eventually the *"end will come!"*

"Do not suppose that I have come to bring peace to the earth. I did not come to bring peace, but a sword."

Matthew 10:34

Christians speak of God's love but there is a war going on to destroy Christianity. We need to be aware of the damage being done and thanks to Christian research groups the message is loud and clear. Use the Sword of God's Word to crush Satan and spread the Gospel. Live each day as if it is your last day on Earth as a Christian. The world will never have true peace until the return of Christ but fortunately God gave us the peace of our eternity with Him until then. Let's share His peace so we and others can overcome the world's chaos?

"The Scriptures teach us the best way of living, the noblest way of suffering and the most comfortable way of dying."[119]
-John Flavel

REASONS TO READ GOD'S WORD

"Nobody ever out grows Scripture; the book widens and deepens with our years."[120]   -Charles Spurgeon

It shows you how much God loves you
It shows you your value
It shows you who you are in Christ
It shows you what Jesus' death meant for you
It shows you how Jesus lived
It shows you God's Truth and His absolutes
It shows you the power in God's Word
It shows you wisdom
It shows you the next steps of your life
It shows you God's character
It shows you how to live a life honoring to God
It shows you how God's Word is relevant today
It shows you how to defend your Faith
It shows you how to show God's love to others
It shows you how to share God's Word with others
It shows you how to disciple and mentor others
It shows you how God's Word is eternal
It shows you God's Holiness
It shows you God's promises
It shows you God's presence
It shows you God's commands
It shows you God's desire
It shows you God's strength
It shows you God's miracles
It shows you God's Kingdom
It shows you God's redemption

It shows you God's shield
It shows you God's forgiveness
It shows you God's gifts
It shows you God's blessings
It shows you God's freedom
It shows you God's faithfulness
It shows you God's love
It shows you God's joy
It shows you God's hope
It shows you God's peace
It shows you God's mercy
It shows you God's healing
It shows you God's justice
It shows you God's wisdom
It shows you God's plans
It shows you God's Will
It gives you freedom from your past, present and future
It gives you the warning signs for the dangers ahead
It gives you courage
It gives you practical answers to life's issues
It gives you a purpose and place in the Body of Christ
It gives you a path to follow
It gives you direction for spiritual growth and maturity
It helps you discover God's Will for your life
It helps you trust God
It helps you discern truth from lies
It helps you recognize false teachings and false teachers
It helps you distinguish between good and evil
It helps you defend and overcome Satan's attacks
It helps you renew your mind and learn the mind of Christ
It helps you fight temptations and lessen your sins
It helps you live a righteous life
It helps you learn how to use your spiritual gifts
It helps you be more God-centered and less self-centered
It helps you be ready an answer for those who ask

It helps you have better relationships with others
It helps you be more generous of your time, treasures and talents
It helps you be thankful and grateful
It helps you worship
It revives you in times of trouble
It connects you to God
It grows your Faith
It feeds your soul with an everlasting hope
It teaches you how to become more like Christ
It teaches you to imitate Jesus' servanthood
It encourages you to produce good fruit
It fills you with joy
It promises you hope for a future with God
It gets you out of your comfort zone
It gives you a community to belong too
It changes people's lives
It corrects you
It humbles you
It reminds you of how much you need God

"The world changes - circumstances change, we change - but God's Word never changes."[121]   -Warren Wiersbe

STOP coming up with excuses for not reading God's Word.
LOOK at the decline of Christianity and look for ways to build the Kingdom.
LISTEN to all the good things that come from reading and knowing God's Word.
BE WHAT GOD CREATED YOU TO BE; a reader and a doer of the Word.

"The Holy Scriptures are our letters from home."[122]
                  -Augustine

GROWTH IN CHRIST
The Sword: Your Offensive Weapon of Mass Instruction

UNDERSTAND "WHOSE" YOU ARE

"In your unfailing love preserve my life, that I may obey the statutes of your mouth. Your word, Lord, is eternal it stands firm in the heavens."   Psalm 119:88-89

God loves you so much He allowed His Son to die on a cross for you. You have eternal value to Him. He left you His Word to let you live in freedom here on Earth and eventually with Him for an eternity. Show how much you love Him for what He did for you by getting to know Him better through His Word. Let the Words and *"unfailing love"* from the Creator of the Universe encourage you with the hope you have in a future with Him.

CONFESS AND PROGRESS

"I have hidden your word in my heart that I might not sin against you."   Psalm 119:11

Have you not been reading your Bible lately? So what! Pick it up, dust it off and begin reading it again. Just get started and tell God you're sorry for not wanting to get to know Him more and ask for His forgiveness. Ask Him to give you a thirst for His Word and enjoy getting to know Him better. Store up His Word in your heart so you can avoid sin easier. God is offering you a way out of the sins that hinder your walk with Him so take His way out!

COMMUNICATE WITH GOD

"You will keep in perfect peace those whose minds are steadfast, because they trust in you. Trust in the Lord forever, for the Lord, the Lord himself, is the Rock eternal."
                    Isaiah 26:3-4

The more you communicate with God the more you know God. The more you know God the more you trust God. The more you trust God the more you have peace from His voice because He knows what is best for your life. When you trust His voice you will know His perfect plan for your life! Find that place of *"perfect peace,"* and rest on the **"Rock eternal."** Allow God to show you how much you are loved.

USING THE SWORD OF THE SPIRIT WITH THE FRUITS OF THE SPIRIT

LOVE: Are you spreading the Word of God with Love? Are you reading about Jesus' love in the Scriptures so you can be more loving to others? Do you know how much Jesus loves you?

JOY: Do your words joyfully reflect the Word of God? Do your words bring joy to others? Do you find joy in your own life when you speak a Word of God over another person?

PEACE: Do you find peace in God's Word? Are you looking at the storm in your life or looking at Jesus? Do you trust God for peace in your own life?

PATIENCE: Are you too busy to study God's Word? Are you too busy to pray and listen? Are you impatiently waiting for an answer from God? Are you listening to yourself more than God? Are you willing to do whatever He asks whenever He asks even if He says, "Wait?"

KINDNESS: Are your words like water to a garden or do they leave plants dry and withered? Do your words help produce fruit in others' lives or do they cut the vine before they can bear the fruit?

GOODNESS: Are you a doer of the Word? If you were unable to speak would people know you are a Christian by your actions? If you were being tried for being a Christian, would there be enough evidence to convict you?

FAITHFULNESS: Do you spend time with God regularly? Is reading His Word a priority? Is prayer a priority? Is listening to God a priority? Is trust in God your number one priority?

GENTLENESS: Do you try to force your opinion of God on others? Is your knowledge more important than the relationship? Do you listen carefully to others or is your mind filled with the next thing you want to say?

SELF-CONTROL: Do you make time for God? Do you have a quiet peaceful place ready to talk with Him? Do you get rid of distractions when you and God are together? Do you focus on Him during prayer? Is your prayer a memorized script used to simply check a box on the Christian to-do list?

TAKE THE MIRROR TEST

When you look in the mirror is God's Word in your hands? Are you reading about how much God loves you? Do you see a loved child of God? Do you see yourself speaking His Word and telling others how much He loves them? Do you see yourself speaking those Words to yourself? He wants you to look in the mirror and hear Him say, "You are loved!" He wants His love to be so abundant in you it overflows from you to others. God is always pouring His love into you, now pour it into others.

> *"God has a plan for your life. The enemy has a plan for your life. Be ready for both. Just be wise enough to know which one to battle and which one to embrace."* -Unknown

DON'T LET GIFT-KILLERS
CAUSE YOU TO BE A GIFT-QUITTER
BE WHAT GOD CREATED YOU TO BE
AND BE A GIFT-GIVER

PONDERING POINTS

What is the Sword of the Spirit?

How and why is the Sword important?

What is the goal of the Sword?

What is the purpose of the Sword?

What is the strength of the Sword?

What is the main weakness of the Sword?

How do we train with the Sword?

Do you have a regular study place and time?

Describe your study place and how it feels to be with God.

What are ways we can sharpen our Sword?

How do we use our Sword to avoid temptation and sin?

What happens when we do not use our Sword?

What can be done about the statistics of Christianity?

What can be done about Christians not reading their Bibles?

Are you ready an answer for those who ask you about God?

Can you explain the Gospel in an easy to understand way?

Can you share how Jesus saved you with other people?

Do you have Faith in the Sword?

What "Reasons to Read God's Word" stood out to you?

What helps you study God's Word?

What keeps you from studying God's Word?

What fears keep you from using the Sword?

"For I am not ashamed of the gospel, because it is the power of God that brings salvation to everyone who believes…"

Romans 1:16

CHAPTER FOURTEEN

THE FIRST DAY OF THE REST OF YOUR LIFE IN CHRIST

"I have been crucified with Christ and I no longer live, but Christ lives in me. The life I now live in the body, I live by faith in the Son of God, who loved me and gave himself for me."
Galatians 2:20

You are a new creation in Christ. Jesus died for you and now He lives within you to help you while you're visiting Earth. This is not your home planet; your real home is in heaven with Him for an eternity. Because He is in your heart you can make better decisions for yourself and others around you. You have the ability and power to help others, through your spiritual gifts, discover their new home despite your past shame and regrets.

"God is able to take the mess of our past and turn it into a message. He takes the trials and tests and turns them into a testimony."[123]
-Christine Caine

"I will give them an undivided heart and put a new spirit in them; I will remove from them their heart of stone and give them a heart of flesh. Then they will follow my decrees and be careful to keep my laws. They will be my people, and I will be their God." Ezekiel 11:19-20

If you follow your renewed heart you can choose to sin less and expand the Kingdom of God with your spiritual gifts. You have amazing gifts given to you by a loving and caring God. Choose love and share Jesus with your gifts. Never forget you are important to the Kingdom of God. He loves you dearly!

"God does not change—and neither does His love. He loved you before you were born . . .He loves you now . . .and He will love you forever."[124] -Billy Graham

"Follow God's example, therefore, as dearly loved children and walk in the way of love, just as Christ loved us and gave himself up for us as a fragrant offering and sacrifice to God." Ephesians 5:1

There will be a sacrifice on our part but it will bring you great joy as you discover why God created you. When you use your spiritual gifts to build up the Body of Christ and expand the Kingdom of God you will know why you are here. You will receive great blessings while doing what you were created to do.

"And when we truly believe God and act in faith, we will see victory in our lives."[125] -Sandra Thompson Davis

"Now that you know these things, you will be blessed if you do them." John 13:17

You may be questioning whether you **"know these things."** There was a lot in this book to digest and put into action. Try not to be overwhelmed and just start your journey with your spiritual gifts. It will take time and patience to **"know these things"** but the blessings will be worth it. Your biggest growth will come as you become more like Christ and choose good over evil.

"As we journey through this life - through the easy times and the painful times - God is fashioning us into people who are like his Son, Jesus. That means God is in the process of changing what we desire far more than he is in the process of giving us what we desire."[126]   -Charles Stanley

"Your beginnings will seem humble, so prosperous will your future be."   Job 8:7

You will most likely start small and as you grow in your Faith you will accomplish bigger things. But remember God is about relationships and using your gifts one-on-one can have more of an impact than a stadium event. Never think anything you do is small when it is done for God. The word **"prosperous"** here is more about an increasing power and abundance rather than wealth. As you grow in your Faith you will have more power to advance the Kingdom of God and it may happen with large groups or one person. Just be obedient and follow God's plan for your life, He knows what is best for you.

"Be faithful in small things because it is in them that your strength lies."[127]   -Mother Teresa

"Because of the Lord's great love we are not consumed, for his compassions never fail. They are new every morning; great is your faithfulness. I say to myself, 'The Lord is my portion; therefore I will wait for him.'"
          Lamentations 3:22-23

Be patient and **"wait for him."** His **"great love"** for you is preparing you to use your Gifts. Stay in His Word and expect something **"new every morning"** no matter how small it may be. Trust His Faithfulness to direct your path and put His love into action. Always look every day for ways to please God.

"One phrase that got me through many difficult times in my life was: God's delays are not God's denials."[128]

-AJ Winters

"Therefore, since we are surrounded by such a great cloud of witnesses, let us throw off everything that hinders and the sin that so easily entangles. And let us run with perseverance the race marked out for us, fixing our eyes on Jesus, the pioneer and perfecter of faith. For the joy set before him he endured the cross, scorning its shame, and sat down at the right hand of the throne of God. Consider him who endured such opposition from sinners, so that you will not grow weary and lose heart." Hebrews 12:1-3

People are watching you live out your Faith so be a good example. Keep your eyes on Jesus and strive to become more like Him. Even in His death He had joy in the fact He was saving the world and you in it. If He can die for you then you should *"not grow weary and lose heart"* as you follow God's Will for your life. This life is a race and it will take endurance to finish it but Wow; think about what the finish line will be like.

"God never said that the journey would be easy, but He did say that the arrival would be worthwhile."[129]

-Max Lucado

"He who was seated on the throne said, 'I am making everything new!' Then he said, 'Write this down, for these words are trustworthy and true.'" Revelation 21:5

Jesus promised to make *"everything new"* and He is using you to accomplish His promise to the World. Your spiritual gifts are uniquely designed to help you carry out this promise. Do not be afraid of the future He has for you. Let His perfect love drive out your fears and become what God created you to be.

You are a special child of God with a purpose to build up others and expand the Kingdom of God.

"No matter what has happened to you in the past or what is going on in your life right now, it has no power to keep you from having an amazingly good future if you will walk by faith in God. God loves you! He wants you to live with victory over sin so you can possess His promises for your life today!"[130]

-Joyce Meyer

"I pray that the eyes of your heart may be enlightened in order that you may know the hope to which he has called you, the riches of his glorious inheritance in his holy people, and his incomparably great power for us who believe..."

Ephesians 1:18-19

When I talk with the speakers on Tres Dias weekends I tell them to be real and leave your audience with hope. If something bad happened in your life tell them how Jesus got you through it. Give praise to God for leading you to where you are today. So I want to leave you with hope!

I've been through a lot of trials in my six decades on Earth and I'm still standing. God saw something in me a long time ago and trusted me to carry this book to its completion. I've grown a lot through the process and God has been faithful to finish the work He began in me. If I, this filthy sinner, can be used of God you can also be the mind, hands, feet, heart and mouth of Jesus. Jesus left you a perfect example; now follow ***"the hope to which He has called you!"***

"What you are is God's gift to you, what you become is your gift to God."[131]   -Hans Urs von Balthasar

Take the first step of your leap of Faith; ask God right now to grow the seed of Faith that is already inside of you. Take the next step in your journey and be blown away by what God will accomplish through you.

You are fearfully and wonderfully made to do miraculous good works while you are visiting this planet. Get everything done you can get done before heading to your heavenly home. Never stop, never give up and never stay down after a fall. Get back up and move on to the great things God has planned for you. You are a loved child of the Most High and have been given amazingly fantastic gifts to build up the Body of Christ.

STOP using excuses to avoid using your spiritual gifts.
LOOK at all God has given to you for you to have a future with Him.
LISTEN, God is calling you to greater things because He loves you.
BE WHAT GOD CREATED YOU TO BE and use the wings God gave you to fly to new heights. You have power within yourself you never knew you had. Let God show you the power He gave you and use it for good.

I'll end with my translation of what the angels said to the disciples at the ascension of Christ in Acts 1, "What are you standing there gawking up at the sky for, get busy! You know what you've got to do; you have no excuses, move on."

"I've read the last page of the Bible, it's all going to turn out alright."[132]
                                                    -Billy Graham

THANK YOU

Iwant to thank you for being a part of a 20 year old spiritual goal. I have traveled many a road to get this information to you and I've had many times when I grew weary of the battle. Without the support of family, friends and church I would not be writing this to you. I pray the information in this book transforms your life and gives you the kick-in-the-buttock you needed to move forward in your relationship with Jesus. I have several bruises in that area so I understand.

In all my battles I believe the greatest weapon we have is dwelling on God. When we draw close to Him we are transformed, renewed and protected. No matter what, stay close to God and His Word. He loves all of us so much and He wants to constantly remind us of His love for us. His love cast out many of my fears and helped me carry on despite many hardships. I cannot wrap my head around how much the Creator of the universe loves me, but He does. Rest in God's love for you and you will find peace beyond understanding.

Grateful,

Dr. Mike Miller

REFERENCES

Chapter One

1: qtd. in www.azquotes.com/quote/880815
2: qtd. in www.azquotes.com/quote/1498217
3: qtd. in www.christian.net/resources/50-great-quotes-about-life-and-living-to-the-fullest/

Chapter Two

4: qtd. in www.brainyquote.com/quotes/bede_griffiths_186637
5: qtd. in www.quotefancy.com/quote/539770/Alfred-Brendel-The-word-LISTEN-contains-the-same-letters-as-the-word-SILENT
6: qtd. in www.azquotes.com/quote/1404445
7: qtd. in www.quotefancy.com/quote/2129304/Charles-Haddon-Spurgeon-God-never-loses-sight-of-the-treasure-which-He-has-placed-in-our

Chapter Three

8: qtd. in www.quotefancy.com/quote/2155534/Henry-T-Blackaby-The-willingness-to-obey-every-word-from-God-is-critical-to-hearing-God

Chapter Four

9: qtd. in www.gracequotes.org/quote/it-is-not-great-gifts-that-god-blesses-so-much-as-it-is-great-likeness-to-christ/
10: qtd. in www.christian-quotes.ochristian.com/Cornelius-Plantinga-Quotes/

Chapter Six

11: qtd. in www.azquotes.com/quote/949770
12: qtd. in www.brainyquote.com/quotes/john_d_rockefeller_119902
13: qtd. in www.dailychristianquote.com/charles-r-swindoll-28/
14: qtd. in www.azquotes.com/quote/912372
15: qtd.in www.brainyquote.com/quotes/florence_nightingale_121022#:~:text=Florence%20Nightingale%20Quotes&text=So%20never%20lose%20an%20

opportunity%20of%20urging%20a%20practical%20beginning,seed%20 germinates%20and%20roots%20itself.

16: qtd. in www.goodreads.com/quotes/154682-have-you-no-wish-for-others-to-be-saved-then

17: qtd.inwww.quotemaster.org/q8a4fe0990df5441b6a9e0d85fedd02b0

18: qtd. in www.gracequotes.org/author-quote/d-l-moody/

19: qtd. in www.azquotes.com/quote/447510

20: qtd. in www.azquotes.com/author/11361-Blaise_Pascal/tag/faith#:~:text=Faith%20 is%20a%20sounder%20guide,but%20faith%20has%20no%20limits.&text= Faith%20embraces%20many%20truths%20which%20seem%20to%20contradict %20each%20other.&text=There%20are%20three%20means%20of,by%20 reason%2C%20and%20by%20custom.

21: qtd. in www.azquotes.com/quote/532442

22: qtd. in www.christianquotes.info/quotes-by-author/henry-drummond-quotes/

23: qtd. in www.azquotes.com/quote/355229

24: qtd. in www.goproject.org/the-power-of-prayer-joe-knittig-ceo/

25: qtd. in www.quotefancy.com/quote/1343609/John-Newton-How-sweet-the-name-of-Jesus-sounds-In-a-believer-s-ear-It-soothes-his-sorrows

26: qtd. in https://www.brainyquote.com/quotes/charles_dickens_163892

27: qtd. in www.azquotes.com/quote/710987

28: qtd. in www.azquotes.com/quote/857800

29: qtd. in www.searchquotes.com/quotation/According_to_Scripture%2C_virtually_ everything_that_truly_qualifies_a_person_for_leadership_is_directl/375793/

30: qtd. in www.allchristianquotes.org/authors/521/Tony_Merida/

31: qtd. in www.quotes.pub/q/harmony-is-produced-in-ministry-when-everyone-seeks-to-be-a--376400

32: qtd. in www.goodreads.com/quotes/3206451-ministry-s-not-an-option-for-a-christian-it-s-a-privilege

33: qtd. in www.goodreads.com/quotes/475528-personal-ministry-is-not-about-always-knowing-what-to-say

34: qtd. in https://www.allchristianquotes.org/quotes/Wanda_E_Brunstetter/9175/

35: qtd. in www.allchristianquotes.org/authors/231/Jacqueline_Jackie_ McCullough/17-32/

36: qtd. in www.azquotes.com/quote/1351597

37: qtd. in www.azquotes.com/quote/1211638

38: qtd. in www.inspiringquotes.us/author/5380-j-i-packer/page:2

39: qtd. in www.goodreads.com/author/quotes/21025.Henry_T_Blackaby?page=2

40. qtd. in www.brainyquote.com/quotes/benjamin_franklin_383997

41. qtd. in www.quotefancy.com/quote/805701/Francis-Chan-Don-t-fall-into-the-trap-of-studying-the-Bible-without-doing-what-it-says

42. qtd. in www.goodreads.com/quotes/560173-the-word-of-god-i-think-of-as-a-straight

43. qtd. in www.currentschoolnews.com/articles/charles-spurgeon-quotes/

44. qtd. in www.heartlight.org/gallery/7501.html

45. qtd. in www.azquotes.com/quote/1364637

46. qtd. in www.christianquotes.info/quotes-by-author/sinclair-b-ferguson-quotes/

47. qtd. in www.brainyquote.com/quotes/richard_cecil_129226

48. qtd. in www.azquotes.com/quote/1320127

49. qtd. in www.goodreads.com/quotes/202361-true-wisdom-consists-in-two-things-knowledge-of-god-and
50. qtd. in www.azquotes.com/author/13978-Charles_Spurgeon/tag/wisdom
51. qtd. in www.gracequotes.org/quote/it-is-not-great-gifts-that-god-blesses-so-much-as-it-is-great-likeness-to-christ/
52. qtd. in www.goodreads.com/quotes/9457478-god-has-given-a-spiritual-gift-to-the-church-in

Chapter Seven

53. qtd. in www.goodreads.com/quotes/7484482-oh-that-we-would-hunger-to-be-filled-with-the
54. qtd. in www.brainyquote.com/quotes/john_c_maxwell_383606
55. qtd. in www.brainyquote.com/quotes/saint_augustine_148546
56. qtd. in www.azquotes.com/quote/114856
57. qtd. in www.leadership.lifeway.com/2016/09/19/best-quotes-from-spiritual-leadership-part-one/
58. qtd. in www.brainyquote.com/quotes/rick_warren_395865

Chapter Nine

59. qtd. in www.christian-quotes.ochristian.com/Zac-Poonen-Quotes/page-2.shtml
60. qtd.in www.christian-quotes.ochristian.com/Affliction-Quotes/page-2.shtml
61. qtd. in www.christianquotes.info/quotes-by-author/john-c-broger-quotes/
62. qtd. in www.goodreads.com/quotes/1278716-it-s-not-how-much-we-have-but-how-much-we
63. qtd. in www.gracequotes.org/author-quote/william-secker/
64. qtd. in www.brainyquote.com/quotes/blaise_pascal_159870
65. qtd. in www.quotes.pub/henry-blackaby-quotes

Chapter Ten

66. qtd. in https://www.goodreads.com/quotes/51034-refuse-to-be-average-let-your-heart-soar-as-high
67. qtd. in www.brainyquote.com/quotes/martin_luther_king_jr 121315
68. qtd. in www.christianquotes.info/quotes-by-author/harry-ironside-quotes/
69. qtd. in www.azquotes.com/quote/304052
70. qtd. in www.azquotes.com/quote/874630
71. qtd. in www.acts29.com/ten-things-for-every-church-planter/
72. qtd. in www.azquotes.com/quote/430800
73. qtd. in www.azquotes.com/quote/662659

Chapter Eleven

74. qtd. in www.azquotes.com/quote/307485
75. qtd. in www.azquotes.com/quote/800805
76. qtd. in www.brainyquote.com/quotes/john_wooden_386192
77. qtd. in www.goodreads.com/quotes/132988-unless-god-has-raised-you-up-for-this-very-thing
78. qtd. in www.quotemaster.org/q3b4eddd444de0d74f1f3dbd9a972e4a4
79. qtd. in www.azquotes.com/quote/763273
80. qtd. in www.christianquotes.info/quotes-by-author/warren-wiersbe-quotes/
81. qtd. in www.azquotes.com/quote/694525
82. qtd. in www.azquotes.com/quote/162942
83. qtd. in www.azquotes.com/quote/903828?ref=idols
84. qtd. in www.gracequotes.org/author-quote/d-l-moody/
85. qtd. in www.azquotes.com/quote/418407
86. qtd. in www.christian-quotes.ochristian.com/Satan-Quotes/page-8.shtml
87. qtd. in www.azquotes.com/quote/307473
88. qtd. in www.goodreads.com/quotes/856252-some-people-have-a-warped-idea-of-living-the-christian
89. qtd. in www.azquotes.com/quote/569788
90. qtd. in www.sermonquotes.com/corrie-ten-boom-2/11179-worry-not-empty-tomorrow-sorrows-corrie-ten-boom.html
91. qtd. in www.crosswalk.com/faith/spiritual-life/inspiring-quotes/30-christian-quotes-about-thankfulness.html
92. qtd. in www.quotefancy.com/quote/899632/Rick-Warren-Fear-is-a-self-imposed-prison-that-will-keep-you-from-becoming-what-God
93. qtd. in christian-quotes.ochristian.com/Charles-Stanley-Quotes/

Chapter Twelve

94. qtd. in https://crossquotes.wordpress.com/2016/05/20/ray-stedman-10-really-good-quotes/
95. qtd. in www.brainyquote.com/quotes/mother_teresa_121373
96. qtd. in www.goodreads.com/quotes/tag/faith-in-action
97. qtd. in www.quotefancy.com/quote/2617124/Darrell-W-Johnson-The-God-who-has-claimed-us-for-himself-if-Father-Son-and-Holy-Spirit
98. qtd. in www.azquotes.com/quote/877332
99. qtd. in www.wow4u.com/rickwarrenquotes2/
100. qtd. in www.goodreads.com/quotes/9326206-trusting-god-does-not-mean-believing-he-will-do-what
101. qtd. in www.turtlequote.com/positive-trust-god-quotes/
102. qtd. in https://www.brainyquote.com/quotes/william_carey_191985
103. qtd. in www.azquotes.com/quote/680228
104. qtd. in www.azquotes.com/quote/862335
105. qtd. in www.christian-quotes.ochristian.com/John-Hagee-Quotes/
106. qtd. in www.azquotes.com/quote/1222900
107. qtd. in www.azquotes.com/quote/798623

108. qtd. in www.br.pinterest.com/pin/398498267011558599/
109. qtd. in www.goodreads.com/quotes/9240587-imagine-what-god-would-trust-you-with-tomorrow-if-you
110. qtd. in www.graciousquotes.com/germany-kent/
111. qtd. in https://twitter.com/stevenfurtick/status/959582497322553344?lang=en

Chapter Thirteen

112. https://www.azquotes.com/quote/661876
113. qtd. in https://www.christianitytoday.com/ct/2009/mayweb-only/120-42.0.html
114. qtd. in www.goodreads.com/quotes/7484490-we-need-to-encourage-new-believers-to-feed-on-god-s
115. qtd. in www.azquotes.com/quote/799440
116. qtd. in htwww.azquotes.com/quote/761478
117. qtd. in www.azquotes.com/quote/1121591
118. qtd. in www.azquotes.com/quote/45932
119. qtd. in www.azquotes.com/quote/764575
120. qtd. in www.azquotes.com/quote/363783
121. qtd. in www.azquotes.com/quote/1368787
122. qtd. in www.azquotes.com/quote/455743

Chapter Fourteen

123. qtd. in www.goodreads.com/quotes/734741-god-is-able-to-take-the-mess-of-our-past
124. qtd. in www.azquotes.com/quote/880864
125. qtd. in www.wow4u.com/quote-of-daydec2020.html
126. qtd. in www.wow4u.com/qgod7/
127. qtd. in www.brainyquote.com/quotes/mother_teresa_121373
128. qtd. in www.wow4u.com/qgod7/
129. qtd. in www.quotefancy.com/quote/865710/Max-Lucado-God-never-said-that-the-journey-would-be-easy-but-He-did-say-that-the-arrival
130. qtd. in www.azquotes.com/quote/198172
131. qtd. in www.goodreads.com/quotes/170462-what-you-are-is-god-s-gift-to-you-what-you
132. qtd. in www.brainyquote.com/quotes/billy_graham_150656